Dear Dorothy
Years have pass
you desiring to ser
tried also — we are both on the some page
to try to make a difference. God Bless

I Love You
This Much

Pat Brahman

I Love You
This Much

A Journey With the Holy Spirit

Pat Brahman

To order additional copies of this book, contact:
Xlibris Corporation
1-888-795-4274
www.Xlibris.com
Orders@Xlibris.com
17443

Contents

PART 3

The Chastening

TO THE CONFUSED
AND
EMOTIONALLY DISTRESSED

Acknowlegement

To Mary Kelly
for without her lessons
There may not have been a book.

Also to my dear husband who has
Been so patient with me while I was writing.

To my children who tired of hearing for many years,
"Everything is going to be okay. Mommy's writing a book"!

Cover photo by Chris Quinn

PART 1

The Fall

"The sinful nature desires what is contrary to the Spirit,
And the Spirit what is contrary to the sinful nature."

Gal: 5:17 (NIV)

Chapter One

"I Take Thee . . . . "

Youth gone in one stroke.
Ambition. Worldliness.
Darkness all around.
Inner anger not yet voiced.
The yearning in her heart kept her going.
Young love so tender.
Maturity always just around the corner . . .

It was the 1960's . . . a time in which the moral codes knit
into the fabric of our American society were dropping the stitches
of truths and unraveling the spiritual blessings which our country
had been showered with up until this time. Even the religious
were hiding this "new morality" under their candles. "God, where
are You in all this?", I pleaded as I sat silently in my kitchen,
beer in hand, listening to the radio attempting to sooth my wounds
by breathing in songs of love which haunted and fed my soul all
at once. I would watch the dial on the old parlor radio that had
belonged to my grandmother. It lit up the dark kitchen where I
often sat into the deep night hours after the kids went to sleep. I
had found myself in the one predicament that I knew would never
fall on me. I was now a divorce'. It had been a case of fearing for
the moral safety of my three little children and my very own sanity
as well. Not only was my husband involved in the mess, but so

13

was the police moral squad involved . . . so was the cagey prosecuting attorney, one of my ex-husband's more unscrupulous political buddies. And last but certainly not least were the priests who were involved in the big cover-up. Homosexuality was not yet a household word.

Just nine years previously I had had the world by the tail. Everything up until that point had always worked out quite well for me. I had had a good job, a supportive family and a boy friend in the service. Then I walked into it. A Dear John "good-bye" to my high school sweetheart and a "hello" to an ambitious young man five years my senior. He was a man of the world having been on his own and had been "around. He was experienced! I felt safe with him. I remembered that mischievous twinkle in his dark brown eyes, a sort of forbidding twinkle, the likes of which I had never seen before. He had great talents of dealing with people: a very outgoing personality. I had felt as though I was the luckiest girl in the world.

He took me on an exciting trip. Of first importance, I gave birth to our two sons, Robert and Blake, born 11 months apart. It had all happened so fast. I looked at it as Catholic tradition. No, it was more than that. It was Catholic law! Birth control was out! These little boys were nurtured amongst the excitement: from the frightful evening when Bob had been stabbed in the back by a hitchhiker whom he had picked up . . . to the marvelous experience of his having run for public office as representative of our district. Life with Bob was never boring. He had managed to raise himself to places of recognition when he became president of the Young Democrats of our county and the president of the Kennedy for President Club. I had been so proud of him.

Now, here I was, alone feeling very forsaken. I squirmed in my chair drawn back to the music not even daring to go on with my thoughts. They were wandering back to the time when I got the first hint that something was very wrong in my marriage. Up until then I had been in complete denial of any problems. The fact that I'd received very little tenderness from my husband in our love making just stayed buried into a matter of conscience that told me "no matter what, I was to accept my husband for better or worse". I just figured that's the way he was due to his fast lifestyle and huge energies. I knew he had a lot on his mind.

It was just after my grandmother's death that I began to realize that I was a part of something much larger than myself. As usual, I'd been lying in bed waiting for Bob to come home. I was alone a great deal in the evenings. I believe I was in a slumber mode when I heard a sweet woman's voice talking to me in a dream like I had never had before. I was semi-awake with my eyes open, seeing things in pale transparent colors. A street dimly lit appeared before me. There were trees . . . big leafy trees all up and down the street, and strange looking brick houses: rows and rows of houses all hooked together. I saw myself standing on a curb spewing ugly anger . . . a horrible hatred. Then the soft voice whispered to me again. "There's a plan for you." The whisper turned into a glowing circle of light. My grandmother's face, only much younger than I had known her, was staring down at me. "Be careful, dear. There's a plan for you. Be very, very careful." I was a little shaken. In fact, I felt somewhat sick and went to sleep a little drugged with fear telling myself that it was just a stupid dream.

These months later, my mind was worn out from going over the particulars of the nightmares that occurred right after that dream, of those times when my beautiful bubble had burst. Now I sat in my kitchen day after day, hour after hour taxing my brain, my emotions, my very soul. The picture of my husband's eyes haunted me that day when I had lost hope that our relationship would ever be a healthy one as man and wife. Those eyes! They loomed up before me. The memory of that day would forever pierce my heart. I was sitting in the psychiatrist's office. I could hear my husband's huge sobbings, then screams of anger from behind the huge wooden closed door. It was a forbidding door, one that warned me that I never wanted to enter into its chamber. Bob had gone there as a promise to me when I had, quite by accident, happened on the problem.

We had moved our little family to a new strange place far

away from home. Bob's company had sent him across the country first. Later on he had finally sent for us. Our family now consisted of two boys and a girl. I had given birth to a precious little girl, Betsy, just weeks before he had left. He barely knew his little girl when we arrived. I was so happy that we were all together once more. Bob had found a temporary place for us to live in a trailer court. We were awaiting the arrival of our furniture so that we could move into the pleasant, yet odd-looking row houses in the city.

I had been sitting on the step of the trailer breathing in the freshness of the cool air this particular spring evening. There was a pasture that was just down a path from our little domain. Bob had explained to me that it relaxed him to go down there to play with the horses and watch the beauty of the sunset. I was always stuck at home because I couldn't leave the kids. I had the urge to join Bob, anyhow. The kids were asleep. I gingerly made my way through the brush, careful to walk around the slimy bogs. I caught a glimpse of a shocking sight . . . lovers up on a small knoll. The evening dusk had silhouetted their forms against the sky. It was my husband and the young boy who lived a couple of trailers down the road. I had called out in disbelief. "Bob, is that you?" I loathed the memory of my husband sneaking back to the trailer on his belly hiding behind the scrub brush, hopping from one bush to the next. I was both embarrassed for him and in a state of trauma myself.

I had confronted him that very night. I entered the trailer finding him nervously sitting there looking very embarrassed and fearful of what I might do. It was then that he had promised me that he would see a psychiatrist if I would promise not to tell the boy's mother. I had been devastated for I knew nothing about homosexuality. Society still frowned on the hushed-up life style that had been smothered under the ashes of secret perversions, abuses that hadn't yet been brought to light.

I'll never forget Bob's eyes as he had stood before me outside of the psychiatrist's office on escaping from his chamber of horrors. They were red and swollen from crying. The blue veins in his pale face stuck out under the whiteness of his skin. Lines of torment cut deeply into his face. "Here I am", he had painfully sneered, " . . . this is me. Take a good look!" Then the pupils of his eyes became very black, like black pins that suddenly ignited into flashes of fiery darts spewing out hatred. "I can't change! I'm not coming back here. You do what you want, but I can't change!"

The music of the times on the radio as I'd try to distance myself from the memories which plagued me were playing songs which perfectly expressed my inner feelings so bringing it all back before me. "Are you satisfied, *really* satisfied . . . ?" the song questioned me. It was as if Bob was asking me, this question causing guilt to overcome me from having finally given in to a divorce. I hadn't known what to do. I didn't trust the priests anymore. Bob had made sure of that. It was as if he had given his will over to Satan himself from the moment I had found out his secret. "Some of my lovers are priests!" he had informed me. "In fact, there's a French priest right downtown tonight waiting for me." My own husband had seemed to enjoy watching me squirm. "There's more guys doing this than you think, ever since I was a kid . . . ", he had attempted to fill me in on how he had started in this life style. "My mom remarried for a short time when I was about nine or ten years old", he blurted out his defense.

I remembered a talk I had had with Bob's mother shortly after we were married. She had moved into our little house while we were on our honeymoon. At least I had been told it was our little house. It turned out that Bob and his mother had bought the house with his mother's money. He hadn't forgotten to tell me, but had kept from me the secret that she would live with us on weekends. Up until that time she had a live-in housekeeping job. Quite to my surprise she had quit her job and moved in bag and baggage while we were gone. The little Slovenian lady had had a terrible tussle in sharing her only living son with another woman.

This particular morning she had sat me down to have a chat. Bob had been out all night, again. I had just naively thought that he was out with the boys. I had promised myself that I wasn't going to be possessive of him like his mother was. That morning she shared with me her pain as she explained in her thick Slovenian accent that I was just barely learning to decipher. "Bobby's a bad boy. It may be partly my fault." She was trying to explain Bob's behavior to me. Now I understood what she had been trying to warn me about. I thought it was just more of her possessiveness, trying to make trouble.

She began to describe to me the most horrible week in her own life. It was the week in which she had experienced the death of her first son, Marion. She cried of the week that she had sat in the hospital day after day while they amputated his leg. She could hear her little boy screaming from excruciating pain that floated up to her from way down the hall. She couldn't escape it. The doctors and nurses would come in to her shaking their head saying that they would have to amputate it again. This happened several times until the little guy couldn't take anymore and died.

She shared with me the happenings of the day before Marion had gotten so sick. As he sat on the floor playing he had asked, "What's it like to die, Mama?" She wept as she relived that precious day, his 6th birthday. It was the last day she was able to live in peace before the pain from which she'd never recover. His foot became infected from the cheap dye in a pair of shoes they had bought him during the days of World War II. She described how she and her husband started to fight all the time. He would accuse her of not having watched the sore on the boy's foot closely enough, and she would accuse him of not buying some better quality shoes. Bob's parents had divorced from many years of fighting over Marion's death that had occurred before Bob was ever born.

As I would sit in my darkened kitchen trying to shed some light on the happenings of my marriage and the relationships therein, I found more insight each time I tossed the nightmare over in my mind. At the time when I learned of these family revelations I didn't yet have the insight to fully understand, for I hadn't yet experienced deep sorrow. But now, I saw her pain so much more vividly.

During the first year of our marriage Bob and I had taken his mom to the gravesites of her two sons. It was a short time after our first son, Robbie, was born. I hadn't yet learned of her second son who had died. That day I learned all about how he had died in infancy, again, before Bob was ever born. He had lived to be just 10 months old having been harmed in a skirmish that Bob's mother and father had had over Marion's death. The baby's brain had been damaged from the assault through the womb, an accident of reckless anger. That little boy had lived just long enough for his mother to hold him lovingly in her arms, only to lose him in death.

"Oh, God." I heaved a heavy sigh prayer as my consciousness became emersed in pain for her as I sat there feeling so alone and helpless taking another sip of the beer anesthetic. There were no thoughts, only pain for that woman. "Oh, God." My mind began working again only with more depth and understanding, reminding myself that Bob had been born after this very sad chain of events. His mother, by this time, was over-protective and shared all her love with this very, special son. His father departed not able to cope any longer with a wife who had become obsessed with her sons, in death, as well as the one who had lived.

Bob's defense for his behavior had taken place during his mother's second marriage. His mother had married a second time when he was about ten years old. He had relived those years with contempt. I had been unable to help. I had been unable to see past my own pain as he had divulged the darkness in his past to me, attempting to explain his behavior. I had ached to understand why. He had gone on with his story: "The old man used to get drunk and throw beer bottles at me. I'd hide out back in a ditch that was there, beer bottles flying over my head!" Bob's voice shook as he had recited his story. "I escaped the crap by going to church where I became an altar boy. It was like a refuge for me. A certain priest there liked me and showed me how to please him. He said he thought of me as a son, as if he were my father. (More than just his priestly title).

"Fathers don't act like that, "I had retorted. I remembered how I ran from the room holding my head from being just plain horrified.

Taking advantage of that shocking moment, off he had gone into his dark, spooky world, there in a new land where I knew no one. By now we had moved into town into a brick row house. I sat there alone on the front steps waiting up for him until the wee hours of the morning. I was in a daze attempting to figure out how my life had become so rotten. I reflected on my wedding day looking for a clue to what might've happened. Had he purposely tricked me? It had been a beautiful wedding. My three bridesmaids had worn icy-blue taffeta ankle length dresses, each of them carrying arm bouquets of roses that were shades of color a little paler than the usual deep red rose. Wrapped around their waists they wore light-rose colored cummerbunds. I felt the tears as they began to run down my cheek while I dared to remember the rest of it. Now, this big truth which I had just been evilly enlightened with had made our wedding a big farce. There had been three priests on the altar that morning. Two of them, I had been told, were Bob's "special" friends . . . blessing our marriage! "Oh, my God . . . " Years later, here I was, at my kitchen table, my head laying on my arms sobbing out the pain which was just as vivid as it had been on the day I had found out the truth. I sobbed from the realization of the whole mess. *"I don't believe we were even married in the eyes of God!"* my heart spoke to me. *"I was taken! The whole thing was a fraud!"* I pulled myself together reaching out for another beer from the refrigerator. It was the only way I could have peace. These thoughts tormented me night and day.

Events that had followed the days of enlightenment had only made things worse. I remembered back to how helpless I had felt. He knew he had me where he wanted me. "Where are you going?" I remember pleading with him one night to stay home. I was so lonely and frightened.

"It's none of your business, you filthy cunt," he grabbed his coat and ran out to the street.

There I was alone again. Whenever I'd be upset at his being out all night he would always turn the tables on me. Somehow or other he would twist things around until finally I would find myself saying, "I'm sorry." He had power over me that I didn't understand.

I had taken to walking around the block after the kids were in bed, sort of like pacing. My nerves wouldn't allow me to sit still. One night I had decided to cross over the street and walk around the block across the street which led onto the avenue. Just as I had approached the corner to turn and go down the other side of the block, Bob appeared in his car. I ignored him. I guess I just figured that I'd ignore him like he ignored me. He revved up the engine in his car and tore around the corner. I knew he was furious. I also felt he had no right to be so mad. There was a limit to what I could take as a wife, as a person, period. But, then, suddenly I became frightened. Maybe he'll turn me in for leaving the kids alone. I hadn't even thought about that. Feverishly I ran around the remainder of the block, across the street to the house. He was tearing up the stairs to the house when I grabbed him by the shirt. "I'm packing, you little slut."

"You're not leaving here again," I tugged at his shirt.

"I'm a man," he screamed. "This is a man's world. I'll do what I want and you, or God Himself, can't stop me."

My fingers were clutching at his throat. I remembered the surprise I felt when I found out how strong I was in my frenzy. I was choking him. It was as if another person was inside of me, watching me squeeze my fingers tighter and tighter. I knew I could kill him . . . the snake! He was choking. Suddenly there became a consciousness of a surprisingly bright light all around us. It was more than just the streetlights. Then I noticed the row houses setting up on the grassy banks with trees lining the streets. They stood there as a warning. My mind traveled back to that dream I had had after grandma died. "I'll kill you!" my heart had chanted. The trees were all in a line in front of those strange row houses, like I'd never seen before. My soul screamed out in moanings from deep within . . . "I possess the strength of hatred!"

The realization of the dream, the realization of what I was doing caused me to release my grip. Then, a cool silence took place. He stared up at me unable to believe what had just happened. "I saw this coming," my voice quivered. I had a strangeness about me. He was even frightened.

It all seemed like a lifetime ago. I had been so far away from home during those tormenting times as if we had been sent into a foreign country. I had become so homesick. Would I ever get to go back home? Would I want to if I could? My pride was so hurt. What would my family and friends say? What a waste. I remembered how excited I had been when the opportunity had presented itself to learn what it was like to live in a different place. The day before we had boarded the airplane to travel the full width of the nation I had felt a special need for solitude and guidance. I sighed just thinking about how naive I had been then, how excited at the promise of a new adventure . . . no idea of what I was getting into. That day I went to the church to make a visit. There was no one in there but me. It was a huge empty cathedral-like structure. Only a special warmth was there that day, a special feeling of comfort. The candles flickered through the red cups that sat in front of the altars in golden-like racks illuminating the statue in front of which I knelt. The sweet face of Mary, Jesus' mother, smiled down at me through the means of that statue which helped me to realize her beauty. This was the church I had grown up in. It had seemed like such a protective place. My first Holy Communion and Confirmation had been administered to me here, at the very railing that I was leaning on. It was where I had married Bob. It was then I chatted with God, "Are we doing the right thing? I've put our house up for sale, and tomorrow we'll be gone! My first jet air-plane trip . . . and of course a first for all the kids, too." I remember gazing up at the colorful stained glass window: a picture of the angel Gabriel talking to Mary. He was telling her that she was to become Jesus' mother. It was a reminder of my little baby girl who had hardly seen her father . . . "By tomorrow we'll all be together again," I signed off to my heavenly Friend, my God, and walked into a new life.

I had lived in the same city all my life, and here I was, back in my home town, still here in a different house, a different kitchen, a little wiser, a lot sadder and confused. I found myself trying to think of some of the less traumatic experiences I had had in that foreign place. I was actually able to smile. My eyes were gazing on the beer I had popped the cap off of, but my thoughts were with that far away city. I thought back to the many customs there which had been so different than the ones here at home. The grocery men expected money after they took the groceries to the car; the postman stopped by at Christmas time with his hand out expecting a gift. At Halloween time the children were invited into the homes they visited and given punch and cookies: a regular party at each house, and on and on.

My mind brought me back to the particular lonely night of the many when I had been waiting for Bob to come home. I had noticed that sometime around sunrise the parking strips up and down the street had been laden with interesting clutter. I surmised it was trash day. "I wish I'd known," I remembered swearing to myself under my breath realizing all of the junk I could've freed myself from. This wasn't at all like a trash day of my past experiences, but more like a garage sale. People had put out boxes of old clothing, books, nick-knacks and you-name-it. The headboard of an old bed leaned against a tree. Bundles of newspapers, neatly tied, were rustling in the cold morning breeze. As the sun was bringing a new day into being, suddenly there appeared a commotion down the street. First I watched little boys pushing grocery carts up the block filling them full of newspapers. A truck screeched around the corner, stopped quickly. The driver then piled the new found treasure on the back of it, and on to the next pile of choice junk until it finally reached the old bed which lay in the yard next to ours. Throwing the bed on board he climbed aboard the truck once more, and with a lurch started up, stopping at the next pile, and the next all up the street. There were more kids and more trucks . . . a parade! An elderly little man had joined in. He found an old hat in a box. Brushing the dirt off of it he poised it on his head slightly cocking it over one eye. His face lit up.

I chuckled as I recalled how cute that little scene had been, happy to retain some good memories of my stay in the famous old city. In fact, that morning that little scene had actually soothed my anxiety enough so that I could actually go into the house and nap. It was about then that I had noticed my nerves had turned raw. It was as if someone had taken a knife and had scraped each nerve ending until it was completely exposed . . . a feeling that still hadn't left me. Drinking beer soothed the cutting pain.

I hadn't seen Bob that day, until he had come home from work. "Woman," he had half kiddingly and half seriously demanded, "you promised to love, honor and obey!" He laughed at me as he treated it like a joke. I had kept myself very busy all that long day trying not to think of the heartache that was warring inside of me. I swore, as I got down on my hands and knees, attempting to clean every speck of dirt from the place. He tried to make me feel dirty by complaining of anything he could find to complain about. With this cruel greeting he had then continued, "Why didn't you polish the boys' beds?"

I had been learning very quickly about how tragedy and comedy were only flip sides of one coin, just as I had been taught in my drama presentation class in school. I laughingly recalled a scene that was far-out. These nightmares had been happening to me, all around me, in this strange city. It happened at a time when the city was feeling the first urges of festivity in the crisp autumn air. There was a quiet knock at the front door, almost in code. It was Sam our next door neighbor. He was a friend of Bob's, in fact, he was the one who had told Bob of their row house which had been for rent. By this time I knew that Sam was also one of them. "Can I come in?" he whispered to me in a sneaky dramatic tone. I couldn't help but notice the suitcase in his hand.

"What are you doing, leaving home?"

"Sh-h! You mustn't let my mother see me carrying this," he slipped through the door. "Where's Bob . . . Oh, hi!" He caught sight of his buddy. "Well, I did it. I got past the old lady somehow," he snickered wickedly as he walked over to the dining room where Bob was seated at the table.

"Great! Let me see what you've got!" Bob had opened the suitcase with great ceremony. "You didn't forget anything, did you?" They both grinned as they bent over the suitcase fingering each piece of clothing.

"I keep this stuff from year to year. Halloween time, you know", he made the excuse to me. "It makes my mother terribly mad. That's why I have to sneak around like this. See? I even shaved my arms and legs. Look here . . . " he brought his face closer to me so I could see clearly. "Do you see any eyebrows? I shaved them, too. They were too frizzy."

"What in heaven's name are you guys up to?" I already knew the answer.

"Sam's going to dress up here. He's got a date tonight," Bob winked. "Watch him. Maybe you'll learn a little about putting on makeup. He's a beautician, you know, and a darn good makeup artist."

I knew they were just trying to make me mad. I figured I'd just play along with their little game and see where it led. "Let me have that wig," I toyed with them, "I always wanted to try one on." Standing in front of the mirror I tried to arrange it properly all the while attempting to appear unshaken. "I don't like it. I guess the style suits you much better."

The guys raised their eyebrows at each other wondering what I was up to.

"It's OK if I get dressed in your kitchen, then?" Sam asked.

"Sure. Be my guest. Doesn't everyone get dressed in the kitchen?"

He humbly thanked me as he awkwardly slipped into the kitchen gingerly closing the door behind him. There were a few awkward suspenseful moments . . . moments in which neither Bob or I said a word. We just waited in silence. Then Sam called out the door. "Are you ready for the style show? Are you? Huh?"

"We're ready," I teased back in a "saccharin sweet voice".

"Here I come," he peeped around the doorway. "Ready or not . . . "

Out the door he pranced . . . a six-foot tall floozy. He had on a short sexy black dress, his legs bowed, ankles wobbling . . . wearing a pair of very high-heeled shoes. "Aren't they chic?" He twirled around the room. "Aren't I beautiful?" he squealed delightedly. His head hit the chandelier. "Oh, you naughty!" he scolded the light fixture grabbing on to it to keep from falling. "What do you think, Pat?"

"Well, let's face it. Your gams leave something to be desired, but all in all you look lo-o-vely." I made fun of him very subtly.

"Do you think my dress is out of style this year?"

He was so ridiculous I couldn't keep from laughing. "Oh, basic black is always in," I waved my hands to him, flopping them in dainty fashion. He reminded me of a chicken strutting around the room without her feathers. "You'll either knock them out or knock them dead," I added.

"I do look pretty sexy, don't I?" With his little finger he smoothed the painted lines above his eyes. "Oh, Sam. You're gorgeous!" Just then his smile faded as he plopped himself down on a footstool. "Oh, drat these things," he swore flinging his left leg up in the air. "My girdle won't reach my nylons and they keep slipping loose. It's one of those merry widow, one-piece things. No give. It sure pulls in my waist, though." He arose to get a good look in the mirror. "This is a gas," he tittered, " . . . isn't it?" he turned to Bob.

"It's different, all right. Let's go out for awhile and see how it goes over," Bob grabbed Sam by the arm.

My heart skipped, or sank, or something, for now I knew what they'd been up to. They wanted to see just how much I could take. "What are you going to use for a coat?" I continued to play their little game. I figured I'd just shock them and make them wonder what I was up to. *I'll not get mad, no I'll not get mad* . . . I repeated to myself over and over.

"Here it is." He pulled out a mangy fur jacket. Part of the fur was so matted it appeared to have holes in it.

"Oh, Sam! You can't wear that old thing. You look so beautiful; you'll mess up the effect. Here, wear my stole." I pulled out my phony gray fur from the closet. "It looks much better with the dress, anyhow."

"Thanks, Pat. Wow! I'm hot to trot tonight!"

They rushed through the door hollering, "Don't wait up for us."

I slammed the door on the two creeps barely making it through the ordeal. I tried to tell myself I didn't care but deep down I was hurting probably more than I had ever in my life. I think that the reason why I hurt so much was to see my husband, whom I knew had some wonderful qualities, cheapen not only himself but our relationship in this way. But then suddenly, the sight of Sam in that outfit became very funny. I started giggling which soon gave way to hysterical laughter, then uncontrollable tears. Sam looked so silly: so tall, so awkward. Some gorgeous broad!

They received not the love of the truth
That they might be saved.
For this cause God shall send them
STRONG DELUSION
That they shall believe a lie:
That they all might be damned
Who believed not
The truth,
But had pleasure
In unrighteousness.

2 Thes 2:11-12 (KJ)

Chapter Two

City of Brotherly Love

Bob had taken pity on me. I was now drinking down my sorrows in this God forsaken state of confusion feeling mighty stupid for actually having believed that at that time. I was finding out the clarity that hindsight offers to a person . . . or was it experience? After a chug-a-lug of beer, I dared to mull over the period of my enlightenment concerning Bob's strange lifestyle. "Let's go out on the town," Bob had actually offered to take me out on a date.

We had started the evening out having cocktails at a hotel bar in town. There were several guys there that he knew. We were invited to sit with a very pleasant fellow whose hair was cut in a short butch and was looking mighty suave in his colorful red vest. "This is your wife?" he then politely introduced himself. I supposed that he was one of them. Evidently, I was now getting somewhat used to the idea.

The nicest part of the evening was going to the famous Peppermint Lounge. I guess I appreciated it so much because it was something nice that Bob did for me. For one thing, I had never experienced live entertainment before. And a delightful experience it was! The group was made up of singers who were of color, and they were really swinging! They even called some people up on the stage to help them sing their hep music. Being black entertainers, their music was a cross between soul and rock and roll. One of the guys even motioned for me to get up there and join them. Deep down I really wanted to (something inside of me was dying to become awakened), but I was glad that Bob had shook his head no because the three young women who climbed up on the stage were delightfully singing their soul music which was second nature to their roots.

Saving me probably from a very embarrassing moment up on the stage, he decided it was time to show me the surprise he had saved for later—the "piece de resistance"!.As I thought back to that night after all the things that took place, I now realized that he had waited until I had become tipsy then driven me to a quaint little tavern, all as in a plan. All I remembered were the red and yellow shutters that decorated either side of the windows. A thatched roof sloped down to create an awning above the red and black door. "This is cute," I giggled a little tipsy giggle. "It has personality!"

"Yeah, and then some!" Bob's eyes showed a mischievous sparkle. "I come here quite a bit. I'll introduce you to some of my friends."

As we made ourselves used to the dim lighting inside we were greeted at the door by a sickening sweet voice saying "Hi!". I looked up into two eyes fluttering long false lashes at me, a cigarette protruding between big lips coated in a thick layer of purple lipstick. "Hi, there sweetie," the voice repeated. On looking closer I saw that it was a man's face . . . rouged and powdered. His long black hair hung immaculately in pageboy style. A wide silver cummerbund was tied around his waist which had a blouse tucked in it. It was a white blouse . . . an off-the-shoulder thing covered with white sequins. He had on black slacks: ordinary men's slacks. It all seemed so creepy! I cringed as we allowed this person to seat us at a booth. His tall six-foot body had towered over me in his black high heels. "Ish," I remember whispering to Bob. "What was that?"

"You haven't seen nothing yet," he laughed. "He sure is something, isn't he? I knew you'd get a charge out of this place. Let's order a beer," he signaled the bartender. "Two beers here."

"Yeah, OK," I muttered obediently. "I'll try anything once. Well, not anything . . . "

"Here you are, sweet pea," that voice surprised me from behind this time. Chills went up and down my spine. I then saw that "he?" was poised with pencil and pad in hand ready to take an order.

"That's the waitress?" I asked Bob. "That . . . *it*?"

"What are you doing in here with her?" the "it" stooped down to whisper to Bob.

"That's my wife," Bob grinned as he pointed across the table at me.

"You're wife? You've got to be kidding. That's crazy man, crazy." "It's" long hairy arm reached across the table showing his huge hand which was adorned with bright purple nail polish. The gaudish hand placed a table setting neatly. My stomach squirmed as the "it" walked away swinging his hips from side to side.

"Boy, he thinks he's a sexpot, doesn't he?" I tried to laugh it off as I bravely looked around the dimly lit room. There were couples scattered here and there sitting in booths heads bowed in intense conversation. On the dance floor were two figures dancing close. Then I realized, "Those are two guys dancing together!" I bellowed out loud.

"Shhh!" Bob held his finger across his lips. "Sure. They're in love", he whispered. "Actually, they're married," he explained with a chuckle. "They're in here all the time."

"Oh, brother," I blurted out my biggest fear. "Is that the type of things you do when you're out all night?"

"No, I'm not like that," he confided. "See those girls over there?"

"Is that a girl?" I squinted attempting to see more clearly in the dark room. This was the previous shock in reverse. One girl was dressed like a girl in pants, but the other one looked just like a man: men's shoes, a man's belt, man's haircut, man's shirt . . . more than that, mannish actions. "Are they like that, too?"

"Sure. They're what you call lesbians. They live together

across the street. Do you want to meet them? They could explain more to you . . . "

"What do you mean by that?"

"You, know . . . maybe they'll like you . . . "

"Do you want me to be like them? No wipe that out. Forget it," the fear of hearing the answer to that question was too much. I quickly chugged down a couple of last gulps of beer. Bob didn't say anything. I was feeling very conspicuous for I was the only different one in the place. "Everyone else seems to be more married than we are," I rashly commented. "I can't believe this is happening. I just can't believe it. Let's go!" I grabbed my purse. "I've had enough of this place."

It was a downhill battle after that. To this very moment it sickens me to think of how we clashed head on, each one thinking that his own agenda was the most important. I had felt that my body had sickened him and that he had tricked me to marry him so I could produce him children. I felt betrayed! I became violent! One night in a rage I ripped my clothes off saying, "I make you sick, don't I?"

He had reacted with a hypocritical emotion, "I never thought my wife would behave in such a way!" I thought I was losing my mind. He knew he was upsetting me and enjoyed it for he had never forgiven me for finding out his secret. It was a part of his life that either I had no business in, or he would rub my nose in it trying to make me wish I had never found out.

The climax was one night when he pretended to want to fondle me as a woman (which he never did). The change in behavior had given me hopes that perhaps he was going to try to overcome the problem. My heart melted as I had turned over to kiss him, wanting to stop the stupid war and let him know I was willing to try."I think I'll go over to see Sam!"

He shot up out of bed. I can't express how I felt. He had made a fool of me. He had been cruel to me. I screamed. I tore into a rage standing up on the bed and flinging myself on him like the scenes in the cowboy movies when the hero jumps off the table onto the bad guy.

"Why, why . . . why do you do this to me, you goddamn fairy?" I struggled in the memory of the whole ugly scene. I figured that I must've been almost crazy that night as we fell to the floor struggling. He slapped my face. "You fairy, you fairy, you fairy," I laughed at him. I continued asking for more, "You little creepy fairy," I laughed again and again. I could still feel the sting for he had slapped me over and over because I had laughed hysterically in his face over and over. "Keep it up, you little fairy." Finally he had had enough. He got up standing over me, breathing hard.

"I'll see you sometime."

He got dressed and slammed out the door. I lay in a daze but feeling unbelievably happy. I remember thinking, *at least he has some feelings for me, even if it is hatred . . . he hates me.* It was some kind of relief or was it just a release? Whatever it was I remember laying there feeling a sense of contentment.

But, the next morning I weathered a frightful experience. It was then that I knew I had to get some help. I could hear little Betsy crying. It was time to go get her. I could barely remember that the boys had already left for school. They must've gotten themselves off. I wondered faintly if they had heard the commotion the night before. *We can't go on like this.*

I shook my head as I groggily walked into her room and stood there beside the crib. A terrible helplessness overcame me. I couldn't pick her up! The thought of even touching anyone at all made my stomach queasy. I was so frightened wondering what in the world was the matter with me. I winced thinking of the night before. I felt so helpless. I had to take care of my baby. I prayed, "Oh God, help me! If you're there, please help me. My baby needs me. I can't pick her up. I can't hold her." I sat there on the floor in the corner of the room all hunched up, sobbing, remembering back to the day that she was born. She had been born during the famous Columbus Day storm . . . a storm that ravaged the whole Pacific Coast. "Betsy came in with a storm," I remember thinking it was so peculiar. She was born during a storm . . . not only on her birthday, but in the middle of this storm which was havocking our lives. During my laughter/tears I also remembered that the young woman next to me in the hospital had named her baby Stormy C.!"That's what I should've named Betsy," I cried. "Little Stormy C." I laughed when I remembered the little nun who had screamed in terror over that name.

"Stormy C.! That's a terrible name!" she had told the mother.

"Who asked you?" the young woman sassed. Sister had left the room all in a dither.

Now, in the middle of my life's biggest storm, I sat there crouched on the floor in her room for an hour or so in numbness repeating a little prayer. "Sleep, baby sleep."

That horrendous incident caused a sort-of truce. Bob attempted to become more of a homebody, that is, he stuck around home once in awhile. However, Sam still lived next door. This particular night he noticed that Sam was out walking his little dog and went out to join him. Immediately, my body gave me all the warning signals. My nerves started feeling raw, I was unable to concentrate on what I was doing. I thought I heard a door close next door out back. There was no way I could run around the house to see what was going on over there because each house was attached to the other one. My head told me not to make waves, but my heart told me that something was terribly wrong.

I peeked down the block to see if I could spot them. My heart sank as I realized that they had disappeared. I continued to hope that they had just gone around the block. After an hour or so I walked around the block, myself. They were nowhere in sight. I was positive that they were together in Sam's house.

Then I got a bright idea. Maybe I could hear something through the wall from Betsy's room. I knew that the bedroom was there because Sam's house was exactly the same as ours was, only the floor plan was in reverse. I went into little Betsy's room to see if I could hear anything. I could barely hear men's soft voices talking but couldn't quite make it out. I wanted to believe it was just my imagination. Then I remembered an old trick that I learned as a kid. I found a water glass in the bathroom just across the hall and held it to the wall. The voices were speaking very softly. In fact, I heard more than I had wanted to hear. I fumbled the glass! It fell to the floor. Then I heard a loud "Shhh" and a commotion like someone shuffling around. I knew I had blown it. In a frenzy, I banged the glass against the wall hoping to flush them out as a bird hunter does with his prey. As I ran for the stairway, I could hear a jumbled sound of footsteps scrambling on the other side of the wall . . . the footsteps loud and frantic. I nearly slipped from running so fast. Out the front door, then I leaped one giant jump over to Sam's—from our porch to Sam's porch. My fists banged on the door. I uncontrollably shouted, "Open this door! Open this damn door!"

"What's going on here? We just got home . . . " Sam's mother hesitantly opened her door.

"Where are they?" I whined.

"What are you talking about?" she answered quietly.

Suddenly I felt very foolish. "You know they were up there. They were together in the bedroom."

"Dear, what are you talking about?" She led me into her front room. "There's no one there. Do you want to take a look?"

"Yes, I do," I shyly took her up on it. The woman calmly showed me to one room, then another room, much as a mother would show a child that there was no Boogieman in the house. The bedroom was very neat. Almost too neat. "See?" she pointed to the bed. "No one's been there."

"I heard them running down the stairs," I stammered. Then I began blubbering like a baby from embarrassment. I honestly felt as though I was losing my mind.

"You were just hearing things, dear. Go home and try to relax. I'll sit with you until you calm down."

She followed me to my house and did just that. Nothing much was said, just an older woman trying to be supportive to a younger woman. After awhile she left. But all was not well. I started to cry. I was all mixed up. *What if I had been hearing things? Or maybe he's trying to drive me crazy. Oh God, I can't stand it!.* I literally felt like pulling my own hair out of my head. *For better or worse!*

I began laughing hysterically. *Yeah, live in hell!* For the first time in my life I began to doubt the existence of a God. The doubts were overwhelming. It was all such a nightmare. I couldn't quit sobbing. I knew I needed some help. *Maybe if I go talk to Father. Maybe he'll talk to Bob, or something.*

One glance in the mirror before I left the house told horror stories. My eyes were all red and signs of broken blue blood vessels had appeared under them. I was a little frightened to go to see father because I had never met him. I just went to church there every Sunday staying to myself in my state of anxiety. I knew that he didn't know me from Adam. The kids were sound asleep. I wasn't thinking very straight. I had never left my children alone, but I figured Bob must be nearby somewhere.

The rectory was all dark. It was about 9:30 in the evening. The house sat way back behind some large overgrown bushes and trees which caused a spooky feeling as I slowly walked up to the door. A little light shone from the parlor which gave me confidence that the hour was not too late for such a call. One soft knock and the door opened. "What do you want at this hour?" the priest asked gruffly. "It had better be important."

"It is, Father. It's my husband."

"You bothered me because of that? Lady, you go home and make up with him. I'm nearly ready to go to bed."

I remember feeling like I was in a daze. I was too upset to be embarrassed. I was too upset to argue. I just turned and left. As I started back down the walkway he called out after me. "Come back tomorrow," I know he had begun to regret his attitude.

"Don't worry, Father, I won't be back. Just don't worry about me ever bothering you again with my little problems. I won't ever be back!" I walked out the gate. He waved his arm a little then quietly, rather sheepishly closed the door.

That night I walked away, from the Church, from God, Himself. I walked for blocks, many blocks. Thoughts of the children ran through my head just long enough to convince myself that Bob was home by now. It seemed to me that everyone else was doing as they darn pleased. What difference did anything make anymore? I felt a relief as I reached a well lit tavern and I swung through its friendly doors. "A beer please," I ordered from the friendly bartender. "In fact, make it three."

"All at once?" he shared a teasing grin.

"Yeah, might as well. They won't last long." I was talking real brave, but then my phony sureness turned to tears that began streaming down my cheeks. I chug-a-lugged the beers.

"A beer for the lady," a fellow nearby had watched the beers disappear. He hailed the bartender.

"No, thanks," I shunned him, nose in the air. "I'm not the best of company tonight."

"Come now, it can't be all that bad," he pulled up a stool.

"Oh, yeah? Try me." I felt very much like a mystery woman, no name, no address, just a sad, confusing story. His friendly nature finally prompted me to take advantage of the opportunity to just let it all out. By the time I finished my ramblings, the bar closed. The evening had absorbed the hurt that I had been feeling for weeks: endless, torturous weeks. I looked on this nice fellow as a good friend. What a comfort he was even though we were both feeling our booze. Fate had made us friends. He was someone who cared.

I ended up at his apartment. It was a comfortable place, not at all fancy, just a well lived in room with a bed off to the side. He kicked off his shoes cuddling up to me as he chit-chatted probably nonsensically. We enjoyed just being silly, laying there giggling over stupid jokes, making stupid statements about the sad state the world was in. A sip of beer, then a kiss . . . a long kiss. "Come on, let's take off this dress of yours," he started to undress me. He had already managed to shed his pants "for comfort".

"No. I don't think so. I can't trust my judgement tonight," my eyes pleaded with him. "I really do like you. Don't mess it up."

"I won't push you," his voice was very tender as he leaned over to kiss me.

My mind floated away in the warmth of his caresses. My brain was going in circles, trying, trying to beam in on something . . . a message. What was it? Yes, a voice from the past. Words, familiar words began to emerge into my consciousness. I could hear them. They kept coming, drowning out the sighs of heavy breathing. "Be careful, dear. Be very, very careful," they whispered to me.

"Grandma!" I suddenly cried out as I sat up straight in the bed. Quickly, strongly I pushed him away. "I have to go home! I'm sorry. I have to leave!" I busied myself gathering my belongings putting them back on my body where they belonged.

"Oh, come on now. We were just getting comfortable," he pleaded.

"I'm sorry. I have to go. Don't worry, I'll walk home."

"No you won't," he sprang to his feet. "I'll take you. It's no bother." He stepped into his trousers. "I like you, you know," he gave me a little kiss on the nose. "Come on. Everything will be OK."

I arrived home about 5 o'clock in the morning to complete quiet. The kids were safe and sound in their beds. Bob was sound asleep. He didn't even notice that I had come home. I sneakily slipped under the covers and lay down beside him. "Hi," he greeted me. Then he rolled over and went to sleep. He never even asked me where I'd been.

The next day after Bob had taken off quietly to go to work, I saw the kids off to school and then decided to go to the store. I put Betsy in the stroller and started down the street. A car with two men in it began driving very slowly next to me barely keeping up with my fast pace which was getting faster and faster. I became a little nervous at first, but then I looked in the car. There he was . . . my friend!.I remember smiling to myself as I noticed that the car was an official gas company car. Knowing this about him reassured me that he was a responsible guy. I quietly liked him all the more.

"Is everything OK?" he leaned over the front seat to the window.

"Yeah, I guess." Then I could've bit my tongue. The dutiful words just rolled out. "I've decided to try to stick it out, I think."

"Oh," he replied slowly.

"I have to try," I pleaded for him to understand.

"Yeah, I guess . . . well, good-bye."

"Good-bye", I wanted to cry as the car drove away. I knew I would never see him again.

The leaves were piling up in the parking lot showing that Jack Frost was busy painting beautiful fall days. I had realized that the kids did know that something wasn't right at home, but they didn't know what it was. The first real sign of their distress was when Robbie had made a horrible scene one day at school. A matter of acting out his helplessness over a situation that he only perceived, but knew nothing about. He had taken all of the Sister's books and materials that were neatly placed on her desk and wiped them off of her desk in one big swoop. We had enrolled him in a parochial school that was very close by. Blake had been going to kindergarten in a public school being as how the Catholic schools didn't have kindergarten. Bob did take the responsibility of taking the afternoon off from work to go to have a talk with Robbie's teacher. However, of course, he didn't tell Sister what really was going on.

There were also fond memories of the kids at that time, though. I was thankful I had some good memories of this period of my life. I giggled a little as I remembered back to Halloween time. I had been so embarrassed when the boys' had been invited into the homes for punch and cookies. Robert was dressed as a witch which was OK, but I had dressed Blake up as a scarecrow. The straw that my expensive china dishes had been packed in on the long trip to the East Coast had prompted my creativity. I had stuffed straw down his neck and up his sleeves. What a great idea until I saw the trail of straw he had left in each home as he was invited in. There I was dying from embarrassment saying, "I didn't know you invited them into your homes here. Back home we didn't do that."

It was also good to think about some of Bob's strengths. It made me feel less of a fool. He was a good disciplinarian. Bob had brought home a couple of pumpkins for the kids. There was one very very large one and a small medium one and a itsy bitsy one for Betsy who had just had her first birthday. She was a very pretty little dishwater blonde with a very quiet demeanor, content to just watch the "big show" which her brothers put on for her day after day. Robert, the oldest, had been using his "big brother" strengths of manipulation quite a bit, lately, not wanting to share. One thing that Bob and I did agree on, which was quite rare these days, was that little Blake should get the big pumpkin for a change. Robbie was quite offended at first but did take it quite well, eventually. However, Blake was in a state of shock. "My b-i-i-ig pumpkin!" he cackled. "I'm going to take my big pumpkin up to my room". He rolled it over to the stairway. It was almost as big as he was. He grunted and groaned as he pushed the pumpkin up each step. "My b-i-i-g pumpkin," he said over and over in a comical manner. It was the first sign of what a good sense of humor he had. It was a lesson of love for both of them.

Except for these little excerpts of family life the empty days and empty nights had become the norm for me. The cold war between us had brought into our lives a daily routine with as little communication as possible. The telephone broke the silence. The emptiness turned into shocking news. "She's dead. She died early this morning." Bob's mother had been very sick, but still it was a shock to hear of her death.

"Let me have the phone," Bob cut in. He talked very low taking it all in slowly. By the time he had hung up the phone he was very upset, groping his way out to the front porch to fall into a lawn chair out there. I followed him out there for I knew the unusual bond that they had had.

"Are you all right?" I sat down beside him trying to break through the silence. Instead we just sat there together in a colder silence than ever. As the night crept in on us I attempted to fill in the stillness by counting the stars flickering overhead. Huge sobbings suddenly broke the deadlock.

"She's gone!" His feelings began to flood. He could hardly catch his breath between the anguished sighs. Then abruptly the sobbings stopped. "You might as well have killed her," he poked me in the chest.

"I what?" I asked sharply.

"You killed her. If you hadn't married me she'd be alive right now. She never was the same after we got married."

"Oh, Bob. You're not ever going to make me believe that. You're the one who asked me to marry you. I didn't kill your mother. If you remember, you wanted to get away from her possessiveness." I tried to remind him of the way it was.

Bob had two older sisters besides the two deceased brothers. The oldest one had been born in the old country a good decade before he came along, and the younger sister was just a few years older than Bob. Evidently she was born in the middle of all the turmoil. "Remember when you and your sisters had asked me to bathe her? They told us that she had wanted me to do it. She knew that I cared about her."

I didn't tell him what really had happened. Her children had been treating her like a little baby. I could sense why she wanted me to bathe her. She wanted to do it herself. The rest of them had hurriedly placed her in the tub, washing and drying her and then setting her out in her cleanliness to sit around doing nothing. They thought "doing for her" was a loving gesture. She hated it! I remember the fun we had had as she played with the soap as a little child would do. She slowly rubbed the soapy suds over her body rinsing herself off from the drippings of the wash rag as she held it over her head. She was having fun. Her mind had been getting more and more demented, her language going back to that of her childhood. I remembered how she had smiled up at me saying, "You. You're the one who always understood." At that moment there had been a special bond between us. I had even grown to love her. And, believe it or not, she had even grown to love me.

The last time I saw her was just before we had left the West Coast. We had brought little Betsy to visit. By that time Josephine had ended up at the mental hospital. I had always felt it was from lack of purpose. She was calling everyone Patti that day. The nurses, the attendants, even the custodian woman who was busily mopping up the floor near where she sat. I felt then and still do that she was trying to tell me she was sorry, for now I knew that she had known Bob's problem all along.

I began to focus in on the conversation with my bereaved husband. "I did dislike her an awful lot in the beginning, she was so possessive. But Bob, I did grow to understand her. I think I even grew to love her." After that I just sat down on the front steps knowing that I had said enough. A fullness welled up in my heart as it reached far off . . . far off into another reality. It was as if my soul had united to death, to life . . . to all.

> "Why had he hurt me so much? Where was his soul?" It was in his beginning, influenced by his mother.
>
> Her actions would say to me, "Why did you take my little boy away from me? He's all I have in the world to replace my pain. I want to hold him to my breast forever and ever. He's my baby."

All of the happenings, the sufferings began to make a certain sense. A cause. A purpose. The words kept flowing into my heart authored by the unknown . . .

> She handed her world to me. She began to feel useless. It was a slow death. She became more and more helpless. "I want to be of some use," she had begged. I saw that she was growing in spirit through her suffering. The enemy took all of her worldly possessions. She looked down on him as she raised herself up over the suffering with wisdom. "I will use this time to know God." Her desire had saved her. The enemy had jailed her. "Please don't leave me all alone," she had pleaded, but found that she wasn't alone. Her God, her Friend, was there to help her. She had become as a beautiful child.

Suddenly I was brought back to the present for Bob had left and gone upstairs to be alone. It was late. As I climbed into bed with him hoping to be able to relieve some of his pain by just being there beside him he gave in to his deepest emotions. "Mamma", he cried. "I'm sorry I left you. Please forgive me. Oh, I'm so mixed up!"

He cried like a baby. More and more I became aware that his cruelty stemmed from his confusion: he felt guilty about things which weren't wrong, and he felt no guilt about things that were very disturbing to God. His head buried into the pillow. "I wish I had never heard of sex. Sex!.Sex!.Mamma, please, I just want to be buried next to you. Mamma, Mamma."

His ability to finally express the trauma he had felt within gave him strength to cope. The family made it possible for him to fly home with the aid of what little money his mother had saved in her lifetime. While he was gone I tried to get myself together a little bit more, hoping against hope that with my new understanding of his problems and his having buried his mother, that somehow things would be different. I just attended to the kids and forgot about all of the problems. Actually, I functioned quite well having been freed from the constant turmoil of emotional pain I had felt while he was with us.

The day finally came, though, when he called from the airport announcing that he would be taking the 5 PM subway. I was surprised to find that I was even anxious to see him and that I had missed him. I still had hopes that there was something left of the man whom I thought I had married. I think that I had new hope that the worst was over and we could start anew. I raced down the sidewalk to greet him as soon as he came into sight. I just wanted him to know that we were there for him and that I wanted to try to make things work. Bob was a little surprised at my new tender feelings, also.

Things seemed to be OK for awhile until one night as I waited up for him, the first time in a couple of weeks, I heard something at the front door. I opened it to find Bob standing there bloodied from head to foot. "Someone jumped me!" He fell into the house. I helped him into bed half dragging him and half encouraging him. Then I washed him up. I knew he had received his injuries from probably announcing his affections to the wrong party.

All the while I tended to him I began remembering back to the night when he had been stabbed by a hitchhiker. It was as if a brick had fallen on my head to knock some sense into me. "I'll bet the guy who stabbed him was disgusted at Bob's unwanted advances!" The incident clarified inside of me. My mind raced to the scene in the hospital . . .

I had been eight and a half months pregnant with little Blake, our second son, that horribly upsetting night. In fact, the nurses were all set to wheel me up to delivery until I made them understand that I was there to see my husband who had been stabbed. I will say that he had been very concerned about my condition during that ordeal. However, a few days later after he had become a celebrity, since the whole incident was on the front page of the newspaper, his whole demeanor had changed back to his cocky old self. I happened to be visiting him when a plain-clothed policeman came to question Bob about the incident. I remember at the time that I had felt that there was something amiss. I didn't know what it was—just a feeling. Bob was getting a little huffy about all the questions until finally he blurted out, "You know, you're talking to a pretty important guy, here. I'm going to be running for public office this next election." Bob winked at me. It was the first I'd heard of it.

He did just that, too. Quite frankly I was surprised as to how well he did in the election. I should've known then. Whenever we had gone to a function as husband and wife, he would always disappear and leave me standing or sitting there all alone. He would disappear for hours. The night of the Kennedy's Inaugural Ball put on by the Young Democrats for the county, I had sat in the kitchen of the huge ballroom with the Secretary of State and his wife sitting on the counter waiting for Bob to show up. They had been so nice. I had just told myself he was "politicing" since he was the president of the Young Democrats Club. Now I pondered it over in this more enlightened state, *I wonder if they knew what Bob was up to? Maybe they all knew.* My mind then raced to the memory of the Governor's Ball. As we had made our way through the receiving line the wife of the Secretary of Insurance had leaned over to me whispering, "You're the prettiest one here tonight". At the time I was very pleased, I also knew it wasn't true. But now, now I knew why. *They all knew!* I had stood there on the sidelines that whole evening waiting for Bob until finally, he showed up quickly whisking me out of there, away from it all. For some reason that night was the end of his political career.

As I began piecing the memories of our marriage together I became aware that Bob was a very sick man. This last episode had warned me of the danger that we were in. Bob was evidently completely out of control with his addiction.

Things happened so fast that it was as if I was in a daze. I wrote to my mother. It's so humiliating telling her about Bob's problem, but not about the priests. I just can't bring myself to divulge the "terrible secret".

Looking back at that time my thoughts were blurry. Even these years later, sitting alone in my kitchen rolling thoughts around in my brain hour after hour I began to realize that, perhaps, I still hadn't recovered from the shock of it all. Or maybe it was the fact that my drinking for that evening had clouded my thoughts that were racing through my mind.

Recalling the politics that we'd been involved in brought to memory a very special day, one in which everyone who lived in this country remembers with clarity, a calamity which this country would never recover from. It occurred right at the crucial time when we were back there on the East Coast experiencing the breakdown of our marriage. I was stirring the dough of a cake I was preparing for little Robbie's 6th birthday as I was watching TV. The newsman broke into the program to say, "President Kennedy has been shot!"

Almost as quickly, I heard a knock on my front door. It was a friend from across the street. "Did you hear the news?" she held her hands to her mouth in horror. I had been so thankful, especially that day, for a friendship that God had evidently arranged for me at that time. This young woman from across the street had begun to hover over me. She had known of the pain I was going through because she was Sam's ex-wife. I was so grateful for the day when she had unveiled her secret to me. She was now remarried and had several children. She had divulged to me the terrible emotional pain Sam had experienced when she was married to him. He had actually stuck his head in their gas oven and turned the gas on trying to end it all. This new trauma, the commotion that was going on in front of the whole country, had brought this new friend to me where we could share the shock of the times together. I've always felt guilty for not having written to her after I left there, but things were so awful and I was so confused, it had all been so difficult.

After a few days when the death of the president had settled deep down in our groanings, Bob suggested that we go to the capitol to pay our respects. Hours become very blurred. The days become more and more difficult. There was trauma everywhere. We arrived at the capital about 3 AM. Bob was telling the officers overseeing the huge crowd of people that he had come clear from Washington State with his family. Exaggerating as usual, he filled them in on the fact that he had been the chairman of the Kennedy for President Club (allowing them to believe that it was a statewide club instead of just for the county). He showed the officer his honorary sheriff's badge he had received when he had run for public office, probably more impressed with himself than by anyone else.

The officer gave me a glare as though I were nuts for taking the three little kids, Betsy all bundled up in her stroller, there in freezing weather in the wee hours of the morning. He let us pass through, anyhow. We managed to get inside of the capitol after carrying the stroller up all of the steps to see Kennedy's casket. (I just found out, 30 years later that this was Betsy's first memory. She described to me the huge steps wishing she could run up them like her big brothers did. It's hard to believe because she was just barely one year old!) As we got close to the casket Bob snapped a picture (even though it was against the laws of the moment). I found that I'd lost Betsy's bottle. I located it in the possession of the security officers who were nesting underneath the steps of the capitol building.

Hundreds of people were standing in line for hours and hours being astonishingly quiet. The reverence was impressive. I had feelings of guilt from getting in front of them, but I was also happy that we didn't have to stand out there for hours with a little baby to worry about.

The drive back from the capitol was splotchy. I remembered counting the pennies to pay for the many toll bridges and turnpikes. It was during that trek that I discovered why they call the highways "free" ways out west.

When we got home there was a letter from my mother. She was devastated about my problems, (but not as devastated as if she had been informed of the whole truth). Her advice was to go see the parish priest. I took her up on her advice. This time I dealt with the handsome young priest. He was friendly, but rather passive. He didn't even bat an eye when I told him about the problem, and what Bob had told me about the priests being involved. He swept my shocking statements under the rug advising, "You need to find some activity for yourself." This was his only consolation.

I joined the bowling team at the church that he helped to arrange for me. Snow was piling up in huge drifts. I remember having to walk over huge snowdrifts in order to get from one street to the next just to get to the church's bowling lanes. I remember very little about the women, or the bowling. I just remember they were very good to me.

Some God forsaken hour during this time little Blake came into the house frozen, his face blue, falling to the floor crying, "He sat on me, he sat on me!".I found out that a young boy in the neighborhood had buried him in the snow, then laid on top of him. I was frantic and angry. I approached the boy's mother. I received very little understanding or kindness. They, the neighbors, had begun to snub me!

I got another letter from Mom that contained the address and phone number to call a priest who was extremely good at counseling in the downtown area. In order to get there I had to learn to take the subway. I was thankful I had the opportunity to experience the subways that I had only seen in movies. I was amazed as to how neatly they were planned right underneath the heart of the city. I was so relieved how very caring and friendly the priest was... someone to lean on. He explained to me that it was not Bob whom I hated, but the things that he did. I baked fruitcakes for Christmas being careful to give one to Father. I get caught not only in the Christmas rush, but I get stuck down on the avenue with too many packages to carry. A huge snowstorm causes traffic to come to a stand still. Bob refuses to come and get me. I took the taxi home.

Happy memories of the kids on Christmas morning came flooding into my heart: Robert with his train set, Blake with his Viking ship that actually sailed across the room and Betsy's sweet smile as she held her first little baby doll.

The holidays were over. I found a "private" letter in the mailbox addressed to Bob. Feeling entitled to open it due to the situation I was in, I found it an enlightening experience. I'm glad I opened it . . . it was from a lover. I felt helpless in the matter so I went to see my counselor priest. He asked if he might be able to talk to Bob. Bob refused at first, but then he finally did go to see the priest.

The next thing I knew, Bob came dashing through the door actually on time getting home from work. "Guess what?" he danced me around the floor. "You won't believe it . . . we're going to move!"

I winced. The astonishing news made me a little afraid to find out where it would be . . . "Timbuctu"? I retorted in jest.

"Nope, guess again," he teased. "We're going back home. I'm being transferred back home!"

"How did that happen?" Sarcasm took over. It seemed very peculiar that he got himself transferred just as soon as he went and talked to the priest . . . *something's fishy* . . . I warned myself. I knew that he had told the priest about his secret attempting to thrust some "shock therapy" on Father.

"I think I got in a little over my head at work. They decided they needed me back on my old job."

The phone rang. It was the priest wanting to make an appointment to see me. "We're going to be moving back home . . . "

I surprised him with the news. "When?" I cupped my hand over the receiver asking Bob.

"Soon. Very soon . . . maybe in a week", he whispered.

"I don't think I'll be able to see you again." I announced the decision I had to make. "How did it go with Bob?"

"Well, there are some things we just can't do much about . . . " Father sounded very sad, even helpless. "Good luck . . . and God bless your precious little family."

The excitement of Bob's news had put the hidden letter on the back burner until things calmed down. Then I shared the news with him. "I have something that you'd better look at." I had found just the right moment. "Has this anything to do with the reason they're sending you home?" I threw it across the room at him.

He began to chuckle nervously as he read it. However, he also blushed. Thinking back to all the hours I had spent with my husband I think it was the only time I had ever seen him blush. "Oh, that nut! He's just a tease," Bob tried to pooh-pooh the incident.

"What's the 'love Tom' part mean?

"Lots of people sign their names like that," he explained. "He's just giving me a bad time."

"Who is he?"

"He's a salesman who comes in from an outside company to sell to our company."

"They found out, didn't they?" I blew up at him.

"Found out what?"

You can't lie out of this one!

"Let's just go back home and start over. Pick up the pieces. I'll really try, I promise."

I didn't pry any farther. Going home was enough. A relief. A new start.

Husbands ought to love their wives
As their own bodies.
He who loves his wife
Loves himself.

Eph 5:28 (NIV)

Chapter 3

"Til Death"

After the hours of guzzling and thinking (the purpose of the guzzling was to stop the thinking) exhaustion would at last set in. My hope as I would climb the stairs to my bed was that I'd be able to rest and wake up the next day refreshed. As I entered my room, as usual, reminders of the months of the recent year stared me in the face. The window over my bed still haunted me. I heaved a huge sigh as I climbed into bed realizing that my thoughts were still not going to turn off. I knew I was lucky to be alive. Those frantic days of the divorce swirled around in my memory: the hole in the window, the hammer that lay on my pillow, Bob had been so out of control. His eyes! Oh, Those staring empty eyes that had peered through my kitchen window the day my lawyer had called me, and then even my folks telling us to get out of town. "Bob is stalking us!" he had reported. The mindless man had been seen staring at him ominously in the window of the restaurant where he was having lunch. I told them about how I had seen him peeking at me in a cold stare through my kitchen window, and then as quickly and quietly as the wind, had been gone.

Bob had outburst after outburst after I had filed for a divorce. He had even come stalking me. No, he had actually attacked me at work. I worked for an insurance company as a computer operator. As the janitor was just putting the key in the door to lock up for the night, Bob pushed him aside and barreled through it. Before anyone knew he was anywhere nearby, I was suddenly surprised by a hand grabbing me by the neck of my blouse literally pulling me out into the hallway. "What are you doing?" I begged him to leave me alone. I had felt so helpless in the situation.

"They're talking about me!" he had moaned. "They're all reading about me from the divorce papers!"

It was then that I knew he was out of his mind. Here he was grabbing me right in front of everyone. I screamed, "Somebody, please help me . . . . get the police, or something!" I was lucky. My supervisor was a good-sized man and had no fear, or if he did he didn't show it. Running out to the hall he hollered for some of the other guys to help head the bastard off. Bob hadn't stuck around to see what they were going to do. He made a beeline out of the place and disappeared down the street.

This had been the culmination of the weeks after we, as a family, had come back home after the ordeal in that strange city. Bob had no job when we got back home. Deep down I knew that he had been fired, probably for "cohabiting" with that outside salesman he had been involved with, but the word "fired" was never used. I was just told that there was no job for him when we returned.

Soon after we had arrived back home Bob had found an opportunity to manage a semi-automatic bowling alley. The location of it was impressive. It was smack in the middle of the downtown area across the alley from a very popular department store. I had walked by it many times and had never noticed it. No wonder. The display case in the front window was empty: bare. The place appeared to be closed. However, as we entered the drab walkway that led into the alley, I could hear the crash of bowling pins. It was a clean but colorless little place. Very complete, though. On the right from where we entered were the 20 long gleaming alleys. There were two people bowling. An old man was watching closely, obviously with much enjoyment. All the place needed was customers.

As I turned around I noticed a little room. "What's that in there?" I pointed.

"Oh, that's an old restaurant. It hasn't been run for years."

He had left that matter to me, if I was interested in it. I wiped some dirt off of the windows so I could get a better look. The tables and chairs were all piled up together. A small dusty counter stood on the far wall leading to an old grill.

"Does the stove work?" I asked.

"Sure. Everything in there works. In fact, see those boxes?" he poked me to get my attention. "They're all full of dishes and the freezer is even there. Just think, Hon, two businesses in one! You'll love running it. See the office over there?" He pointed across the aisle. "You can do the bookkeeping there. That'll be your own office. It'll be fun getting this place going. A family business!"

It certainly was an opportunity, and Bob was an excellent PR man. He had promised that he would straighten out and really try. That was not all. The very next day he surprised me as he drove me up to a large old house. The paint was nearly non-existent on its huge four-story frame. There was an overgrown fir-tree in the front yard that overlooked a busy intersection. There was a long front porch. Bob walked up to as if he owned it. He had the key to the house and everything. "The realtor told me that after I show you and if you agree to live here, then I should call him and talk business." Bob was grinning from ear to ear hardly able to contain the excitement of his findings.

The inside of the house had real promise . . . potential for lots of charm. The front room and dining room were large adjacent rooms with the old-fashioned window seats giving the windows an extra friendly feeling. There was a large fireplace on an inside wall leading to a big heavy wooden sliding door, a big wooden slab, which had been refined with picture frame-like designs. The kitchen was a big room of nothing. The sink was placed in the pantry facing to the back of the house. A very long drain board ran underneath a window that overlooked the good-sized back yard. The rest of the wall space in the tiny room was full of cupboards.

The floor plan of the house brought us in a circle so that when we left the kitchen we were back into the entranceway. There was a small room off to the side that we could see when we first walked into the house, a perfect place for a business office. The stairway twisted upstairs to three bedrooms and a bath. A door at the end of the hall invited us out on to a balcony. We stood there gazing over the back yard and the dilapidated old garage. I was awestruck. Bob knew it. "You like it, huh?" He put on his best charm. "It's all for you for sticking together with me through this past hard year." He cozily put his arm around my waist. "The realtor said that we could almost offer any price for it. It's been on the market for over a year and there have been no bites." My heart felt warm. I finally knew that God must be watching out for us, after all.

Bob had made a gutsy cheap offer and it was accepted. It had all been so unbelievable. I had felt a great deal of hope as we prepared the house to move in to. I painted the kitchen while Bob's pin-boys were hired to paint the outside of it. I knew God was with us when during all of the hub-bub, Betsy, then almost one year old, crawled out the window from her new bedroom while the fellows were on the roof painting. I was in the kitchen painting. Suddenly, Al, one of the pin-boys, handed Betsy to me. "Watch her! I just caught her in mid-air! She climbed out the window!" I clutched her to me so thankful she was safe, but under my breath I cried to myself, . . . *and who opened the window in the first place?* I didn't make a fuss over the insinuated accusation, I was too thankful.

At the same time we were opening a new business. I had a meeting with the owner of the bowling alley. We were to pay him a few cents a line. He taught me how to keep the books along with the deal. A very nice and fair gentleman he was. There was even a place for a crib there in the bowling alley for little Betsy. I would stay there until it was time for the boys to get home from school. As leagues were organized and the business surged ahead we decided to take advantage of the whole package. We tackled opening the cafeteria. Bob's sister had been a waitress for years and knew all the ropes. There was but one warning from Bob. "Watch out for her because she'll give it all away. She has no common sense when it come to business."

Donna was a professional when it came to the grill, waiting on customers and knowing whom to deal with for food and beverages. A huge lunch trade ensued. However, as I kept the books I noticed that we were still paying her wages from the bowling alley profits. I knew it would take her awhile to stock up, but there was no relief. I began to investigate by going around to other restaurants in the area to see what their prices were. Sure enough, we were nearly giving the food away. No wonder the staff from the department stores were coming there for lunch in huge droves! I remembered what Bob had warned me about. I told him what I had found out. He laughed. "You're the bookkeeper, you tell her. I have enough to worry about running the bowling alley". I tried very tactfully to explain to Donna. She had a total fit. There was no reasoning with her, no negotiating, no nothing. Just a wild woman emitting venom. "You think you know it all, you'll see . . . you'll see."

Things were never the same after that. Donna found a middle-aged woman to take over the restaurant. She had a dignified appearance and ran the restaurant very well, but I was uneasy about something. I didn't know what it was. She was too nice to me.

The bowling alley was enjoying much success. It was a place where the elderly from the downtown area could come and enjoy watching the younger generation expound their energies on the game. Of course, Bob with his big ideas decided to buy an advertisement on the TV. One day we were in the money, the TV cameras were there taking pictures, the clients happy chattering away, every lane full. Then suddenly the people stopped coming. The leagues canceled out. The business was in the red. Bob began staying away from the business. He would disappear for hours early in the morning before the restaurant opened. He had become a very good friend with our restaurant manager, but I just told myself that she was too nice to be doing anything wrong.

Later on after all was said and done, and my having become more enlightened about such things, Bob had a pattern of finding a "broad" to befriend when he knew he was slipping back into his "female" lifestyle. I suspect he felt that he was reminding himself that he was a man . . . a bi-sexual. At least he wanted to think of himself as bi-sexual.

One day as I was preparing for business I noticed a fellow leaning over the counter just hanging around. "Hi there. Can I help you?" I greeted him.

"No ma'am. Thanks. Just waiting for Bob".

I began wondering what he wanted. Negative thoughts of mistrust were taking over my mind. "Are you from around here?" I had asked him.

"I have a little apartment up the block from here," he answered. "Bob's been up to my place a few times."

"Oh, I see." I tried to remain calm but it was just an act. I found myself shooting questions at him. "How long have you known Bob? Where did you meet him?"

He seemed to be uncomfortable with all of the questions so then he blurted out, "Lady, I came here to say good-bye to Bob, unless he wants to go with me."

"Where's that?" My voice asked as my heart began beating faster and faster.

"I'm going straight. My wife just left me. I wanted to see if he wanted to go into treatment, too. I hear he has a wife, too."

"Yeah, he's got a wife," I stared him straight in the eye smirking. "It's me!"

"Oh, no! I'm embarrassed. I didn't mean to rat on him . . . "

"That's OK. I know more than you think."

However, when I had approached Bob about the situation he just boldly replied, "No one's perfect. We all slip once in awhile."

About a week or so later Bob invited me to go with him to the mental hospital to visit the fellow I had chatted with. I think it was Bob's way of trying to convince me that he was really trying. He knew that I had been sullen since that conversation, not able to face facts . . . just going through the motions of living. Once there, his friend took us for a walk around the grounds. It was like a walk in a park. As we passed the long brick buildings he would point out which kind of patient was being treated there. He appeared to be in very good humor. "I feel great now," he told Bob. "I have a much better understanding of myself. I'll admit, though, I'm still a little afraid to leave. I can leave anytime, you know, since I volunteered. It's up to me to know when I'm ready."

We were making our way around the building when he began pointing to a few open windows. "Here are some of my friends". I looked down into a basement window that was covered with bars. A man was sitting on the floor. Taking a second glance to make sure I was seeing right, I confirmed what I saw. Yes, he was naked. I could see remnants of his clothing strewn here and there in his padded cell. He had his socks in his hand that he was using to dry his tears. He was crying pathetically.

"He's so sad!" I cried out.

"Oh, he cries all the time." Our friend no longer was concerned for him having become used to his behavior.

The sad patient noticed me at the window staring. Slowly, ever so slowly, he came to me blubbering. He was carrying his underwear. His hand reached out through the bars, his fingers moving helplessly. He pushed his shirt out to me through the bars ever so slowly; streams of tears rolling down his cheeks. My heart felt faint. Running around the corner of the building, frightened, I cried within myself, "I never want to see a sight like that again!"

"Hello, there," a voice came to me from behind. I turned around. There was no one in sight. "Can I help you?" I heard it again. Looking around, still not able to see anybody my eyes finally rested on another basement window. A big fat cigar was sticking out between the bars. Behind it was a man's face puffing on it feverishly.

"Hello," I smiled down at him my eyes scanning the window from the top down to the base of it. They stopped wandering when they focused on his feet! They were planted firmly on the windowsill. He was the shortest man I had ever seen!

"I got caught again," he bragged taking another puff from his cigar. "I keep running away, but they keep locking me up. They say I can't take care of myself."

I liked him right away. He was a spunky little man. I was amazed how jolly he seemed even though he was locked up. Still, I was at a loss for words. I had had enough. "Bob", I yoo-hooed. "Hey you guys," I joined the two men who were still standing out in front of the building, talking. "Bob, let's go home." In reality I had wanted to scream for help! There was no one to hear, though.

I continued my every day routine, as usual even though I knew that something was going on behind my back. I heard rumors of how our restaurant lady had been a prostitute for years. I knew that Bob was getting out of control again, but something blinded my mind. I believe I just couldn't face it any more so I had decided to just do what I could do, raise my family and keep my eyes shut the best I could. One night Bob got home very late from the bowling alley. It was usual for the kids and I to eat dinner alone and for them to be in bed when he got home. But this time was later than usual. I could hear his heavy breathing as he walked up the steps to our bedroom. He fell into the bed laying there moaning, "Oh, Patti. I'm so sick. The whole bowling alley is going up in smoke. I just can't make enough money to support us. I'm afraid I'm going to have a heart attack, or something." He was gasping for air. "What are we going to do?"

I wanted to scream at him accusing him of everything in the book. I was racking up more and more proof each day, but I knew it was useless to talk about it anymore. I wanted to tell him how stupid he was to throw away our second chance. I wanted to but I didn't. Instead, I took matters into my own hands. I knew it was only a matter of time. I knew I needed a way of supporting the kids and myself before I made any move. The first thing in the morning I made a phone call to my old employer. Perfect timing. They needed me immediately.

Miraculously (at least he thought that I thought it was miraculous) Bob never complained of being sick again. Now, in retrospect, I knew that he just wanted me out of the bowling alley so that he could have a free reign in his "new business" which I found out about by accident, or was it fate? At any rate, I turned the tables on him.

When I had gone back to work I got the bright idea to hire one of our pin-boys as a babysitter, who was without a home at the time, making him a room in the full basement. The hours worked out perfectly for he worked evenings and I worked days. Of course, things were too peaceful. One night when I got home from work, Dave, the pin-boy babysitter was sitting alone in the living room. His thoughts were far away. "What are you doing?" I had asked entering the front room after a very busy day at work wondering why he wasn't going to work. He had his head thrown back resting it on the big overstuffed chair.

"Oh, I've just been doing a lot of thinking," he said. "I don't know what's happened, but Bob doesn't seem to want me around the bowling alley anymore."

"That's funny," I sat down to listen. It seemed a rather familiar story since it had happened to me, too. I covered up my own thoughts and began to probe. "I know he likes you very much. Are you sure it's not just your imagination?"

"Nah, he hired this new pin-boy. He treats him like he's teacher's pet or something. This kid even has a key to the safe!"

I didn't say anything. I was just all ears, for danger signals were flagging me. I needed to know exactly what was going on.

"There's something fishy going on down there," the young man went on. "Did you know that upstairs in that place there are all kinds of rooms? Sort of like a hotel?" His lips quivered. "He's got a lot of the guys staying up there. Those rooms are filled with a bunch of kids."

"What are you saying? I wrinkled my nose at him. "You mean they're actually staying there?"

"Yeah, most of the time, anyhow. Most of them left home. They've really had some hot parties up there.

"Is Bob in on them?" I stammered. It was horrifying.

"He's running the whole show," Dave confided. "I've been

in on some of it." He started to sob. "Oh, I feel sick from it all! I feel dizzy! He told me that he felt like a father toward me and I . . . well, he really taught me a lot," he confessed. "I think I hate him. It's made me all mixed up. I wish I had never met him!" I followed him downstairs to his room to make sure he was all right. "I'm so relieved you're not mad . . . " the young man looked up at me with thanks.

"It's gotten past that . . . . " I retorted.

Blinding one's mind causes dysfunction. It causes one to escape further from not wanting to know what's happening around them. It caused me to turn from my pain to the only friend I knew. A friend I had met back in Philadelphia, my six-pack of beer. It was the weekend. Everyone was in bed, even Bob. He had come home sighing about how tired he was and had crashed. I was sitting alone sipping on a beer trying to figure out what to do. I could see that Bob's sexual addictions were escalating and all of his promises were going out the window. I could hear the traffic whizzing by the house. "The whole world is passing me by," I began laughing hysterically. "What a crazy world!" I gave the footstool a swift kick while pacing back and forth, back and forth.

Now, a year-and-a-half later I lay this night in the same room, in the same bed that I had occupied on that night haunted by the shameful memory. It had been a night I was not at all proud of, a night when all of the hurt and frustrations had culminated into thoughts of feeling cheated and used. There I was taking it out on the footstool. There he was upstairs sleeping like a baby. *He can sleep. I can't.* It had all seemed so unfair! *He's an animal laying up there in bed not giving a damn about anyone but himself!"* I pulled the label from the beer bottle I had been drinking from. "Hm-m-m . . . a four dotter!" There was a silly game among drinkers that if you get four dots on your label that you were going to make love that night. Making love and having sex was all the same among the worldly group of the young. It had all seemed so strangely funny. I threw my head back laughing. "Yeah, that's what this night is . . . sex night! I'll go upstairs and collect my dots . . . " I remember tee-heeing as I climbed the stairs. When I got to the bedroom I teased, "Bob, it's my turn . . . I'm here . . . "

His eyes opened. "Huh?" They slowly focused on me as I stood there looking down on him swaying a little from drink.

"I'm here . . . do you think you're man enough?"

"Do you think you're woman enough?" he snickered. I could see that he was enjoying this new flavor of behavior from me. But inside of my own thoughts I was thinking more in terms of, "You act like an animal, I'm going to make you feel like the animal you are. You, you . . . beast!" I was riding him! I remember singing, "I'm back in the saddle, again." Suddenly he had realized that I was more out of my mind than in a playful mood. He became petrified.

"That's enough", he blurted . . . "that's enough!"

"Not for me, it isn't," I teased him. "Can't you take it?"

"I think I'm going to be sick. Please, let me up," he crawled out from under me, and on all fours crawled toward the bathroom to vomit at the same time crying out, "Have I done this to her?"

I've learned that in marriages, after a disgusting and painful experience takes place, there becomes a moment of wanting to make things better, wanting to make things up . . . even though it may be short lived. The next Sunday Bob had come running up the steps to the house all excited. "Let's take a nice ride to the park . . . what do you say?"

He was in a truce-like spirit. It had sure sounded good. Good fresh air. That's what we all needed, emotionally as well as physically. "Come on, kids." I had hollered. "Daddy's taking us to the park!"

"Yay!" They tumbled down the stairs and into the car. To our surprise there in the back seat of the car was Don and his crippled younger brother. The kids weren't prepared for the sight of braces that were on Don's little brother's legs. They stared at the awkward looking cages that were wrapped around the skinny little calves of the underdeveloped legs. But then, after they took it all in they began to play with him as though they had seen nothing.

At the shore we found a place to squat. I put a blanket down on the sand. The kids scurried off for a bout or two with the waves. Bob took off with his friends carrying the crippled kid on his back holding him by his legs, which were wrapped around his waist. I had already been warned about Don from Dave, my babysitter. On down the beach they went. I just sat there deep in thought daring to think of future plans as I sifted the itty-bitty morsels of sand through my fingers.

It was a beautiful aloneness. The sand felt soft and warm. The sound of waves splashing over and over brought peace as I stared up into the vast blue sky . . . no clouds, no nothing. I closed my eyes and nearly drifted off to sleep. Only now and then a motorboat would interrupt the lull and I would sit up startled, to watch as everyone shouted and waved it on. The kids were jumping up and down right along with the rest of them. "Go away! The waves are wrecking our sand fort," they had yelled with delight. As the waves splashed up on the beach Betsy got all wet. She started to cry. I brought her back to the blanket to sit beside me just idling there with my arms clenched around my knees thinking about how young and carefree they were. I reflected on how little they knew of pain, yet the beauty of the deep sky and the soft sand escaped them, too. Suddenly, Bob had come out of nowhere plopping the little crippled kid next to us. "Stay with him a minute, will you?" He ran off toward the water. As I waited I nervously began to notice the waves as they crept up closer and closer. I was beginning to fear that we were getting closed in. I couldn't stand that closed in feeling. Glancing up the beach I spotted them: Bob and his friend. I watched the strangeness between them as they walked along. They were in ecstasy. They were lovers trying to be alone, yet acting so nonchalant about it. In a fleeting instant they disappeared. I had never liked this particular pin-boy. He had always reminded me of a little crook; a finger in every pot. In fact, I suspected that he was the one that Dave had told me about, having a key to the safe. He was like a little snake crawling through my life. *How many like Don? How many like Dave?* I sauntered over to the water glancing at our own two little boys. They were so far removed from what was really going on. *What'll I tell them when they get older? It won't be long before they'd be teen-agers.* I threw a rock into the water. *Old enough to catch on. Old enough to . . .* Oh, God, Bob wouldn't dare! Would he?"

I was paid back for that day of kindness (actually another day of being taken advantage of) with another revolting episode. I had found myself sitting alone, as usual, only this time in the dark. The kids were all in bed and Bob still wasn't home. It was getting to be wee hours in the morning. Abruptly, the sound of cars came screeching around the corner. Then there was a siren. I parted the curtains back to peer out the window. I couldn't see anything out of the ordinary, but I could sure hear plenty. The cars were screeching around corners a couple of blocks away as the sirens kept whining away. Suddenly, down the side street they flew near the house. I still couldn't see them. Instantly all was silent. I figured that whoever it was must've got caught. I settled back down trying to figure out just where my thoughts had left off when there came a loud pounding on the door. I barely got the door opened when Bob and still another pin-boy, a tall handsome red haired kid, pushed their way in closing the door quickly. This was a kid that I had always liked. He had the nicest smile. He was very mannerly and helpful at the bowling alley. In fact, he was the one who had caught Betsy in mid-air when we were painting the house. "I brought Al home with me," Bob had announced. "His mother locked him out of the house".

"Where's your key?" I asked blocking the way to the front room.

"I misplaced it somewhere . . . "

"What have you guys been doing? Was that commotion just now anything to do with you guys?"

They both started to snicker. "We got rid of them down the block. I invited him to sleep on the couch tonight."

"Now you take your filth into our home!" I screamed. "You black devil! Go back to the gutter where you came from!"

Pushing them out the door I slammed it behind them. The

chair caught me as I shakily fell into it. This is it! I felt a relief. Finally, I had done it. Sitting there in silence I breathed in a new freedom from my new state of mind. I could still relate to how good it had felt. There had been no-one . . . no-one in the world, it seemed. I just sat there frozen, not moving. Hours went by. The sun began to shine into the room through the front window. There were no tears. There was no laughter. There was only death, death of the soul.

> "He took me to his world, the world of the lost. 'See? This is my world,' he grinned. 'This is a man's world. We have no use for women. We only use them to get the things we want. Your body sickens me because I only like that which reflects me. I crawl on my belly in the dirt and slime of society. I love to involve the young especially because they look up to me as they would a father. I will turn them into my children. I love to play God. Men are strong and the women will follow. It will be my world.'
>
> As I walked through his world I saw others springing up all around. They would sneer and laugh at me. 'See what fun we're having? We're so happy and gay! We like to take anything we can get, any way we can get it.'
>
> I was sickened. "Oh, God. Let me out of here. Where are you? Have you forgotten me? Please, please let me out!"

I didn't see Bob until the next evening after he had closed the bowling alley. He came home being very demanding, bossing me around like a madman. I had attempted to ignore him and went up to bed. He followed after. Suddenly I felt an arm pulling me out of bed, dragging me to the stairway and on down the stairs. My body bump, bump, bumped down the stairs as he dragged me into the kitchen to watch the show. He went into a rage throwing the electric frying pan across the room, then the toaster. Dishes were flying . . .

I escaped. Into the night I fled getting into the car. My doubts and fears were now very valid. My decision was very real. I found myself sitting on the church steps in such a state of shock that for some time I don't think I knew where I was. The church was all locked up. I so wanted to make a visit remembering the feeling of a loving Presence there. I had missed that peaceful Presence. I had wanted to pray to Him, the very Jesus whose death was depicted in the Stations of the Cross, which adorned the cold stone walls of that grand old church building. I knew He was still around somewhere, if only I could reach Him. Yet, I did feel somewhat close to God just sitting there on the steps thinking and praying, mulling over my predicament. *"Dear God, I know I've tried. I've searched my soul. Didn't I try to understand? I tried to believe in You with all my heart, yet, all of it turned out so sour. Why? Oh, why? Am I to be alone forever? I can't marry again? Why not? Your ordained don't know what it's been like. Only You do. I've been living in a hell, and my children are in danger. Dear God, please understand. I can't go on. You have not shown me the way. I must divorce him so that I may save my own being, or else I'll die forever. Amen."*

When I arrived home, Bob had left, bag and baggage. Once in bed my body thrashed around knowing that my mind would soon take me on a trip I didn't want to take. Things had definitely gotten out of hand. I had felt that not only we, his family, were in danger but also the pin-boys. I remembered gathering together all of the names of the pin-boys from the bookkeeping records and marched on down to the moral squad at the police department. "I'd like to report some information I happen to have," I had blurted the words out to the policeman at the counter.

"What kind of information?" he leaned over his desk to give me extra attention. I handed him the list of names . . . at least a dozen of them.

"What's this all about?" he said.

"I don't know how to tell you. It's about a bowling alley here in town. It's just awful what's happening there."

"Oh, yes . . . . " he said slowly. "I have an idea you want to talk to a detective." He very meekly walked me to the plainclothesman's office. "Hey, John. I've got a lady here who wants to see you," he peeked around the corner of an office as he introduced me. "It's about a bowling alley . . . " The officer raised his voice as if flagging the explanation.

"Not the Fairy Bowl . . . " the detective raised his eyebrows.

My heart saddened to know that others knew about it and were nicknaming it. "I used to work there . . . " I explained. I then detailed the whole story and handed him the list of names. As his eyes scanned the page of names he became exited.

"This is incredible!" he remarked. "The first two names mentioned here are out at the mental hospital right now. I know of three more on this list. They're in custody. In fact, they're being held right upstairs as we speak! They ran away from home. We haven't been able to get anything out of them. Maybe this'll help. Oh, yeah, and this one here. I don't believe it. This kid was sent to Texas to live with his uncle." He excitedly swirled around in his office chair grabbing some papers out of a file. "We'll take care of that hell-hole!" I glanced at where the man's finger was on the page. It was Don, Bob's favorite pin-boy.

Here, a year-and-a-half later, I still would lay in my bed weeping over the mess, often, unable to turn off the grief. I remembered back to that night that I had made my final decision, the ugly word "divorce" had raised its ugly head. Little did I know it would stir such hatred in Bob. I had hoped that it would free him, free us both from a relationship that wasn't working out. He had become so out of control that I had to move in with my folks waiting for the day when he would calm down. The evening that Bob had been served his divorce papers the phone rang. I picked it up to a very hateful voice. "Hello, bitch? I got your little surprise today. I thought I'd give you one in return."

"Oh, is that right?" I had answered. "I'm afraid I've had enough of your little surprises."

"This one's a lulu!" he laughed heartily. "You won't even recognize the place."

"What place?"

"The house."

"What have you done?" My hands quivered as if I was old and feeble. "What did you do? Burn it down or something?"

"Oh, no . . . nothing that drastic. I just had myself a little fun."

The only thing I had known to do was to hang up on him. Immediately I was taken home to behold a mess. Glass was shattered all over the place. The front window was completely smashed out. The pane in the front door had a big hole in it. I walked around to the back to find that the window in the back door was also broken. I was horrified when I had noticed where blood had trickled down from a jagged edge in the window of the door. I surmised he must've broken the windows with his fists. Carefully I slipped my arm through the jagged glass remains managing to get the back door opened without cutting myself. The minute I entered the front room I could see the destruction there. The screen on the TV set was shattered. Blood was smeared all over the set and drippings created a trail clear on over to the front door. "He's nuts!" I cried out.

I had decided to spend the weekend home cleaning up the mess and getting the glass doctor over to fix the windows. Then I had another surprise late in the morning. A strange, very well dressed man appeared at my door. "Hello", he tilted his hat. "Are you Pat?"

"Yes," I had answered a little stunned.

He was very business-like, carrying a briefcase and all. "I'm from the CIA," he had introduced himself flipping a badge in front of me. "I've been informed of your divorce proceedings. I wish that I could talk to you about some of your husband's dealings at the bowling alley."

"Oh," my heart flip-flopped. "I'm no longer connected with it." I hoped to end the conversation immediately.

"Ma'am, we think you'll be able to help us in clearing up a court matter which we are prosecuting."

"Now what's happening? I sighed.

"May I come in and talk about it? I have my secretary out there in the car", he motioned to the street where I could see a woman sitting, apparently waiting for a cue. "She'd like to take some dictation of our conversation."

"Gee, I don't know . . . I guess," I shrugged my shoulders feeling rather helpless in the situation.

The woman in the car came trotting up the walkway awkwardly lugging a typewriter.

The question and answer period revolved around a soldier who frequented the bowling alley. He had gotten into trouble over his homosexuality and pimping. It seemed that Bob was named as one of his outlets. "Have you ever seen this man?" He flashed a picture at me of a man in army fatigues.

"I'm not sure . . . " I really wasn't. "Guys look so different in civilian clothes. He does sort of look like a guy that hung around down there looking mighty important."

"Do you think it could be?"

"Oh, yes, it definitely could be. He has the same build and all." I looked at the picture very thoroughly. "Yes, it does look like him."

"That's all we need to know," the man began picking up his papers. "Now. You've done this for us, is there anything we might be able to do for you?" After a moment of thought I remembered a story Bob had told me about when we were first married.

"Can you find out why Bob was discharged from the navy? He told me a story about how he was on guard one night, and shot this guy who had escaped from the stockade, and had paralyzed him. That was why he was discharged from the navy because the guy's family was going to sue, and they got rid of the records so there wouldn't be any evidence. Does that sound fishy?"

"Yes, ma'am. That does sound very fishy. I'll see what I can find out for you." He jotted down some notes while his secretary finished typing the transcript of the entire conversation. Then, just as suddenly as she had set up her equipment, she dismantled everything. I had just sat there aghast, shaking my head in astonishment at the whole scenario. "This is far out . . . really far out".

Bob really got crazy then. It still amazes me that fear didn't take over me at that time. Either I was just plain stupid or in a state of shock. I really didn't realize just how much danger we were in until one afternoon. It was shortly after Bob had dragged me from my office, which I mentioned earlier. My attorney had called me directing me to go home with a private detective that my folks had hired to protect me until Bob had calmed down.

He was a friendly man, quite a few years my senior. He drove me home and with briefcase in hand escorted me into my kitchen. The lock on the front door had been broken during one of Bob's rampages so now we entered through the back door. "I'll sit with you for a few days until they feel it's safe," he consoled me.

It was a relief to feel that someone cared, even if he was being paid for it! He then opened up his briefcase and pulled out some sandwiches. "I can fix you something to eat." I offered. I had to laugh for I thought it was funny that he had camouflaged his lunch in a briefcase.

"I always come prepared. Never know what's going to happen next in this line of work."

He was such a pleasant person, always cracking a joke trying to make me feel better. In fact, he was actually interested in what was happening in my life giving an open ear to each tale I had to tell. I had been experiencing a shut-off from people around me for they didn't know what to make of the mess I was in. Perhaps it was fear or perhaps it was just weariness from their feeling helpless to come to my aid. This man wasn't helpless. He was trained to do a job.

As we had chatted he remained very alert not only to any clues of Bob's personality, but at the same time, with an ear ready to pick up any noises from the street in case of a car driving up to surprise us. The phone rang. He immediately went to the phone with an ear on the receiver while I answered in case of the need for him to witness what was being said. Bob had used the phone in the past to threaten me and frighten me.

"I have some information for you concerning your husband's discharge status," the voice belonged to the friendly CIA man. The friendly detective breathed easier but was still very interested in the subject matter. "It seems that your husband had received an undesirable discharge. There was no mention of the story he told you. I suspect it was because of his homosexual behavior. That's the type of discharge they use for that kind of problem."

I was pleased with the message for I had been trying to find any information or a hint of any kind to prove Bob's homosexuality before our marriage so that I could get an annulment. I felt that I had been deceived not only by Bob, but by the priests, as well.

The private detective hovered over us all week. My sister-in-law had watched my children in her home because I couldn't have a baby sitter in the midst of all the trouble. Nothing much happened for about a week until, one day, Bob had started to act even more strangely. I would find myself going over those few days in my mind, over and over. It had all happened so quickly!

It's a beautiful Sunday morning. I'm sipping on a morning cup of coffee. Through the kitchen window a morbid face is peering in. His lifeless, glazed eyes: Bob's eyes . . . black, very black . . . piercing through me. The door is unlocked. I run to lock it racing him to the door. Gasping sounds come as he breathes. He's clawing at the door whining, "The people . . . the people, they're laughing at me. The phone keeps ringing . . . it's ringing and ringing! It's all your fault! Everyone knows about me. They've been reading all about it . . . in the divorce papers! I'll kill you! It's all your fault! I'll kill . . . . " Then, he's gone!

The bell, telephone bell, saves me. It's my folks. Bob has also been stalking my lawyer. "We're taking you and the kids to Aunt Aurea and Uncle Bud's farm. You've been put under our 'protective custody'. Things have become too serious!"

Mom and daddy tried to make light of the whole thing for the children's sake. "We're all taking a vacation!" they cheerfully announced. It was all happening as in a dream. I seemed to be just watching the whole scenario. The kids were riding in the back oblivious to what was really happening. There were long periods of silence until we arrived at the farm. Each one of us was deep in thought. I was thinking that the kids know more than we cared for them to know.

We were received quickly and whisked off for a picnic deep into the woods. It was a sweet picnic. I finally found a sense of peace. I walked towards the water and found solace just sitting on a log trying to breathe in the beauty of the sea. Aunt Aurea joined me. We entered into deep conversation.

"Will you marry again?" Auntie was very concerned.

I had thought it all out before I had even made a move. "Yes, but next time it'll be a small town guy. Someone who knows how to do things God's way."

My aunt's words were strange words, but full of love. "I think there is something for you at the mill." Her smile, a strange far-off smile, was puzzling to me but made me feel so much better. Her words gave me hope.

The weekend had been peaceful, so peaceful, that our uneasiness had almost faded away. We had come back home after two very pleasant days at Auntie's farm. We began to unload all of our belongings carrying the luggage up the stairs to our bedrooms. It was then that I noticed a cold draft in my bedroom. My folks had followed the kids and me into the house checking to make sure that everything was in place and that we'd be safe. As I had cautiously peeked into my bedroom I saw that the curtains were fluttering from a strong breeze which was blowing. The window . . . there was a big hole in it! Glass was shattered all over my bed. On my pillow there was a hammer! My heart cried out. "Oh, God, when is this ever going to end?"

The visit to the farm had been over too soon. I had to come back home just to face the same old things once more. As I stood there frozen in my tracks, my head was going through the motions of coming home . . . we were all silent once more wondering if the house would still be intact as the house comes into sight. We pulled up in front searching for any sign of disturbance. All was well. What a relief! The kids were piling out of the car. I hollered, "I'll carry this luggage up to my room," I called to my mom, "Why don't you guys come in for awhile?"

"We'll just come in for a minute, until we know everything is OK."

Mom was walking into my bedroom. The curtains were blowing in a breeze! There was a big hole in the window. She stood there unable to move, also. I wanted to scream, but couldn't. There it was laying on my pillow . . . the hammer! The terror of it all was running through us both realizing that if we hadn't gone away I would possibly have been killed! "Oh, Mom," I cried, "why does he hate me so much?"

A man that is a heretic
After the FIRST
And SECOND
Admonition,
REJECT;
Knowing that he that is such
Is subverted
And sins
Being condemned by himself.

Titus 3:10-11 (KJ)

PART 2

The Call

"But you are a chosen generation, a royal priesthood,
a holy nation, a peculiar people; that you should
show forth the praises of Him who has called you out
of darkness into His marvelous light . . .

1 Peter 2:9 (KJ)

Chapter 4

Friends or Fools?

My confidence had waned since the episode of the hole in the window. The moment that my folks and I had found the hammer lying there on my pillow, a phone call was made to my friendly bodyguard. He came to my aid immediately. He quickly scrutinized every aspect of the scene before him. "Things are coming to a head!" He rubbed his hands together as though relishing the idea. "I think tonight's the night!"

"How do you know these things?" my mother asked, astonished at how he could assess things so accurately.

"Oh, You get so that you can tell . . . it's the way he does things. His M.O."

The kids had gone to bed in the early evening tired from the long trip from Aunt Aurea's farm. I was left alone with my bodyguard. He instructed me to get ready for bed just like I would normally do. The lights were left off as we sat in the dark front room just listening and waiting. It was near midnight. "Are you scared?" my bodyguard checked me out. "Here cuddle up close to me. It'll make you feel better." I did just that. It felt so good for a comforting strong arm to hold me and to have someone who actually cared about the fact that I was shaking from fright. The romance of the intrigue and the danger assisted us. He kissed me. It was a very passionate kiss. "I've been trying to figure out how that creep could treat such a lovely woman this way. You're lovely, you know . . . " he kissed me again. *No*, I whimpered to myself, *I didn't know anything of the sort.* I had felt anything but lovely since Bob had turned on me for finding out his secret. The minutes became timeless. The problems of the time became minute. Our passions became all important.

As we lay there relaxing afterward, abruptly there came a noise on the front porch. My bodyguard-lover arose in a flash sneaking up to the door, his back to the wall . . . like in the movies. "Sh-h-h", he wanted to make sure I didn't say anything. "It's him!" I hadn't heard a thing. It had all happened so fast. He peeked out the glass door. There was Bob just ready to beat through the glass with a big club. "Hey, buddy, what the hell do you think you're doing?" my protector hollered in a deep loud important voice. Bob didn't expect that. He turned and ran to the car speeding away as fast as lightening. "That son-of-a-bitch has finally done it . . . " my lover" went to the phone to call the police. "I think we've got the bastard. I'll be right down there to make a statement," he told them. "Send a patrol car to watch the house. The lady is here with three kids. I don't think he'll be back, but just in case . . . . OK?" Out the door he went. He looked back over his shoulder saying, "Take care now, hon. Don't answer the door for anybody! Call the police if you need me."

After he was gone it took awhile for me to get a grip on myself and evaluate the events of the day. It had been almost unbelievable. My emotions lie somewhere in between deep gratitude and feeling very cheap. I was so thankful that he had been there to protect me . . . but deep down was a gnawing realization of my vulnerability. Who was going to protect me from my protector?

Now, a little more than a year later, that window over my bed brought back to mind not only those frightening times but a fond remembrance as well. After the whole ordeal of Bob's rather crude or even childish attempt in trying to kill me was over, I had called employment security to see if they knew of anyone who would like to live-in and baby-sit for me. It had gone so smoothly the short time that Dave had lived with us while he babysat that I felt it was the solution. During all of this agony my sister-in-law had stepped in and took care of my children, picking them up and delivering them back to me after I got home. She was beginning to feel the pressure. I knew I had to make some kind of arrangements. The kids were holding up so well under all of this stress that I began believing that there was a God after all looking over us.

After I arranged to interview a young woman that they recommended, I went into a deep quietness. I guess I collapsed emotionally. My actions became only actions of duty. My functioning was so removed from reality that I have no idea of how the kids came and went. Shortly after the separation, Little Robert, my first-born, had tried to take on himself the family worries. He would check the furnace to make sure it was turned down at night, he would check the gas in the car to make sure there was enough in it. I do remember telling him that his job was to go to school and learn to read and write really good so that he could get a nice job some day for his family when he grew up. I assured him that "mommy could take care of everything". Now, in the state I was in I suppose that he took over as overseer realizing that mommy had more than she could handle. I guess they were OK for no one complained. The interview I had arranged for had escaped me as well as all of the other memories during this time of shock and disbelief.

The day came for the young woman to call on me for the job. I suppose it was on the weekend for I hadn't even gotten dressed this day. I have no idea where the kids were. I suspect they were visiting their father. He was out of jail the day after he had flipped out so badly. I suppose they wanted to go with him, I don't know. Perhaps this was why I was in such a state of withdrawal, worrying about them and wondering why I let them go. The light couldn't make it through the windows for these days I kept the drapes tightly shut to create even a more depressing attitude. There was an empty quietness, not even the TV or the radio were playing. A knock on the door brought me out of my silent solitude and back to reality. I was in my nightgown as I opened it to the stranger. I had no idea that I wasn't even dressed, or that I was going to give an interview.

"Do I have the right house?" a young woman, in her early 20's, stood before me. Her eyes were a-twinkling. Mischievous eyes they were even though she put forward a very dignified and business-like manner. I was immediately drawn to her warm smile. "I was supposed to have an interview for a baby sitting job. It's one o'clock, isn't it?"

"Oh, yeah . . . I forgot all about it." I managed to gather myself together long enough to invite the candidate in. "I'm afraid I haven't been feeling well lately". I brushed the hair from my eyes as I tried to focus in on what I was supposed to be doing. I motioned the young woman to a seat. As oblivious as I was these days to happenings around me, I could see that the applicant was probably quite poor, also. She had a rope-like belt drawn around her waist causing the hemline of a rather shoddy soft blue dress to drape higher on one side of the skirt than the other. "I have three children . . . " I began the interview.

"I love children," the interested young woman interrupted as she introduced herself as Carolyn (her formal name). She became a little nervous as she realized her rudeness. "I didn't mean to cut you short . . . look, I need a job very badly. In fact, I need a live-in job . . . that is, if it could be arranged.

"Umm. I suppose that could be arranged." I didn't want to act too elated. I was relieved that someone would want to stay in my spooky old house. I giggled to myself as I realized that she didn't know about what had been happening around there. It had become spooky to only me. Suddenly I was a little embarrassed over the shoddiness of the house as I lifted my eyes focusing them on the ceiling where some bare wires hung from the ugly hole left from an old light fixture which had once proudly hung there. It was as if I was seeing it for the first time. "Well, let me show you the house as crappy as it is," I pulled myself up out of the chair.

"It's a very large house, isn't it?" Carol remarked brightly as she followed me into the dining room.

"The table leg is broken," I sighed feeling very helpless about it as we passed by. The tour led us into the kitchen. Piles of dishes were stacked in the sink that was filled with stagnant water. I repeated so as to give the excuse of why the house was unkempt, "I don't feel too good, you know."

"I know how it is," Carol replied gently. "What kind of illness do you have?"

"Well, . . . I'm not really sick, I guess. I'm just upset. I'm in the process of getting a divorce."

"Oh, I see." Carol peeked up the stairway. "Are the bedrooms upstairs?" she inquired. "C'mon. I'd like to see the kids' rooms," she started up the two flights of stairs which curved on up to the second story leaving me trailing along behind. "Are the kids school age?"

"Yes, the boys are. My little girl is just two years old. They're on visitation."

On inspection the rooms were reasonably picked up although the beds were unmade. She found the master bedroom. Her eyes settled on the broken window. "What happened there?" she asked.

"Oh, that. The kids broke it by accident." I lied. I felt it imperative to cover up the trouble that was around me. I was afraid the truth would scare her away. Other babysitters had sensed trouble in the house and only lasted a week or so.

Carol took it all in. Then, looking closely into my eyes with deep scrutiny she offered, "I could start right away." Hurriedly she added, "I'll go get my things and move in tonight." She took over the situation rushing me down the stairs and to the door. As she left she gave me a warm wink. "I really like it here . . . broken windows or not." She then stared me straight in the eye. "There's an air of mystery about it." Then I knew that she knew that I had lied. I sighed in relief as she gently closed the door. Now I had someone for moral support.

My memories of Carol brought with them a flood of happenings. Sleep came and went, I think. My head never turned off, thinking, thinking about the days that followed that unusual interview. What a barrage of emotions. What a relief! I had been made alive again. I was feeling laughter. Tenderness and tears had followed.

Tossing and turning all night brought the morning time much too soon. My memories were still much too vivid. Here was another day of trying to function, another day of pretending that I had matters in hand. So much had happened since those nonsensical days I had had with Carol. I was OK as long as my body was doing something. Once down stairs in the kitchen my mind would once again take over. I brought a cup of coffee near the fireplace to sip on until the children woke up. The fireplace reminded me of when Carol had first come to live with us. She had brought with her much needed silliness and laughter.

I focused in on the day that we had taken the kids to see the movie, Mary Poppins. She lived in a world of fantasy much as Mary Poppins did. She even pictured herself as the famous English nanny after we got home from the movie. I still chuckle as I relive the moments when she had opened up my umbrella and tried to climb into the fireplace pretending that she was going to fly away.

Carol had rosy cheeks that brightened her full face. Her hair was naturally wavy, and its color coal black . . . as black as her eyes. The fact that she was a little overweight and a little unkempt was a plus for me for I hadn't been into trying to keep an immaculate house anymore. I didn't feel a bit uneasy in this kind young woman's presence. She had an inner prettiness that I liked. But there was also a undercurrent of something I couldn't get a clear handle on, an undercurrent of unmanageable impracticality. This impracticality was the very thing that had made her fit into my life at this time. One never knew what was going to happen next.

After a couple of weeks of no major incidents the calm was suddenly broken by a loud clattering on the roof. Just then the phone rang. I had raced downstairs to the phone at the same time being frightened over the strange noises on the roof. "Hi, good-bye . . . " a voice said. That was the beginning and the end of the conversation. Carol came running downstairs, ashtray in hand, puffing away at a cigarette.

"Can I have one of them?" I grabbed one from her quickly. By this time the noise on the roof became louder. It was no longer a clatter, but huge bang—banging sounds. "I'm going out to find out what's going on. If I ask you to call the police, call!" I ordered.

Quietly, I snuck out into the yard where I could see what was going on. There was Bob with his little "pin-boys" crawling all over the house. Just then a carload of more "pin-boys" came screeching to a stop in front of the house. They were all screaming and making noises cheering loudly. *Don't act scared whatever you do, Patricia,* I warned myself. Attempting to cover up my fear I hollered, "I see Santa Clause came early this year." Silently I motioned for Carol to call the police.

"Yeah, what's it to you?" Bob snided. He stood there against the night his body weaving like a drunkard while his little army was crawling all over the house like an army of ants.

"I can't call out. That guy never hung up on the other end . . . " Carol whispered to her frightened friend-employer.

Just then the neighbor next door hollered out, "Do you want us to call the police?"

"Thank God. Please, please . . . " Carol grabbed me by the arm quickly pulling me into the house locking the doors behind us. It was quiet. We sat there in the dark smoking cigarette after cigarette, moving from one room to another, ashtray in hand at all times peeking out the windows wondering what might be next!

Finally we heard a voice say, "OK, you guys. That's enough. Anyhow, I think the police are coming." Gradually the noises subsided and they heard the final car pulling out.

"I guess it's no fun if we don't act frightened!" I laughed it off sounding very brave, but still shaking like a leaf.

"Yeah! Knowing that the cops were going to come didn't hurt, either," Carol grunted. Whenever something exciting was happening she would exude little grunting sounds that would gradually turn into a giggle.

" . . . but Bob has no respect for the law, anyhow. He loves to see just how far he can push them."

The most amazing thing, though, during the whole ordeal was that the kids didn't even wake up. They had slept right through it.

It was perfect timing for the boys' birthdays were less than two weeks apart. One night when I came home from work, Carol and the kids surprised me for their birthday. "Meet Duke!" They proudly introduced me to the new member of the family. He was shepherd brown and Doberman black. "Mom!" The excited little boys shouted in great jubilation. "Carol took us to the dog pound and let us pick out Duke! Isn't he great?"

"Are you sure he's safe?" I quizzed Carol as to how much she knew about dogs.

"He'll be a real good watch dog . . . " Carol knew that would be a great selling point for me to accept the idea. " . . . and the shepherd in him will make him a good loyal pet."

I was sold, even though somewhat reluctantly, thinking of expenses and all. A handsome dog Duke was, though, and immediately he made himself at home in our hearts. He evidently took his job of policing to heart, for every night after everyone was in bed he would make his rounds from room to room to check that we were all tucked in for the night. In the morning we would find him laying on his back, legs in the air, on the armless sofa with his head dangling backwards to rest on Betsy's little overstuffed rocking chair. It was his favorite place to relax. Our first encounter with his comfort zone brought laughter ringing throughout the house for it was the silliest thing that we had ever seen.

The joy which Carol had brought to me and my family had helped me to begin functioning again. With the laughter had come the tears. I was no longer a zombie. In fact, I was even able to be the slightest bit creative—with a push from Sister. I had enrolled the boys in the Catholic school that my folks had sent me to. My heart took backward flip-flops when Robert handed me a note from Sister, his teacher. "What now?" The last thing in

the world that I needed was instructions for me to make Robert
an angel costume for the Christmas pageant. The instructions
were very clever, but quite frankly, my exhaustive state had left
me with very little confidence in creativity of any kind. My ability
to concentrate was minimal for I had so many things on my mind
that somehow it had shut down and now I was becoming just a
happy dimwit. I managed to do my job at work for I was in another
world then. But when I came home I was back into trauma-land.
Quite frankly, Christmas was the last thing on my mind. "When
does this have to be done?" I asked my anxious little son.

"Sister said we have to have it Monday."

"Oh, my gosh! This is Friday! How am I going to make it that
soon?" I stomped around the house. Feeling ashamed after seeing
Robert standing there very still, afraid to move, wanting so badly
to be an angel, I gathered myself together. "I need a sheet, a
hangar, aluminum foil . . . . " To my amazement it was fun. Viola'.
It took shape very quickly. "Here, try it on," I attached his wings
on him with great pride and a relief that I hadn't disappointed
my little boy. He'd been through too much, also. He was one
happy little dude.

The festive mood at the office was becoming more and more
manifest. My co-workers arranged for a party at a nearby hotel. It
was a time for everyone to let their hair down. I was certainly in
the mood for a drink. However, as that evening progressed, I
could see that Bob was right about one thing: Things are not as
they seem. All kinds of behaviors are brought to your attention
once you're considered to be a divorcee. There were many things
going on under cover. In fact, I was propositioned more than
once from people I had worked with for years. It was a very
disturbing time, learning to face the facts of life.

As I sat near that fireplace remembering, the sight of our first
Christmas with the crib scene of Jesus' birth lovingly placed on
the mantle came very clearly in mind. It was the signal that
Christmas was indeed here. The cards which we had received
from people, who had no idea of what was happening to our little
family, were hung along the rim of it . . . *and the stockings were*

hung by the chimney with care. It was a warm memory. Friends are so important especially when things go topsy-turvy. However, I was to realize later on that when most acquaintances, whom we call friends, hear of divorce in the family they often back away. It seemed to me it was from fear, sort of like maybe that what we had was catching.

Unexpectedly, though, one of my high school chums, Wynne, looked me up over the holidays. In fact, it was Christmas Eve. She had been teaching school in Germany. Her life sounded so fascinating to me. However, Wynne felt that I was the one leading an interesting life. She met me at the pub across the street where she had confided rather drastic fears that she would never find a husband. I hoped that my story would make her be thankful for her blessings and not to worry. She was still much more naive than I was for I was learning many things very fast. Disturbing things. Hurtful things. Sinful things.

Under that backdrop of these distressing findings, I received still another lesson. Out of the blue who should decide to pull up a chair and sit at our table but the prosecuting attorney?!!—a friend of Bob's from his political days. "Hmmm", I squirmed, surmising . . . *something is up. He's been put up to something.*

He was his charming self until a few drinks down the line. Then he slovenly leaned over the table saying to me, "If you go to bed with me at the hotel up the street, I'll give you a diamond for your navel."

I nearly choked on my most recent sip of the hot rum drink that my school chum had talked me in to trying. Wynne just sat there like nothing was happening. I whispered to myself, *Do you suppose she didn't get the drift? She's as naive as I used to be.* Dumbfounded, I remarked, "Where's your wife?"

"Oh, she's home. I suppose she's waiting for me. What's this? Is this Christmas Eve? Gees, I don't even have a gift for her yet."

"You didn't buy your wife a Christmas gift?"

"No, I'll dig up something at the last minute."

"How about that diamond you offered me? Why don't you

give it to her for her navel?" The words had come out of my mouth like jewels.

Wynne caught on to that one. She began to laugh. In fact, we both couldn't contain ourselves after that. It was time to exit leaving him sitting there crying over his glass in seemingly despair.

It was Christmas Eve—and I was late. When I got home I still had the chore of assembling the gifts I had bought for the kids. I had waited to the last minute to see how much money was left from household expenses and food. Things were tight, but as always, I had enough left to buy some nice gifts that were inexpensive, mostly because they needed to be assembled. I was also somewhat concerned if Carol would react unfavorably at my being so late. I had made one babysitter extremely nervous one night right after I had started divorce proceedings. It was before Bob had received the papers, when he had attempted to use his charm on me to make me change my mind. He had invited me to the pub. (I still think he did it to mess me up with my babysitter). I still cringe at the stupid remarks that I had left him with that evening. "I'm so sorry Bob. I'm sorry if I hurt you. I just couldn't handle your problems." I had felt ridiculous when those words had gushed from my mouth before they had gone through my brains. But then, again, I had felt that perhaps they had swished around in my heart for a time. Anyhow, this time Carol wasn't the least bit upset.

"I figured that something had come up. Everything's OK," Carol had soothed my conscience. Just the night before she had gone out with Jim, the boyfriend I had never met, and they had walked along the avenue looking in the jewelry store windows at engagement rings. I could tell that Carol's hopes were high that he would ask her to marry him. Evidently, Carol had felt that it was my turn to have a night out. It was a relief. It was so hard to try to have a private life of any kind worrying about babysitters.

I promptly got down on my hands and knees knowing that I still had a big job to do even though I was a little tipsy. It was now or never. First was the wooden high chair for Betsy's doll. It was all in pieces. I needed a carpenter. No, I needed to be a carpenter. I studied the directions following each detail carefully. There was just one thing they left out. How the heck do you hammer those little nails without making them bend? Finally. I did it. "That calls for a beer!" Carol promptly and dutifully went to the refrigerator and handed one over to me, getting one for herself at the same time.

The next project was for the boys. It was a cardboard office building with "elevators that actually worked!" (with rubber bands). "That's if, I can figure out how", I confessed to Carol hoping that she would be able to help. Carol stayed by my side making silly comments, in charge of keeping me supplied with beer, as I nervously assembled the gifts. It was at that time that I found out that Carol might've been fun and jolly, but didn't have one practical bone in her body.

The highlight of Christmas was the brand new bikes that Bob bought the boys along with a little kiddy car for Betsy. He couldn't pay support, he was planning to file for bankruptcy, but he could play Santa Clause. The scrimping and saving and working that I had done was nothing compared to the flashy new expensive gifts that Santa Bob was able to give. I hid my anger in a six-pack of beer and another and another. I didn't care if I could afford it or not.

Carol's most favorite topic, though, was Jim, her boyfriend. You could tell that she loved him deeply for her eyes sparkled with great happiness when she spoke of him. I began wondering if he might be a figment of her imagination, for I had never seen him or heard him call her on the phone. I was glad when one evening Carol asked if she could invite Jim over to visit her from time to time. "After all, the kids are in bed by 8:30 or 9:00."

"It's OK with me as long as you watch yourself around the kids."

"We'll watch it," Carol promised. "It's just that I miss him, and I'd like to be able to see him during the week."

The holidays turned into normal days that turned into weeks. When I'd arrive home, Carol would be sitting there alone, but very excited. She would tell of funny little things that she and her boyfriend had said, all the fun games and good times that they had had together. But still I had never seen him. I began wondering if Carol was just making him up, if he was another of her fantasies, especially after she showed me his picture. He was extremely good looking: a blonde Tab Hunter type. "I'd like to meet him sometime," I finally hinted mainly for proof of his existence.

"All right. I'll ask him to stay tomorrow night until you get home."

She seemed happy that I had shown an interest.

Sure enough, when I got home that night there he was sitting on the sofa next to Carol. Carolyn had told the truth. Not only was he very good looking, but very tender in the way he behaved. They popped popcorn and later sprawled out in front of the TV creating a very relaxing evening.

Suddenness was a description of what happened in a split second . . . a presto log came flying through the window. Then two or three followed behind crashing again and again through the large front window. One of them had just missed Jim's head making him justifiably irate. He sprang to his feet running to the door. "A red car just pulled out!" he yelled. "What the hell?"

"Oh," I sighed now resigned to these outbreaks. "It's just my ex-husband feeling his oats again. My sister gave the logs to me for a Christmas present. I don't think that this is what she had in mind." Glass was all over the place. I started to pick it up. "There's not a darn thing the cops will do about it. They say that they don't interfere in marital matters. They told me that even if he came into the house, held a knife to my throat but didn't break the skin, that legally they couldn't do anything. He was in jail once already, but he got out on bail." I placed a sack in the middle of the floor as we slowly threw the pieces of glass into it being careful not to cut ourselves.

"I can't believe this," Jim sank down in the chair. "What do they do . . . wait until someone gets killed?"

"I guess so."

It didn't take me any time to cover the windows for I still had huge cardboard pieces that were already cut to fit from the last window bashing episode.

"Does this happen often?" Carol even appeared to be a little nervous this time. She raised her eyebrows at him in "I told you so" fashion. He nodded back.

"Once before," Patti explained. "He used his fists that time. I figured I'd save the cardboard, just in case. The whole thing is beyond me . . . I guess I'll just have to live with it."

During the holidays my friend-sitter and I had discovered that we both liked to drink. Once that was known and I condoned it, we became not only friends but were now unwavering drinking companions. Carol had happily furnished much of the holiday cheer from her meager paycheck. During work hours Carol and Jim would have their romance and squabbles. During my hours free from my job we would sit by the hour chattering. I loved to listen to the week's episodes of the two lovers all the while playing rummy and sipping on a beer. I found out that even though Carol didn't have much common sense, she sure had card sense. She could win at any card game. The kids went to bed early, these wintry days, probably exhausted from the emotional happenings. They never complained, just lived through it all like I had to.

Carol confided in me one night. "You know, it's our anniversary. Pat, could I have an advance on my pay so that I can get myself a white dress and buy Jim a white dinner jacket? I found a jacket at the second hand store. Can you help me with it?"

I certainly didn't have much extra, just a little, probably because Carol bought all the booze. I sat down with my bills and wangled a way to help her out. I was so very glad I did for it was the greatest memory I have of the two of them.

The night of their anniversary I had given Carol permission to have the kids play in their rooms or go to bed early so she could put on her little party. I wanted them to have some privacy for her special dinner. I had purposely tried to stay away shopping and browsing around town for as long as I could. I found the two of them sitting at a candlelit table after just finishing a steak dinner, restaurant style: with salad and baked potato, which Carol had prepared. She was wearing the brand new long lacy white formal gown that she had found at a very good price. Jim was so handsome in his dinner jacket! His blonde hair was even blonder in contrast to the whiteness of the jacket that glowed from the candlelight.

When I arrived home they had invited me to sit with them and have a drink of wine poured very formally in wine goblets. I don't know if it was the drink or if it was the emotion of the evening but suddenly the two of them were on the couch, Jim's head on her shoulder sobbing hard. "I'm not good enough for you," he was blurting out to her. She tenderly stroked his hair as he cried like a baby. It was then that I knew that there was more to this story than met the eye.

There was one problem that was now in the back of my mind. Perhaps watching the romance in Carol's life made me wonder if maybe the Catholic church would give me an annulment since I had been so deceived. It seemed the right timing. I had decided that I had enough confidence to tackle this tricky problem. I went to see Father. I had done a lot of thinking trying to accept the facts which Bob had told me concerning the priests in his life with a grain of salt. The salt had been rubbed into my wounds, but I chose to reason that the priests, after all, are only human. I didn't mention anything about the priests that were involved. I hadn't even told my folks about the priests' involvement because I didn't want their faith to be harmed. I sometimes wondered if it was God that they believed in or the priests. My priority was that maybe the church would free me from my marriage bond.

Father was angry. "Why didn't you come to me sooner?" he scolded.

I explained that I had been to the priests back east and was told by my counselor priest that there wasn't much hope.

"I can't give you much hope for an annulment, either" the young priest had replied. Quite frankly the conversation was very difficult for he blushed every time any word with the name "sex" in it was mentioned. "You have three children. Therefore, your marriage has been consummated." His words were straight from the book he had learned from. *Of course it's been consummated,* I swore under my breath. *We've been married for over eight years.*

"Father, I *know* I'm not married in the eyes of God. A person just can't be married one-sidedly. God can't honor deceit."

"We need to have proof of his homosexuality before your marriage."

"I don't have any, Father, my mind was spinning. *I know he had something to do with some of the priests. What would Father think if I told him? I don't have any proof. He'll think I'm awful.* "I only have proof of his recent actions."

"That's not enough. I'll make a report, though, and we'll see what happens."

He was not consoling at all. It was all business . . . no mention of the cruelty which had made it all so impossible. No mention of the pain from having been so deceived. No mention of how sick it all was.

I walked home slowly, not even wanting to go anywhere. It all seemed so unfair. Itwas so upsetting. I had to think. Where was my conscience in all of this? *God, I know I did the right thing to get away from Bob. Why can't they see it? It's so hard to explain to Father. He's so naïve . . . "*

That day was still painful to me as I sat there by the fireplace—another scene coming to mind. The reminiscing never ceased. My head never turned off. There I was remembering the most vivid fireplace scene in my memory. I had arrived home from seeing Father to find Carol and Jim cuddling together before a glowing fire. They had pulled the davenport up in front of the fireplace. I fell back into a chair nearby feeling mighty alone and exhausted. "My feet are killing me," I kicked off my shoes. "That darn church stuff is killing me too."

"What happened?" Carol asked.

"Not much. As far as they're concerned I'll be married to him for life." I burst into tears.

"Come on. Sit down here by the fire and have a beer. Relax." They were so sweet as they tried to console me.

"No, no . . . " I backed off. "I don't want to butt in. You guys look so cozy."

"Come on," they coaxed. "Loosen up a little . . . " They set me at ease with their joking and silly stories of their courtship. After a few beers were guzzled things didn't seem nearly as bad. We were all very relaxed as we gazed into the glowing flames of the fire saying nothing. Of course, the drink had also taken its toll on us. The quietness became pulsating. There was a faint feeling of something amiss. Carol suddenly excused herself, "I have to go upstairs to the bathroom. I'll check on the kids while I'm up there."

Jim took the opportunity to slowly place his arm around the back of the couch . . . around me. "I'm glad we've been able to help," he squeezed my shoulder.

"I do feel much better," my mouth formed a serene smile, "but this church stuff just doesn't make much sense to me anymore. I feel so lost!" At that he leaned forward to kiss me, a sweet tender kiss. Through a deep sigh I confessed, "Jim, I needed that. I've been feeling so alone . . . " He took that as a 'go' sign . . . "but I can't hurt Carol." I shoved him away waving my hands in front of him to ward him off. "Let's just leave it right here."

"OK," he whispered. "I don't want to hurt her, either."

Carol re-entered the room. "You two having a good time?" she spewed out the words coldly.

Oh, oh . . . she heard us, I moaned silently. *Darn myself, anyhow.*

"OK, Carol," he whimpered. "So I kissed Pat. So what? It was innocent."

"If that's what you want, I'm not going to stand in your way," she ranted.

"OK, if that's how you're going to be. That's what I want," he screamed.

She threw his picture at him. Then his white dinner jacket,

which she had saved from their anniversary night, went flying. It splatted him in the face. "I'm just a born loser," she screamed hysterically. "Go ahead, you two . . . I've got to get out of here."

"Carol," I begged for her to listen to me. "Come on out to the kitchen with me. I want to talk to you."

As we got out there I confided to her, "No one's asked me what I think of this whole mess. Carol, I'm terribly sorry. I feel awful. It was just a little tender moment . . . Jim was just trying to help. I don't want Jim. You two belong together. Forgive me, Carol, please."

She grunted.

"Come on, Carol, . . . "

"Well, I know it was just a little kiss," she admitted, "but it hurt . . . "

Her eyes pleaded. She wanted to trust me. She wanted me for a friend.

"I know." I looked her straight in the eye.

Jim came into the room. "Carol," he butted in, "I want to talk to Pat a minute."

"Be my guest," she stomped out of the room.

"Pat, I think I love you," he blurted out.

"Oh, you do not, Jim, you . . . you . . . don't even know me."

"You're the girl of my dreams," he rattled on. "I want to take you up to bed right now and . . . "

"Oh, shut up, you . . . you marshmallow," I pushed him away. The soft sound of the front door shutting quietly blared in my ears. "Carol's leaving!" I cried as I ran into the front room. A lone note sat there on the table.

"Good-bye. I hope you'll both be very happy."

It was written in an emotional scrawl. "Oh, no!" I flew out the door. Not a sign of her. The streets were empty.

"She's gone, Jim. She's disappeared! I'm worried. You know, that girl really loves you with all her heart."

"I know, Pat," he said quietly as they returned into the house to talk. "I don't deserve a love like that. I know I'll always hurt her. I just don't know what to do about it."

"Why don't you try being a man?" I tried to reason with him. "Jim, don't take advantage of her." We sat there wringing our hands, talking, trying to figure out what to do, still slugging down, now, sobering beers. In time we fell asleep on the sofa side by side.

It was what seemed hours later that Carol returned. She entered the room with a snooty, "My, but don't you two look cozy?"

"Carol, we've been so worried."

"Don't worry about me," she snapped. "I just almost jumped off the bridge, that's all. But I decided it wasn't worth it."

"You're right Carol," he agreed.

"You bet I'm right!" she yelled. "Good-bye Jim." She held the door open for him to leave. Jim sheepishly closed the door slowly behind him.

"Don't look so down," her voice cracked in a dulled anger as she tackled our friendship. "It's all right. It's not your fault. This deal was doomed right from the beginning. Pat, there's a lot about Jim and me I never told you about." She motioned me over to sit at the dining table to tell her tale of woe . . . .

"I met Jim at the U.S.O. where I used to go and try to cheer up the guys who were going to Viet Nam. In fact, that year I was voted Queen of the U.S.O. He was in the army. The first time I saw him was when he handed me some tacks while I was on the ladder hanging up decorations for a dance. I fell in love with him right there on the spot. There was a sadness about him. He was quiet and withdrawn. I found out he had been married and had been stationed in Hawaii. He was all mixed-up."

I was all ears. I was finally getting an explanation for that gut feeling that told me that there was more to their relationship than met the eye. It had such depth, yet was so fragile . . .

"I know I was good for him," Carol rambled on. "He fell in love with me too, but would never admit it to himself."

"How can that happen?" I questioned. "Doesn't he know his own feelings?"

"He's too confused," the tearful young woman confided. "We wanted to be together so we moved into an apartment. I told my mom and friends and sisters and everyone that we were married.

We really were happy. Then it happened. I got pregnant. Pat, I got real scared!" She wept so meaningfully, her emotions were right on the surface. "He was married and I was afraid to tell him. My sister helped me. She lives in California. In California you can have abortions in the hospital. It's all legal and everything."

"Carol, you didn't!" I scolded.

"I did," she admitted, " . . . I did. I had it done. You know, I've felt lousy ever since."

"Does he know?"

"Nope. He never will, either. I just have to handle it myself. I'll never do anything like that again."

"Carol, you have to put it all behind you. Do you think this is the end?"

"Yeah. I know the way he is. He'll never change. He doesn't love me. At least, not like it should be. This little episode really finished us, but good."

"Carol, I'm so sorry."

"Don't be," her voice sounded flat. " . . . there'll be a time." Her eyes chilled me right to the spine.

I tried cheering myself with wine,
And embracing folly—
My mind still guiding me with wisdom.
. . . I saw that wisdom is better than folly, just as
light is better than darkness.

Eccl 2:3 & 13 (NIV)

Chapter 5

"Do You Wanna Dance?"

My heart still sighs as I think about how fragile relationships can be. Looking back one never knows how things are going to turn out despite right intentions. I was still wondering. *"Is there a God? Why are all these things happening? Why? Why?* I was becoming more and more confused even then. Carol saw that I was beginning to lose ground and she feared for her own heavy emotions at this time, also. She knew how to pick herself up and try for the moon. Carol took things into hand. One night she approached me with her bright idea. "Don't you ever go out?" her voice was full of warmth and concern.

"Out where?" I hadn't even dared to think of where or how or who I might meet next.

"Out on the town . . . "

"I wouldn't know where to go," I answered stupidly.

"I think you need to get out for an evening," Carol shook her finger at me, " . . . or else you're going to crack up or something. What do you say we go out this weekend? I already asked your mother and she said she'd baby-sit."

I was secretly grateful even though it sounded so crazy. I giggled to myself, *My babysitter gets my mother to baby-sit for her.*

It was a calm March night. The adventure started almost immediately. I felt very gussied-up since Carol helped me put on eye makeup—even eyeliner! Off we went out the door feeling a freedom that I hadn't felt for a very long time. Near disaster was lurking around the corner as we stepped off of the curb. A car swerved around the corner at a rather dangerous speed nearly running us over. We awkwardly scampered out of their way in our high heels shaking our fists at the two guys who were in it. The car turned around and stopped beside us. "Do you want a lift?" they hollered.

"Not with you," I stuck my nose in the air trying to appear very independent. "I'd rather ride a bus any day."

"Where are you going?"

"We're not sure, yet," we giggled in unison. "Just out for the evening."

"Come on with us."

"No, thank you. Good bye."

"Stuck-up dames," they laughed as they jetted away.

We climbed aboard the bus which came along just in time, chattering and giggling all the way downtown. Not knowing where to go once we got there we took in a few cocktail lounges, but there didn't seem to be much excitement going on except for the leftover St. Patrick's Day decorations from the popular "green beer day".

"Do you like to dance?" Carol asked very carefully not wanting to appear to be a floozie or something.

"I haven't danced very much since high school." I got a sick feeling thinking about the dances that Bob had taken me to only to ditch me and disappear. "I can slow dance, but this new fast stuff . . . . I don't know."

"Come on." Carol coaxed, "I know a place down the block. Maybe we can find a little action."

We trotted on down toward the skid row area of town. The only time I had ever been to skid row was to visit Bob's sister who had been a waitress down there somewhere when we were first married. "Now, we'll be OK as long as we stick together," Carol proceeded to show me the ropes.

The street was bustling with servicemen everywhere . . . and bums. There was a cheap amusement place on the corner advertising girlie pictures and tattoos. Its flickering sign reddened the street as we walked past several shabby pawnshops. We came on an attractive brick facade. Music rushed out at us. It was peppy and inviting. "This is it," Carol said as we started in the door. A policeman stood at the door, a familiar face. He was the husband of one of my best friends, in fact, my maid-of-honor at my ill-fated marriage ceremony.

Embarrassing memories haunted me as soon as I saw him. He had helped by giving me a ride home one night after work around Thanksgiving. I had felt that he knew about the bowling alley and wanted to find out what was going on. Evidently, Bob had found out about the lift, somehow, and had threatened him. Bob had called me up and told me, "I took care of that policeman boyfriend of yours. He won't be giving me any more trouble." I never did find out what Bob had done to him. All I knew was that my former bridesmaid friend wouldn't even speak to me when she had called that Thanksgiving morn to announce the fact that our friendship was over.

I blushed when I saw him as he held his hand out for I didn't know what. With a professional demeanor, he smiled a warm, but "stay away from me" smile. "Your I.D.?" He pressed.

"Oh, ID. Driver's license OK?" He nodded me on in. He knew me and how old I was, but I ignored that fact.

Passing the inspection we went on through the turnstile. The place was packed. We couldn't see too well at first in the dimly lit room. A psychedelic light flashed on to some western singers doing some silly antics on the stage. They were as drunk as their customers, but they never missed a beat of music. All in all they were very entertaining, however, it probably depended on how badly one needed to escape problems through laughter.

Carol noticed an empty booth. "Come on, Pat. Over here," she ushered me down the aisle. Almost immediately we found ourselves dancing, short little ditties, very little conversation, probably because the night was yet young and the drink hadn't livened things up yet. I was getting a little nervous about protecting my belongings while I was on the dance floor. "What do you do with your purse?" I asked for help from the pro.

"Oh, come into the bathroom. I'll show you." Carol gave me a lesson of how to wad up the money and tuck it down into my bra. "It'll be safe there," she winked.

As I undertook to accept the next dance suddenly I found myself tripping on something that was on the floor. My partner stopped to pick up a $20 bill. In fact, the whole dance floor was covered with $20 bills . . . money that I had so carefully been saving toward food and rent. "Oh, no!" I held my hands to my head, then crawled on my hands and knees in search for them. Couples stood there laughing at me, but believe it or not, one by one they handed me a morsel of good will until I got back every last cent. The mishap actually became a blessing . . . a little bit of faith in human-hood, after all . . . which I badly needed.

The evening wore on. Now, new guys were walking in off the streets already acting loud and tipsy. The next few chumps that asked us to dance were very drunk and full of propositions. I became very insulted and disgusted. "These guys are after just one thing. What do you say we leave?" I complained to Carol.

"As soon as we finish these beers," she tried to prolong the agony even though she was tired of it, too. As we mulled over the problem of whether we should stay or not, I slowly became aware of a sudden strange glow which warmed me up all inside.

"I feel sort of spooky . . . " I whispered to Carol.

"What do you mean?" Carol frowned from puzzlement.

"Do you see anyone watching us?"

"No," Carol looked around. "Where do you think it's coming from?"

"I don't know, I just feel it." It was only a moment when there was a soft tap on my shoulder.

"You wanna dance?"

I looked up to a face that seemed strangely familiar, and yet I was sure I'd never seen him before. I timidly nodded a "yes" shakily following him onto the dance floor. His shyness was appealing. He heaved a quiet sigh. I smiled my best Mona Lisa smile. His voice cracked as he broke the silence with, "Do you come here often?"

"Oh, no. This is the first time I've been here." I winced.

Oh, oh. He's going to hand me a line . . . like the others. He asked me some other pertinent questions. My suspiciousness took over. "Listen . . . " I straightened him out then and there, "I came here to dance." My hands began waving frantically. "If you have anything else on your mind, then go ask someone else to dance with."

He chuckled with delight giving me a big squeeze.

"It sure is refreshing to meet a nice girl for a change." His dark brown eyes sparkled huge stars. His black wavy hair shimmered under the wandering colored lights which flashed on and off over us as we glided by the bandstand.

"Are you married?" He pumped me for more information.

"I'm in the process of getting a divorce." I answered even though I didn't really want to talk about it.

"How many kids you got?"

"Three," I smiled proudly.

"Oh," he gulped deeply. Then he caught a hold of the moment, "Oh, well, no matter. I like kids."

We began to get into some serious dancing. The music seemed brand new as though I was hearing it for the first time. A sweet kiss, meaning to be an innocent kiss, became a necking session as if no one else was around. Lighthearted and silly he attempted to do the twist. He was game, but I just didn't have the courage. We had to give it up.

"Let's go sit down," I panted all out of breath. He walked me to the booth where he had found me and helped me to my seat. He stood there, his feet planted firmly to the floor in an awkward silence. *Please, oh, please, don't leave . . .* I begged any spirit, be it God or angel, whoever might be around to help. I hinted my plea by scooting over to the far side of the booth.

"Can I sit down?" He accurately took the hint.

"Oh, sure!"

Just then Carol came back from an entirely different planet, it seemed. It was as if she was there, and then off into space somewhere. I introduced them. Carol was all busy with happy chatter with whoever she decided to kid around with while Ron and I seriously got acquainted. As he talked he cupped his hands around his beer glass peering into it, slowly spilling out words . . . special words, sort of in little spurts. "I'm a small town guy, myself. I like people . . . " The words were as in a script, just what I wanted to hear. " . . . I know people," he went on. "I'm a quiet guy." I nodded a knowing response as though I knew him all along. "I like hunting and fishing. Back home I can pick up with a rifle or pole any old time." His eyes lit up as he talked about his hometown. "I'm in the service now, though. Back home I work in the mill."

My heart caused my breath to stop as I gasped. The mill! It was all fitting together as in a dream. The strange talk I had had with my aunt that day in the woods floated back to fill my mind . . . My aunt's words! "I think there's something for you at the mill!" Then he whisked out a picture from his wallet. It was a picture of a young woman who resembled me a lot. "This here is the girl that I broke up with. She wrote me a Dear John. Guess she couldn't wait for me to get out of the service." I knew he showed me the picture because he saw the resemblance.

We then quietly resumed dancing each hiding in our own private thoughts. All too soon the music stopped again, only it was for the very last time. The dim psychedelic lights turned into bright lights, a hint that the evening was ended. There was a mad rush of everyone buying a half case of beer to take home. He slowly walked me back to my booth plopping himself in it as he nudged me over trying to hang on to every last second. Carol was sitting across from us. My eyes met those of hers. They were begging her for help. Carol knew just what to do. Ron quickly asked me for my phone number. Then he was gone.

Carol screamed, "half case to go!" to the waitress. "Patti, she added loudly, "we're going to have a party!" Ron heard. He stopped. His body flew back into the seat staying there, hanging on to the side of the booth as though it were trying to get away from him.

"Where are we going?" he asked.

"We'll find someplace," I giggled. Carol winked a we-made-it wink as the three of us walked out on to the street.

"Where's a good place?" he scratched his head. "I could rent a hotel room."

"Oh, yeah . . . that seems to be the thing to do these days, huh?"

"I don't mean nothing like that," he said in disgust, "but it would be a place to go."

An idea hit me. "I know a better place." I was a little tipsy by now and feeling mischievous. "Let's go up to the bowling alley that I used to help run. I still have the key."

"I don't think we should," he halted.

"It's OK," I explained. "My ex-husband leased it. It's all closed up now."

Through the foolish talk we suddenly noticed that Carol was not walking with us anymore. She had disappeared. We looked up the street and then down . . . oh, there she was bending over the window of a car talking to someone. We meandered over to where she was standing, close enough so that we could see who she was talking to. I recognized them immediately. "Well, it's a small world!" I hollered. It was the same guys who had nearly run us over earlier in the evening.

"They're going out to a night spot," Carol explained. "Do you guys want to go?" Ron nodded excitedly, ready for action. We piled into the backseat of the car with me on Ron's lap.

Nothing else mattered that evening except that we were together, not even the late hour of the night and the fact that my mother was babysitting. I had already called her an hour before telling her that we would be home as soon as the place closed. It didn't matter that I had promised her. It was a night as in a dream. We found ourselves in an after hours dance hall. It was full of drunk people who didn't know when to stop, or just didn't want to stop as was our case. Suddenly I could dance to anything! To think that just hours earlier I couldn't dance anything fast. Happiness was such a fun teacher!

He glided me around the floor winking as he twirled me under his arm. "You're a living doll," his lips formed a huge grin as his eyes twinkled stars. The music over, remorsefully we returned to our table only to find that someone had swiped my chair. "Come on. Sit here," he pulled me over to his lap. Looking around us everyone seemed to be on a different plane getting very drunk. We didn't feel the need for more drink. "Let's go out to the car," he suggested impetuously. "We can talk better there."

Once in the car a magic little kiss started the moment. As he placed his arm around the back of the seat he motioned for me to lean up against his body to relax. There were many things to talk about. There were too few minutes to embrace and be close, a kiss, a question and another kiss. Then with an awkward suddenness I backed away from him. Bending over the front seat I crouched, holding my knees, feeling very vulnerable. "What's wrong?" he lifted my chin to turn my tear stained face toward his.

"I don't know. I guess I'm just scared of myself."

"Pat," Ron attempted to explain his intentions. "The only thing I have to offer a girl is a strong backbone. I don't want nothin' from you or for you to do anythin' you don't want to do." He started to gather himself together. "I'll tell you what. I think it's time to call it quits for tonight. I'll call a taxi for you or get you a ride home. I'll send the others out to the car. I think they'll probably run you home. I think they're all right. They're just out raising Cain." He hopped out. Peering back into the car he added, "I'll be going home on leave soon, but I'll call you when I get back." Our eyes met in a bond of trust. "I will . . . ," he gave me a little peck on the lips. " . . . as soon as I get back."

As all good things must come to an end, my mother was full of anger. I explained about the second dance hall that hadn't been in my plan. My mother left the house with, "I will never baby-sit for you again!"

She didn't know. I didn't know. It was the most beautiful

night I had ever had. It was the only night like it that I would ever have.

Calm days followed. I was feeling brand new for calmness was so new to me. I was actually able to sit calmly, mending clothes and doing little things that my nerves wouldn't allow me to even think of before. I was just patiently waiting for that important phone call. The last thing I expected was for Bob to happen on the scene. He knocked on the back door one evening just before the divorce was to be finalized. He was even a little hesitant and shy, with a six-pack of beer tucked under his arm when I opened the door. The back door was the only entry then because the lock on the front door had broken from one of his escapades. I hadn't been able to get it fixed yet. "Can I come in?" he pleaded with his friendly personality.

"What do you want?" I glared back at him.

"I just want to talk. We're almost divorced, you know. I thought for the kid's sake we should try to reach a friendly understanding."

"Oh, come on then." I introduced him to Carol as he followed me into the front room with "This is the Presto-log kid."

"Oh, yeah . . . hi," the nervous nanny mumbled giving me a stern look of apprehension.

We sat down to a forced, but seemingly friendly chat. As the conversation eased he made a suggestion. "Why don't we make a pizza or something? I'm kind of hungry."

"That'd be nice," I laughed haughtily, " . . . go ahead and buy the stuff. If you want to eat, you buy."

"OK, come on then. We'll go to the store."

"Oh no, you don't," I backed off. "I'm not going anywhere with you. You'll probably kill me or something."

"Oh, that," he pooh-poohed. "Patti, I'm sorry about all that. I was terribly upset." I glared right through him remembering about all the nights that he had tormented me so that I had nearly lost my mind.

"I'll tell you what." I felt that he knew he had better get off of that subject, *fast!* "You can drive my car." He had bought a brand new red car, the very one that Jim had seen on that famous Presto-log night.

"Yeah! How did you afford that? You can't even pay support!"

"I filed bankruptcy. I put it in Dad's name so that I didn't lose it."

"That figures." I was getting madder by the minute. "All right, you're on!" I marched out the door. "You'll be sorry . . . " I got even madder as I climbed into the brand new bucket seats putting my hands on the brand new steering wheel. I felt a hateful power as I started up the brand new motor zooming on down the street, swerving into a driveway. I made a dead stop. Then I recklessly pushed it into reverse as hard as I could. Back on the street I stepped on the gas repeating the same procedure at the next driveway and the one after that. I felt like a maniac and wanted so much to be one. He just sat there calmly with his arms folded smiling all the way to the store. "How much money do you have?" I asked him as I slammed the car door instead of screaming a swear word.

"Quite a bit."

"Good. You don't mind if I spend it, do you?" I wheeled a cart through the store darting from one aisle to another dumping food into the basket as fast as it would roll off of the shelf. As I piled a very large sack of dog food on the cart I teased, "You don't mind feeding the dog, too, do you?"

"Go ahead," he chuckled.

A fifty-pound bag of potatoes fit neatly on the bottom rung of the basket. Three cartons of cigarettes came off the shelf very easily. "Everyone has to have a vice, you know," I chided. Oodles of cans and a case of beer went flying into the basket. Meat. Lots of meat. The load grew into two baskets. All of the shopping took about ten minutes. The store clerk, who had known us from years before we had ever moved to Philadelphia, couldn't help join into the spree with laughter. We were all laughing, being mighty silly by this time.

At home the pizza party started out to be jolly, too. The celebration was the ending of the past. Bob was being too agreeable. At one point Carol took me aside. "He's up to something," she whispered. "Be careful."

"I know . . . " I nodded my head. With a wink I added, "I'm having fun. He couldn't hurt me again ever, even if he tried."

After over-consuming the bottle of "cheer", Bob's camouflage wore off. He uncovered what his mission was all about. He backed me into a corner, his hands resting on the wall as his body rubbed up against mine.

"Good grief," I snapped at him, "we must have a little respect." I backed away from him laughing, nearly in hysteria, as I brushed my fingers together at him in naughty, naughty fashion. He sighed and slouched down on the couch. Then he began showing his true spirit. He became snotty.

"I see you've been using your birth control pills," he attempted to fill me with a guilt I didn't deserve. They were still sitting by the kitchen sink.

"I haven't used one pill since you left," I found myself losing it. The birth control pills had just become a fact in the households of America in the past couple of years. I had asked the doctor for help when I had found out about Bob's problem. I had thought that perhaps the fear of getting me pregnant had caused him to turn against me and onto men. However, I had later found out that it had had nothing to do with his problem. My doctor, as many doctors felt at the time, wouldn't prescribe the pill for me now, anyhow, since I was no longer married. The pills sat there in the kitchen untouched. I knew it.

"Boy, have you got big hips," he sneered at me as I walked across the floor.

"All the better to make babies with," I laughed.

He began to whine. "Come on. Go to bed with me. I'll give you my car if you do."

"I don't want your dumb car," I laughed right into his face, "It's too expensive. You don't even have one-fiftieth of it paid for, you dumb shit." He cowered even lower in the chair.

"Can I sleep on your couch? I'm too drunk to drive home." He let his head nod from side to side.

"I'll call you a taxi."

"Don't bother," he got up stomping out the door.

"Boy, he sure sobered up quick, the damn phoney," I laughed. We stayed up for awhile celebrating the victory.

"I'm so proud of you . . . you've got spunk you didn't even know you had . . . " Carol said. She twirled herself around grunting a giggle as only she could do.

"Yeah. I did pull that off pretty good, didn't I?"

However, just as he had always done whenever I had any chance of having a good time, he got even in his own way. It was several hours after his hasty departure that a couple of knocks came striking on the door. It was my poor mother. "Do you have a man in bed over here?" she scowled.

"A what?" I didn't know if I should start crying or laughing. "Mom, why do you say a thing like that?" I let the woman in. She was wringing her hands in nervous fretfulness.

"Bob called. He said he was phoning the children's detention home to pick up your kids because you had a man in your bed."

"Mom," I couldn't believe my ears. "For cripes sake, won't you trust me? Do you want to see for yourself?" A phoney laughter crept into my words.

"I don't see what's so funny," she was hot with anger. We calmed her down as we relayed the story of the evening's events. "That man," she shook her head. "I can't believe it. He's so convincing! Why . . . he can make a person believe black is white."

The divorce was a snap. Bob had at least had enough sense and dignity not to show up. However, it was contested. All my lawyer had to do, though, was to present to the judge documents of Bob's behavior and the sordid facts of why the bowling alley was closed by the moral squad. The judge made a statement to Bob's lawyer who was blushing, big time. He had known Bob from politics, but didn't know to what extent he had carried his perversions. "We must ensure that our community is freed from this type of behavior for it undermines the very fabric of our society," the judge scolded.

That problem was now out of the way. I hated the thought of tackling the next project of importance. It chilled me just thinking about it. I needed to play detective. I needed some proof of his behavior before our marriage. My first phone call was to Bob's best man whom he had met in the navy. His name was Bob, also. Bob and his wife were lovely people. I hated to even tell them what was going on. It turned out that they knew nothing of this type of behavior from Bob. I wished that I hadn't even called them. Next I called the commander of the Civil Air Patrol where we had met. He was a big wig in the police department and I hoped that he might know something. He was very business-like and crabby. "All I know is that any guy who goes around getting little girls pregnant has some pretty heavy problems . . . " I thanked him and hung up fast! I even knew what he was talking about! Had I known all along and had just refused to admit it? I was puzzled about my own behavior in all of this . . .

It was the weekend of SnowCap . . . an adventure which was created for the Civil Air Patrol cadets. I had been a cadet when Bob and I had met. I had actually joined CAP to be near my boyfriend, Eddie, who went on later to join the air force. Bob came from out of the blue to become the commandant of the cadet squadron. He had big ideas! In a very short time the squadron grew from a bare dozen cadets to over 100 under his leadership. SnowCap was a winter survival course that took place up in the mountains in January. The clever leader that he was, he had arranged for a full two page spread in the newspaper of the event . . . pictures of the cadets on their CB's, with stretchers, parachutes, the flag, in formation, etc. I was the adjutant, or secretary, of the squadron, which made me his secretary. A proposal . . . a Dear John to Eddie which had been brewing, anyhow . . . an engagement. We had become engaged in October and were planning our wedding for February.

On this January winter weekend he ignored me almost completely saying, "we need to be business-like". I acknowledged the fact that he had a very big responsibility and went about my business. I had had a big responsibility, too, for I had to keep track of who was going to which maneuver, going to which class, etc by checking out the rosters for the various events, especially for bed-check. Well, the bed check turned out to be a disaster. There was one girl missing. We checked and double-checked and it came out the same each time. I notified one of the officers since I had been unable to locate Bob. About that time the girl was miraculously found by guess who? Bob. The emergency was over. I was feeling mighty exhausted and relieved. I climbed into my bunk while the officers were huddled around the Franklin stove talking over the events of the day and joking around. I had had the honor of bunking with the officers because I was engaged to the commandant. I had been so proud of him and excited about our forth-coming wedding, just a month away.

A few weeks later this young female cadet approached me as I was coming down the church steps after Mass. "Are you Bob's "fi-yan-cee?" This young girl had always appeared to me to be a little slow . . . sort of back woodsy.

"Yes. Do you want to see my ring?" I had proudly flashed the rather impressive diamond.

"Oh," the young girl slowly walked away, head down.

The next time I saw her she was with her mother in our own living room one day when I had come home from work just a month after our wedding. I asked my mother-in-law, who was living with us, "What are they doing here?"

Josephine answered, "Some problem with her daughter."

"Oh," I answered. It was at this point that I could not figure myself out. Had I just buried any suspicions? Was I afraid to find out more? Or was I just too trusting?

Had I just been hiding my head in the sand? I mulled it all over in my mind. Was I really that naive? I couldn't figure out how I could've been so stupid. Remembering back, it was about then that Bob started staying out until all hours during his "night out with the boys". I suppose they were not only his lovers, but his confidants, too. I left it at that. I might as well forget about that incident, it's not going to help me any with the problem of his homosexuality, anyhow.

Since our night out on the town had been so successful Carol and I decided it was time for another night out. I got a babysitter from down the block and off we went, this time in the opposite direction. We went to a dive near the famous park there in the city. It attempted to keep a proper atmosphere, the major rule being that women were to wear dresses. The husband and wife ensemble on the piano and drums, had played there for years. I was just as happy to people-watch as I was to dance. Carol was having her usual blast mingling with the guys: kidding, giggling, and leading them mischievously. I was asked to dance a few times, then a rather extroverted young man, dressed in suit and vest, started to make polite advances to me. "Would you go out to dinner with me?" he asked.

"I can't. I've got three kids," I haughtily rejected him

"That's OK, we can take them, too."

"No, I wouldn't go out with you for all the tea in China." I was downright rude. The poor guy had no idea where I was coming from. This guy, for some strange reason, made me nervous. At first I couldn't figure out why. He was nice, polite, didn't get fresh . . . oh, yes. It was his suit. Bob had always worn a suit. In fact, the guys at work always wore suits, the politicians always wore suits, even the priests and bodyguards wore suits. *He looks like a city-slicker,* I affirmed the reason for my attitude. *Slick as hell.*

. . . Evidently some people
are throwing you
into CONFUSION
and are trying to pervert
the gospel of Christ.

Gal 1:7 (NIV)

Chapter 6

Him

Wandering through my life in memory, I meandered back into the kitchen. It wasn't the homey atmosphere that I dreamed of making when I was a young girl. As my dreams smashed, so did my surroundings. My kitchen had become a lonely place. No family type meals, no happy bustling expressing myself creating delicious smells of baked goods. Meals were now made in haste . . . survival style. The kids loved spaghetti, cinnamon rolls and hamburgers. All that seemed to matter was to see that they were happy and well fed. I slumped down into a chair deciding that it was now late enough in the day to have my first beer. The boys were at school. Betsy was taking her nap. Who would know?

The telephone hung on the wall daring me to remember the times when it was the most important "life-line" that I had had. It had all started while I had patiently waited for Ron, my soldier acquaintance, to call as he had promised. It was not yet an obsession, but it was the "hope-line".

Early one evening the phone rang. Carol had been receiving a lot of phone calls at that time, so I didn't think much of it. This time was different, though! It was for me! "It's Ron," a deep voice trembled over the phone. I could tell that he was worried that perhaps I wouldn't remember him. I played it for all it was worth.

"Ron?" I tried to pretend that I had nearly forgotten. After all, I didn't want him to think that this phone call was probably the biggest wish I had in this life. "Oh. Ron. I have a good friend by that name (which was true.) I thought you were him for a moment. (Which wasn't true—I hadn't even heard from this friend for 7 years, or so). Hi! How are you?"

"OK," he said flatly.

"Did you have a nice visit?"

"It was OK. I've had enough of that home stuff for awhile, though. I'm glad to be back. Does that sound crazy?"

"No . . . well, maybe."

Silence. Finally he blurted out. "I wanna go out."

"Then why don't you?" I teased.

"I don't go out much." Another silence. "Anyway, I don't have no place to go."

"Ron, I told you that you could come here sometime if you wanted to."

"What's the address?" he quickly said. "I borrowed my buddy's car. I'll be right there."

I shook my head in near disbelief as to how cute and funny he was. I just stood there enjoying the sweetness of the moment until it hit me. *He's coming here! Tonight! Oh, my gosh!* I dashed around picking up the house . . . then, too, there was my bath . . . all in fifteen minutes. *Will he look the same? Will it be the same?* I questioned myself all the while.

I nervously peeked out of the curtains, a hundred times it seemed, until finally I saw him pull up in front. Forgetting to act matter-of-fact I ran out the back door. I had forgotten to tell him that the front door wasn't working. All of my fears of rejection or awkwardness disappeared when I saw him. There was that same warm smile and warm twinkling eyes. He grabbed me quickly pulling me over to the side of the house and placed a firm kiss on my lips. Blushing, he murmured, "I don't do that very often. I just missed you."

"I like it," I assured him. I was floating in elation as I led him into the house. "Look who's here!" I presented him to Carol as we walked into the front room hand in hand.

"Hi!" Carol obviously made herself scarce. "I don't want to be rude or anything, but I have some things to do upstairs." She picked up her cigarettes and ashtray, "I have to make sure the kids are in bed, and not into mischief." I could hear her grunting a half-laugh as she climbed the stairs. She was happy for me.

It was already 9 o'clock. Most of my private life had been happening in late evening hours since the divorce. Very polite conversation started off the visit. He had brought a six-pack of beer. It was a common gesture when dating these days. We nursed them as we very politely talked about his trip back home. Abruptly, embarrassment interrupted our peaceful, dignified visit. He burped! Big, loud and sudden gastro shocks! His face expressed emotional pain as it blushed a deep red. We tried to ignore the big blast as we talked on. He burped again. These were loud important burps. "It's the beer," he mumbled. "I'm not used to drinking much." It got worse. I had never seen anyone with such indigestion! He started doing push-ups stating, "they tell me that this is supposed to help hiccups, maybe it'll work with the burps." I had to hold my belly from laughing so hard. "Girls make me nervous," he confessed as he picked himself up off the floor. "I'm not going to drink anymore tonight."

He joined me on the couch trying to forget his embarrassment. "My gosh!" he cried suddenly, "I think I have them licked!" He threw his arms around me giving me a sweet soft kiss. "See? No more burps."

The nervousness finally subsided after the evening's disastrous beginning. A peacefulness came over us making ourselves more comfortable on the couch. Suddenly, he arose to dim the lamp. "You don't mind, do you?" he walked softly back to join me. "I just love you, that's all." It was a very blunt statement. A fact. His face turned a blushing red even his ears blushed as he stretched out his arms to me. "I do," he hugged me reassuringly.

I knew. I loved him too . . . from the very beginning. I didn't dare let him know. He was the first guy I met since Bob. It was crazy. He didn't dare know how deeply he had already touched my heart.

We fell back on the couch holding one another tightly as though not to let the moment get away. After a long while he pulled me up by my arms and sat me on the edge of the couch falling to his knees. "Do you mind?" He very gently undressed me to the waist. Kneeling there, he stared up at me in a calm excitement. "You're beautiful," he kissed my breasts. It was warmth . . . no rhythm, yet flowing motion, fingers and lips moving in tender rhythm. No sound, yet overwhelming sound . . . like music.

The moments, hours passed, it could have been days for time had no meaning. It was a healing experience. A blessed gift. A miraculous togetherness. Eventually, though, time became a reality. We had to face the fact that he had to leave. We didn't want the evening to end. "I'll never hurt you, Pat," he whispered as he lingered at the door. He held me tightly in his arms. It was as if it had all been a dream and it would become unreal if he left. "I don't wanna go . . . but," he turned abruptly, "I have to. Here goes." He dove off the porch. "I'll call," he hollered as he ran to his car.

The next morning I sent my little boy, Robert, off to school with a tenderness that I didn't know I had. My heart had been replenished. I was busying around the kitchen still in euphoria over the night before. I was just getting ready to see Blake off to the morning session of kindergarten. He didn't take the bus because the school was close enough to walk to. I was standing at the back door in the kitchen. It all happened so suddenly! The boards underneath the old faded red linoleum began to part back and forth under my feet. A huge thunderous rumble became louder and louder. Bricks fell from the roof before my very eyes. *Oh, God! It's the end of the world!* I threw my hands up to the heavens. *Oh, God! Don't come now . . . not now when I've just found him,* I pleaded. I was sure that at any time I would see heavenly beings coming down out of the clouds. The rumbling stopped as quickly as it had started. The stillness was interrupted by a "Pat? Pat? Are you all right?" It was Carol coming gingerly down the stairs. "That was an earthquake, wasn't it? It scared me to death!"

Just then little Robert came running into the back door. "Mom! Mom! The ground was shaking!" His face was a sick white.

"It's OK," honey, it's just an earthquake."

"I don't want to go to school," he cried.

"You can stay home today." I knew that there would be no sense in sending him on to school today. The opportunity to learn, for lack of concentration, was dead. However, it turned out that Robert refused to go to school the rest of that week for reasons he couldn't or wouldn't divulge. In fact, it wasn't until he was a grown man that he admitted to me why he had been so upset. It seems that when he had gone to stand at the bus stop, he had stepped off of the curb and on to the very busy street. I had warned him that under *no circumstances* was he to step off of the curb until the bus arrived. He had disobeyed. At the moment his foot had touched the street the earthquake began. He was sure he had caused it.

The excitement of that moment brought with it a wonderfully special phone call, just minutes after the quake. "Hi, are you all OK?" It was Ron.

"We just lost part of our chimney, Robert won't go to school . . . other than that we're fine." My heart held a warm glow knowing that he had cared enough to call.

"Good. Just checking. I've got to go now. Bye."

Physically everybody and the house were OK, but emotionally I had things to straighten out. What with the fact that Robert refused to go to school, I went to see Sister to fill her in on the enormous stressful problems that had been confronting the family. It was only a day or two later, I received an unexpected visitor. It was the young priest with whom I had talked to about an annulment. "Hi, can I come in and talk to you about Robert making his first holy communion?"

"Oh, yes. I was just over to talk to Sister. I'm having trouble with Robert not wanting to go to school, ever since the earthquake."

"Don't push him," he shared his expertise with me, " . . . but set a date and have him stick to that date. I wanted to invite you to attend the First Communion parent group. It'll be a very good overview of our faith and a chance to ask any questions you might have."

"A brush-up course, huh?" I smiled. "Thank you Father. I'd like to go to that."

"Great! What've you been doing these days?" he asked in a pleasant friendly tone expecting it to be just a usual question.

"Oh, besides work and taking care of things here, I've been out dancing a couple of times."

"Dancing?" He was horrified. "A mother of three children has no business going out dancing!"

"Why not? I learned to dance at the Catholic school. What's the matter with that? I happened to meet a wonderful young man . . . "

"Well, I'll have to go now." He was abrupt. "Make sure you make it to the parent group. OK?"

He gathered himself together in order to make a kind gesture of a smile, even though he was upset.

I didn't care what the priest thought for Ron was special and I knew it. I wasn't exactly trusting toward the priests these days anyhow, what with Bob's problems and all. Did they expect that I was just going to go on by myself all my life? I was only 26 years old. According to them, any chance for companion-ship, for love, for a helpmate was over for me. I had already made up my mind before the divorce. I would marry again some day. I knew in my heart that God was with me.

A surprise phone call brought Ron on his second visit. He had managed to get into town early. I was prepared for just such a surprise having an outfit all ready to slip into, just in case he called. He appeared at the back door all bundled up in his jacket due to the crispness in the spring air. His eyes glistened in delight as he held my face between his hands, his eyes scanning my face. He made me feel pretty. I was wearing my favorite red and white striped middy blouse. My red stirrup pants were tastefully sexy as they covered my body gracefully. The moment was breathtaking. In fact, for a moment I thought maybe he had a screw loose for his eyes looked sort of cuckoo, I guess from the excitement of the moment. For a second I felt that maybe I should be frightened instead of elated. But then he calmed down, back to normal, to hopefully enjoy the rest of the visit less passionately.

I led him into the living room chattering away wanting to know more and more about what he'd been doing, and more about his work in the army. We were interrupted by a knock at the back door. Of all people! It was Bob! "Hi!" he grinned mischievously. "I thought that we could make a truce over a six-pack of beer."

"No, Bob. I don't think it would be a good idea." My legs became limp from the fear that he would find out that Ron was there. I gently closed the door in a good-natured manner, nearly squeezing his nose in it, but still able to keep things light.

"Spoiled sport . . . " he guffawed as he quickly disappeared into the dark night. I fled back into the front room.

"Who was that?" Ron asked.

"It was Bob!" I appeared to be melodramatic. Dramatics was one thing that Ron abhorred. I hadn't told him about all of the trouble I'd been through with Bob.

"So?" He had no idea of to what extent this man was capable of ruining a good day. I started to shake. Fears welled up inside of me. What if Bob was lurking around to start trouble? My hands shook. My arms and legs shook. Ron was disgusted. "I think I'd better leave," he quickly moved to the door. "The long bus ride into town was a waste this time . . . " he moaned as he gave me a quick good-bye kiss on the nose. It was then that I realized that he, too, was worried even though he pretended not to believe the gravity of the situation. I was unimpressed, though, as he snuck on tiptoe through the neighbor's fence (just in case Bob was lurking out there somewhere). *He doesn't look like the type of man to be very protective. Maybe he's a wimp . . .* I tried to dislike him thinking that maybe he was crazy, too. But on second thought . . . *no, I think maybe he's just cautious . . .*

His over cautiousness didn't cause him to stay away from me, though. That is, not quite. One early morning he called, "Hi! I just fell out of rank and snuck into the phone booth here. Just wanted to say 'Hi . . . ' "It was his way of saying that it was important that he call me. I loved hearing that deep voice quietly reporting, "Hello?"

But then the next Saturday morning his deep sincere voice came over the phone. "I'm glad you're home." The mere sound of his voice made me tingle all over. "Thought I'd call you before I took the bus into town." *Oh, he's coming over,* my heart pitter-pattered. "I was planning to go down and watch the parade," he went on. The pitter-patters turned into a sinking feeling. *He's just going to the parade! Darn it.* However, I still claimed a little hope, *maybe he'll invite me to join him.* He didn't.

The disappointment caused my mouth to start babbling . . . "I don't think I'd ever better see you again." I twisted the cord of the telephone trembling as I realized what I had just said. *My God! Why on earth did I say that?* The silence was awkward. My mind was in torment. He sounded shattered.

"I'm sorry if I got a little carried away the other night," he stammered.

"Well, I'm glad someone is sorry, because I'm not!" The words shot out of my mouth like darts. There was more silence . . . a long silence. "Ron! Everything is coming out all wrong!" My every limb was trembling. "Will I ever see you again?"

"Yeah, sometime . . . I guess," he answered in an uninterested voice. My knees were weak as I slowly hung up the phone nearly fainting into a chair admitting, *It's all over before it got started.*

Two weeks went by. I had only a vague hope, which hoped against hope, that I'd ever hear from him again. One evening the deep voice "hello" came floating over the wires once more. It was as if nothing had happened. He said he had called earlier, but couldn't reach me. "What time do you get home from work?"

"Oh, 8 o'clock or so." It was a lie. I usually got home at 10 o'clock." I . . . had said that because I knew that 10 o'clock was much too late for him to come and see me. Oh, God I have to sell the company on the fact that it would be good for "them" if I worked a split shift . . . half days and half nights.

The more I thought about it, it was a good idea for the company.

I presented the fact to my supervisor that if I came in part time in the day shift, I could contact the other departments while I was trying to find the answers to the "trouble list" that I had inherited. It was a rather big list for they had just started a new company that was an "easy pay plan" for car insurance. As with any new concept, there were problems. My idea sold! Now I could be home just before 8 o'clock.

The change paid off. Every other night at 8 o'clock sharp the phone would ring. I would be waiting. "Hello?" my voice always sounded as if I wasn't expecting his call. "Oh, hi!"

Sometimes he had nothing to say. It didn't matter. Sometimes he'd even whistle or hum a little tune, then chuckle, "I'm still here. I don't have nothing to say." When he did talk it was comical. The torture he would put himself through trying to communicate . . . . "I bought a large tube of toothpaste today. I've been thinking about coming over to see you. I figure I'll be using more of it now." It seemed that he was only able to talk in riddles.

One particular evening he decided to let me know the seriousness of his feelings. "I sure got hungry tonight. I'm starved. The PX closes in five minutes, but I thought I'd call you."

"Ron, if you only have five minutes, then you'd better hurry up and get over there."

"Oh, that's all right. I like it here. I'd rather talk." But nothing more was said.

Finally I interrupted the silence with . . . "Then why don't you say something?"

"I can't express my feelings very good. I'm so dumb." He was very matter-of-fact about it. "I really am, Pat. In fact, I wanted to be a priest, but they said I was too dumb. I barely made it through high school."

"Hey, you know I'm Catholic too?"

"You are? Oh, wow . . . you're kidding. Really?"

The realization of our similar backgrounds made the conversation a little more intense. "It seems to me that you'd have made a wonderful priest." I clued him in to the fact that I thought he was special. I knew first hand that they weren't getting the cream of the crop into the priesthood these days . . . "You seem intelligent to me. What are you so dumb about?"

"Reading, writing, arithmetic, and . . . women," he snickered.

"You know people." I reminded him. "That's the most important thing. You'd talk to the people so that they could understand . . . in the people's tongue, and tend to their needs." I also knew first-hand that tending to the needs of the people was not the church's highest priority.

The phone calls were nice, but the fact that he never seemed to want to come to see me again preyed on my mind. I was feeling mixed up. What had I done so wrong? He seemed to be comfortable over the telephone with me. Was he punishing me over that big fiasco when he had wasted his time coming over to see me?

One evening my brother, Bill, and a friend of his, Dan, dropped by. "I'm so glad to see you guys!" I was all smiles as I greeted them. A beer and a chair appeared for them all at once as I zeroed in on them, pulling up a chair for myself placing it directly in front of them: eyeball to eyeball. "I've been a little in the dumps," I started out with a warning. "Maybe you guys can help . . . you know, from a man's point of view?"

"Sounds interesting," the two fellows winked at each other. "Shoot! Let us in on the scoop."

"Well, there's this guy I met, see. He came to see me and we had a really neat intimate evening. In fact, we were so close that he even told me that he loved me."

"That's a problem?" Dan asked.

"Wait a minute til I finish. Then we had this misunderstanding the next time he called. I told him I didn't think I should see him again. We got past that, now. He calls me regularly, but he doesn't say anything about coming over to see me."

"He's trying to pull something out of you," Dan said.

"What?" I retorted.

"You know, a guy likes to know where he stands. Especially after he tells a girl that he loves her. What have you told him?"

"Nothing." I stared down at the floor. "In fact, I backed off."

"That's the problem. He's pulling it out of you."

"Oh, yeah?" I thought it over for a few minutes. "I think I can fix that." Suddenly I was feeling angry. I stormed around the room. "How do you call the Fort?"

Carol came to the rescue. Finding phone numbers was her specialty. After calling here and there asking questions she had it. "Here." She handed it over to impulsive little ol' me.

"Is Ron Passardi there, please?"

"Hey," the voice was muffled since the fellow on the other end was probably holding his hand over the receiver . . . "it's a girl for Passardi," he whispered evidently to a buddy nearby. Then back to me, "We'll get him," the teasing voice sang back. It took a few minutes.

"Hello? Who is this?" Ron sounded bewildered.

"Me. Pat."

"Oh, hi. How did you get my number?" he stuttered.

"I have ways," I laughed. "Do you mind?"

"No, I was just surprised."

We talked for awhile over the misunderstanding we had had. At the same time Carol was in the front room making eyes at Bill and Dan. Everything seemed to be going very well, there. My attention refocused in on the conversation. "I'm sorry about the time I said I shouldn't see you again.

"That made me feel bad," he admitted.

I felt relieved. Under my breath I whispered to myself, *I've been right. He was hurt."* I love you," I stated bluntly.

"You what?" he pretended to be surprised.

"I said I love you."

"You luck me? What's that?" Now he was playing real dumb.

"I love you . . . " I hollered louder.

"Oh! You love me." He enunciated each syllable. Silence. That awful silence again. Then . . . "I don't know what to say."

"What do you mean by that?" I felt embarrassed. The sweat started dripping from my forehead.

"Not here, Pat," he answered in a sneaky whisper. "I can't say nothing here, the guys and all, you know. Let's see. Tomorrow's Saturday. I'll call you tomorrow at 5 o'clock. OK?"

I started to cry. "Now I'm sorry I told you."

"It's OK," he said softly. "Don't cry. Everything's OK. Are you all right now?"

"I . . . I guess so."

The time dragged. I could think of nothing else all day as I watched the hour hand on the clock as it slowly made its rounds. The closer it came to the 5 o'clock hour, the more nervous and teary-eyed I became. It was finally time. Ring: it was Ron calling right on time just as he said he would. However, his nervousness was very apparent through his quiet awkwardness. "What's the matter?" I asked him. He sighed in deep exasperation. A stone silence followed.

"Pat, help me. I just can't express my feelings. Please help me."

"I don't know what you want to say," I said tenderly.

"Maybe we should just be friends," he heaved a huge sigh. "I can't be pushed, Pat. I just can't be pushed."

"Who's pushing? Didn't I already tell you I didn't want to see you? Do you call that pushing?"

"No. But let's just be friends, you know, no kissing or nothin'. I think that's half the problem."

"OK, Ron. That suits me."

He sounded relieved. "Good. I'll be over next weekend."

He showed up as planned. As I walked timidly to the door to let him in I reminded myself, *friends now, we're just friends.* I opened it.

"Hi," he started towards me, his arms outstretched.

I turned sharply. "I have the evening planned. Let's play a game of rummy."

"Oh, yeah. That's what friends do isn't it?" He tugged at his sweater. The soft yellow color of it contrasted with his dark hair and eyes making him all the more handsome, even though he had cut his beautiful black Italian hair and changed it into a crew cut. *He's so funny!* I had to fight to hold back a giggle from his efforts to be "just friends". *He's so cute . . . so obvious.*

We sat down at the dining room table to play cards. I was seriously trying to play the game using some of the moves that

Carol had taught me. Through my concentration I could see that the seriousness of the game was not being felt by Ron. Mischievously his knee began to rub against my leg, up and down. I ignored him. Seeing that his moves were not being recognized he decided to concentrate. He won that hand. He threw his head back in proud laughter. Then with a deep sense of pity for beating me, he reached over the table to put his hand on mine. "Here, deal." I handed him the cards.

"Oh, it's my deal, is it?" We played another hand. I won. He leaned over to kiss me again.

"Hey, I thought we were just friends," I teased. My coldness caught him by such surprise, so much so, that he pushed himself back in the chair tipping it backwards . . . almost completely over.

"OK. Here! Cut them!" He slammed the cards on the table. We finished that game. "We'll play again," he dealt them out. We played again and again. I was beginning to get mad.

"I'm tired of this game," I muttered.

"One more time," he glared at me. That game was doomed to be over with as soon as possible.

"Let's go into the front room now," I suggested, hoping it would call a truce. "Carol's in there studying."

"What's she studying?" he asked craning his neck to look at the cover.

"Oh, some book that Father gave her." Carol had gone to see Father after listening to me preparing the boys for their first holy communion. "She's trying to decide what religion she wants to join."

"Maybe I should study that thing a little. You know, I don't even use a missal. I'm bad . . . real bad. Do you know it's a sin even to get mad?"

"Yeah, but there are times . . . " I answered sharply. " . . . like, how about the time Jesus kicked the merchants out of the temple? He was mad. Boy, was He mad!"

"Yeah. You're right. You know, there's times when I get so mad, I go crazy," he slammed his fists into the wall. The outburst was out of place and frightening. *Gee, maybe he is nuts.* I held my hand to my mouth in horror.

"I'm just bad . . . " he smiled a sick smile. *Couldn't be half as bad as Bob,* I mulled over the situation. *He's just upset.*

Carol excused herself. "It's getting late. I'll leave you lovebirds down here," she teased a giggle, grabbing her papers together.

We tried to relax on the couch. Not a word was said. Finally he broke the silence with, "I'd kiss you, only I have a sore here on my lip."

Some excuse . . . I laughed to myself. He was trying so hard to change the "friend status".

"Here," I leaned over and gave him a tiny peck. "Did that hurt?"

"It was all right," he grinned. "Let's try it again." That was all it took. Our passions warmed up past the lukewarm stage. "Oh, oh," he drew away. "We're not friends no more."

I snuggled up to him. "This is better, don't you think?"

"Much better," he sighed. We whiled away our time together with the unimportant important things, which lovers talk about, until he had to leave.

During the week, though, Ron called at his usual time, only with an unusual whining in his voice . . . "I don't know what happened, but we aren't friends no more."

I tried to set his mind at rest. "Why don't you just come to dinner next Sunday? We'll spend some time with the kids and it'll be . . . you know, impersonal?"

"Yeah. That sounds good. I go to friends' houses for dinner lots of times. That's a good idea."

I had fun cooking for a change. It hadn't been fun for a very long time. I was more creative these days since I was being filled with a warmth that I hadn't felt for years. No, I had never felt this kind of warmth. Always before I had needed some sort of set rule or recipe in order to fix most anything. This time I was able to just use a sprinkle of this, a dash of that in the salad dressing, and do my own thing with the chicken. It all turned out so good! The phone rang. It was not a "scheduled" phone call.

"You'd better not wait dinner for me," he tried to be thoughtful . . . or was he being unthoughtful? "I'm going to be late. I missed my bus."

"We don't mind waiting," I assured him.

"No. Go ahead without me."

"We'll see." I felt a pang of disappointment. *Darn him, he's got cold feet.* I pushed the chicken in the warming oven, the disappointment growing into anger. *He's going to have dinner with us if we have to wait all night!,* I promised myself under my breath.

It was still early evening when he peeked into the kitchen. "All done with dinner?"

"No. It's been here waiting for you. Come on, everybody. Dinner time," I sang through the house.

"Oh. I thought you were going to go ahead and eat without me."

"Soup's on," I ignored him as I rounded up the kids.

"Serve the kids first," Ron ordered . . . pouting. "I'm not very hungry."

The dinner became a special happening. It was an experience of closeness between each person. Every moment was an awareness of simplicity: the tinkling of the forks and spoons hitting the plates, a gulp of milk, the warmth of a tender smile across the table. Oneness. Everyone was quiet, but content. His loving eyes glowed as he stared at little Betsy. Her messy face and sticky fingers brought a chuckle as he slurped down a drink of coffee. Betsy stopped eating for a moment, drawn to his smile. She smiling back. It was so simple.

The dishes needed to be done. He sat quietly in the chair watching me tidy up. He appeared to be uncomfortable. His eyes were fixed in a glassy stare. Something was going on. I looked around to see what it was. Little Robert was hiding under the dining table. His eyes were like little magnets. Tears of a happy closeness were slowly running down his little face. Ron couldn't move. He sat there frozen, not knowing what to do.

"It's bedtime," I peeked under the table clapping my hands.

"Scoot!" Off he scampered on up to bed. I went back to drying the pots and pans. Ron sat on a chair watching me.

"You know, back home, I like the kind of woman that can get out and work right alongside of a man." I could tell just how his mind was working . . . trying to talk himself out of our relationship. "I know this one gal that can run the farm all by herself. Why, she milks the cows," his hands acted out the pulling up and down motions of cow milking, "then she'd get out a plow," he got up pretending to be plowing, "bale the hay," he pretended to be slinging a pitch fork, "and carry water from the creek." His shoulders went from side to side like they were lifting a terrible load . . . a pail of water. "She was strong as a bull!"

Oh, brother. I sighed, *He's talking faster than his head is working. He looks so silly.*

"How come you didn't marry her?" I had to laugh.

"I couldn't stand her," he retorted, " . . . but I had another girl," he caught himself fast so as not to appear too foolish. I liked her. I was going with her when I went into the service. She wrote me a Dear John."

"Do you love her?"

"No. That's probably why she wrote me a Dear John. I told you. I haven't told anyone that."

Taking the hint, about his not liking helpless women, I went to empty the garbage. Then going one step further, I decided to exhibit my chore ability as I carried the garbage can out to the front parking even though the garbage man wasn't even scheduled to pick it up for a couple of days.

The closeness of the dinner followed us into the front room where we went to spend some time watching TV. We were like old Ma and Pa. Nothing much was said, just relaxing . . . when Carol blew in. "Look at this," she giggled, "they're playing married!" Up the stairs she ran to her room, as usual, chuckling all the way. I could've killed her. I looked at Ron in embarrassment. Then laughter broke out that brought about a relaxation as we cuddled-up on the couch together. This move always turned into some kind of passionate maneuver as we reached for each other in big "I've missed you" kisses. The passion, as most passions do, turned into his wanting to become even more familiar. He started to unbutton my blouse. The strong Victorian value system took over in my conscience. *Oh, God. This has to be kept right. It's too precious. I can't make a mistake!* I gathered myself together escaping calmly into the kitchen as in a trance. Seating myself at the kitchen table I lit up a cigarette. Tears of deep sorrow from having left the intimate scene were flowing. There were also tears of fear that he wouldn't understand. I could faintly hear the sound of his footsteps walking very carefully to the kitchen door. My eyes raised to catch sight of him standing at the door in the dimly lit room. "What's wrong?" he asked.

"I don't know. I guess I've just been lonely. I don't want us to do something wrong." He knelt down in front of me kissing away my tears, one by one.

"Pat," he looked up into my eyes, "whenever you're lonely, that's when you should pray."

"I do pray," I nodded to him in agreement. He plopped down next to me holding his head in his hands also weeping. I tenderly placed my hand on his.

"I don't know what it is," he confided. "It's just that I can't face the responsibility."

"The kids . . . you mean?" I asked.

"No. It's not that so much. Just everything. I love my home, Pat. I love my folks." That made it clear to me. It would hurt his folks if he married a divorcee. It was against the religion. I understood all too well, because it was also my religion . . . the same one that seemingly failed me, or at least had failed to understand my situation. *If I married him, I would hurt him.* I knew then that I had to resign myself to my fate, whatever it was.

"I know what you mean," I answered him softly. "I know you must go home." My insides screamed in pain. *Oh, God. Maybe if he goes home he'll miss us and come back to us. Please. Please.*

"Do you mean you want me to leave?" he asked a little puzzled.

"If I said I did, I'd be lying." I folded my hands in silence.

God give me the strength, I silently prayed. *I know you gave him to me for a reason. Please give me the strength.* I blurted out the words. Strong words. "Ron, I know you must." Once again the beauty of our togetherness lasted only briefly, then he had to leave.

After a few days the magic phone call hour came. It rang. His voice was sullen. "Pat, I want to thank you for the beautiful dinner, but I don't think I'd better eat there again. You know, the kids might get attached."

"If that's what you want," I knew that Robert's tears had made a big dent in his heart. But the forced coldness in his voice frightened me.

"You don't know me, Pat," he stammered. "I can't ever get married, anyhow. There's something wrong with me."

"Like what?"

"Well, when I get to the point of, you know, going all the way with a girl, I freeze up or something."

"Oh, Ron. It's all in your head."

"How do you know?"

"It's the way you've been raised, sex being a sin outside of marriage and all. Isn't that what you were taught as a Catholic?"

"I don't know what it is, but something's wrong," he said. "I guess I'm just old-fashioned."

"So am I Ron."

"You're an old-fashioned girl, all right, but not as old-fashioned as I am. I'm from waaay back."

"What does that mean?"

"I guess I'm better off alone," he mused. "Pat," he choked out the words. "I think you ought to find yourself another boyfriend."

"All right . . . " I tried to act matter-of-factly. Inside I was livid. "Why don't you just post my phone number out at the barracks?"

"Do you really want me to?" his voice softened into a worried mode.

"Forget it," I screamed. "I'll find someone. Good-bye."

"Pat, Pat. Can we still be friends?" he asked frantically, "Can I see you again?"

"Yeah!" I stammered. "If I'm home."

Again, Carol had come to the rescue. By this time she had met a nice fellow in one of her ridiculous mischievous ways. She had a number of a phone booth at the fort where Jim had been stationed. To fill in the boring times of babysitting and being stuck at home, she would call the number and talk and flirt with whoever answered. Wes was the "answerie" one afternoon. He also loved to flirt around over the phone. Their friendship grew. He had stopped by the house several times with a carload of nice young soldiers, bringing eats and, of course, beer to create a fun evening now and then. "I'll have Wes fix you up with a blind date," she had offered.

"That'll be great!" I brightened up. "I'll give Old Man Passardi what he wants. Dang him."

My anger gave me the strength to get some independence. I needed some wheels. Actually, the most difficult thing that I was experiencing with not having a car was getting the groceries home. On Saturday mornings, Carol's day off, I would take my brood up to the grocery store that was about six blocks away. I had my grandmother's old grocery cart, which Mom had given to me. At the store I would fill the grocery cart full of canned goods. The dog food would be tossed to Robert, the oldest, to carry, then the bag of sugar to Blake and little Betsy would get the loaf of bread, something light and appropriate for such a tiny girl. My little army paraded down the street getting the groceries home, a bystander here and there chuckling to themselves at the sight.

It was time to buy a car. This new development encouraged my decision. I looked in the newspaper for something I could afford . . ., which wasn't much. It wasn't long before I found just the thing, a hundred dollar deal. I called my dad. "Daddy? Can you take me out to this address to look at a car?"

"What kind is it?" he asked.

"A '47 Chevy."

"That's a good year. If the engine is in decent shape it should be a good car. I'll be right there."

A good old car it was. Carol christened her Clarabelle in her wonderful child-like way. Old Clarabelle was just like a friend. When you talked nice to her, she'd perform beautifully. Little Robert, who had a built in talent for responsibility took it on himself to check the gas meter, ask if the water was in the radiator, make sure the air was in the tires, etc. I felt that this facet of his personality was God-given. Ron's rejection left me going on nothing but nerves, or was it hurt? Or was my anger melting and turning into more of a battle mode?

Carol took the project of finding me a date seriously. It fit right into her plans of getting better acquainted with Wes. One night after I had come home from work I witnessed another one of Carol's marvelous touching scenes. The flickering dim light coming from the dining room invited me to peek around the corner quietly, so as not to disturb the moment. Yes, it was as I thought . . . candlelight . . . her favorite ploy. There was her friend, Wes, completely dazzled by her tactics. She had tied a colorful scarf around her head gazing into the bottom of a glass, which sufficed as her crystal ball, and was holding Wes's outstretched hand. "Hi," she greeted me. "I'm telling Wes's fortune."

"Can she really tell fortunes?" Was asked seriously. He was a little lame at times.

"Sure!" I went along with the gag. Carol was so precious and cute as she went through her little rituals. *Very convincing*, I snickered deep down inside of myself, a little envious at her ability to entertain and make a fantastic evening out of almost nothing. They made a cute couple, too. I couldn't help but compare the evening to her anniversary dinner with Jim. Both evenings were very special. Then came the question that car owners are plagued with. "Can you take Wes home?"

"Do I have to do the freeway?" I winced. I had never needed to drive the new freeway, which seemed to be a manifestation of a fantasy from my childhood. The beautiful new highway reminded me of an exposition at the home show in the early 50's . . . a model of the highways of the future with the roads rising up over big cement trestles winding around on down to join one another. Here, already, in the 1960's they were here . . . the great freeways! Anyhow, my little old 1947 Chevy wasn't made for high speeds, and neither was I.

"I can show you how to get there only having to go a mile or so on the freeway," Wes informed me. "I sure would appreciate it. I missed the last bus . . . or I could stay here, but then I'd probably be late for formation."

"I'll take you," I gave in. I just hoped that I would be all right for I didn't know my car that well and it was the middle of the night. However, there was also something that I wanted to find out from Wes. Where were Ron's barracks?

Wes took me on a little tour of the company where Ron worked before showing me his section of the Fort, an entirely different section. As we approached his barracks, he became one of the rest. He asked me to kiss him. This evening was fast reminding me more and more of that horrible evening with Carol and Jim. I refused. "I couldn't do that to Carol."

"Carol said you were looking for a boy friend, I thought . . . "

"You thought wrong. I'm looking for someone with a little sense . . . " I motioned for him to please get out of the car. On the trip home I was so full of mixed feelings. All the way home I was angry. All the way home I was praying that fate would see me home safely. All the way home I was thanking, "Oh, God. I really do love Ron. He's so rare."

The night came when Ron's wishes were honored. Carol had everything worked out for the blind date that she had promised me. We anxiously waited for our dates to arrive when the phone rang. It was Ron. "What are you doing tonight?"

"I have a date," I retorted feeling very satisfied about it. After all, isn't that what he had asked for? "In fact, I'm expecting him anytime."

"Who is he?" Ron asked quickly.

"A friends of Carol's," I answered haughtily.

"Oh," he pouted. "Are you going out or staying there?"

"We haven't decided yet."

"I was planning on coming out to see you."

"I'm sorry Ron. In fact, I'll be going on a vacation this weekend. My first vacation, ever! I'll be gone three or four days."

"Where are you going?" his voice shook.

"I reserved a cabin at my aunt's farm."

"How're you getting there?"

"Oh, I bought a car. A '47 Chevy."

"A 1947? Are you sure it'll get you there?"

"Sure. She's my friend. I named her Clarabelle." He snickered a little for he wasn't into fantasy stuff. "I'll miss you, though." I felt the need to let him know that all was OK, and that I didn't take our friendship lightly.

"Oh," he mumbled. "I'll call again . . . sometime." *He's jealous. It serves him right,* I choked back a ticklish titter. After thinking about it I laughed, *You just do that little thing, call me again "sometime . . . sometime . . . hmmm.* I was elated, ecstatic . . . on top of the world! He was jealous!

The evening was a total success. My blind date was a handsome young man who was engaged to a girl back home. He was looking for someone to have fun with, but who didn't want to get serious. They had a barbecue in the backyard. The barbecue turned into silliness . . . a macaroni fight! Macaroni landed from one end of the yard and into the house, behind the stove, on the hutch . . . everywhere. Beer was flowing, jokes were soaring. I became a clown. It was my way of hiding my deep longing to be with Ron.

Even so, vacation time arrived and I had carried through with my threat. We packed Ole Clarabelle to the hilt: five sleeping bags, a barbecue, clothes, three kids, a big dog and ourselves. We all arranged the pillows to be comfy for the two-hour ride. Even though we were squashed together singing songs made the trip much shorter. I taught them songs from my childhood that I didn't even know I had remembered.

We got about 30 miles from our destination when what should appear but Clarabelle's tantrum? She started to moan, a little signal to me that I should stop and get some oil. I had had the car all checked and the oil changed before we left home, but Clarabelle ate oil like a horse ate hay. Eager to get on the road again before dark, I stepped on the ignition to continue the journey. Nothing happened. I tried again, and again . . . "Oh, no. We're stuck!" My eyes were glazed with fright.

"What do we do now?" Carol asked.

"I don't know. Let me think." I couldn't come up with any ideas. I knew nothing about cars and motors and such. As I pondered over the problem trying to act as if I had the matter in hand, I noticed an old man sitting idly by the door to the station. I got up the nerve. "Pardon me sir. I'm stuck. I think if I had a push, I could get started again. Do you know of anyone who could help me?"

"My God," he swore. "I was just ready to take a nap." He was very crabby. I painfully walked away wishing I had never even talked to him. Evidently his good heart took over for suddenly he called out, "Lady . . . I guess I could push you down that old dirt road over yonder." He pointed to a little winding path, which ran into the brush by the side of the station and then back on around to the highway. " . . . but that's all I'll do. If you don't get it started, then you'll have to figure out something else. I'm going to take my nap."

"Thank you, oh thank you," the whole carload chimed in with such deep relief. The newer old car edged up. We stopped to connect bumpers and together we proceeded down the narrow dirt road. Over a bump. *Screech!* The old man slowly got out of his car slamming his door and walked over to our car window. "We've hooked bumpers," he swore. "Damnit." I quickly jumped out of the car sizing up the situation for myself. "Hell, both sides are hooked. It's going to take me two jacks to get us out of this mess. Have you got one?"

"I have one in the trunk," I pointed to the rusty old rear of Clarabelle. "A lot of good it'll do us now. I can't get the trunk open. Your car is in the way."

"Shit," he said under his breath. Gathering himself together he added, "I'll walk up to the station and get one." He started down the road attempting a short cut through the high dead grass, which had lost its greenness already in the hot May sun. I was feeling so embarrassed over having caused the poor old man so much trouble. *Oh, if only I had just left him alone*, I secretly cried to myself. He was back in fifteen minutes or so. I was feebly trying to be of some help, just wanting to do something!

"Sister," he scoffed, "just let me do it."

"I feel awful about this."

"It's OK. These things happen," he smiled. "I just won't get my nap in today, that's all." After much grunting and groaning and cranking the two cars were finally freed from one another. "I'll go clean up and take these jacks back," he offered. "You try to get your car started and if you don't . . . . "

"If I don't, you just leave me here. I feel bad enough. Just don't worry about us."

He was back quite soon. Confidently he climbed into his car. "Sonuvvabitch!" he shouted. "I changed my pants and I left my car keys in the other pair!" He slammed the door to his car kicking a tire just to let off steam.

"Carol," I climbed back into my car, " . . . we've got to get this car started. That man is getting mad again." I stepped on the gas pedal. Again. And again. It was simply dead. Soon the old man returned.

"I'll have to go around you in order to get out of here," he pointed at a clump of weeds to the side of my car. Slowly he drove up alongside of Clarabelle, almost past the old car until his wheels started to spin. He was stuck!

I ran around the side of my car. There was his car, in a very embarrassing position, its front wheels hanging over the edge of an embankment that had been hidden by the huge tufts of grass. His car was teetering there in mid-air. He stopped his motor. Stepping out on the ground he fell to his knees pounding the ground with his head. He quieted down to lay there and moan for awhile. Then laughter took over. His stomach jiggled from the hysterical laughter, his hands were trying to hold it still. "I don't believe it." The hilarity of the whole ordeal brought tears that rolled down his cheeks." . . . and I was going to take a nap. You girls get the hell out of here," he said good-naturedly. "I'll have to get my friend to get me out of this fix."

I got back into my car. My knees were shaking. I took an important moment to say a formal prayer ending with . . . . *God, make this thing start, please.* I closed my eyes, sort of flying blind. I stepped on the starter. Away we went.

We arrived at Aunt Aurea's just before dusk. Uncle Bud had built the little white house on his parent's property years before. Just past the house was a huge gate that led the way to a large flowing pasture where the cows were seen as dots on the vast piece of land. Past the cow pasture was a winding road that twisted on down through the woods to a beautiful beach on the Strait of Juan de Fuca where Uncle Bud had built several cabins. They were placed here and there near the beach.

Auntie ran out to the car to greet the tired bunch. "I was beginning to worry. It's nearly dark! I'm afraid we're having a little excitement here. You'd better come in the house," she motioned to us.

"What's the matter?" We wanted to hear more about the "excitement".

"A couple of guys escaped from the detention farm just across the water from us. They're armed and considered dangerous. Your uncle and the sheriff are down there scouting out property. They found a boat. I don't think you should stay down there until they get back."

"What a vacation!" I collapsed into a chair. "We sure got off to a good start . . . " Now it was our turn to entertain Aunt Aurea with the crazy happenings earlier in our day. We were all talking at once as Auntie was trying to listen to us all.

"They should be back soon," she shook her head laughing in disbelief of what she had just heard, to say nothing of what was happening all around them that very minute. It was getting dark. The kids were getting cranky.

"How dangerous is it do you think?" I asked, trying to be brave.

"I really don't know what to tell you. There are several other people in cabins down there . . . "

"I'm going on down. I think we'll be all right."

The night was spooky as we settled in. We used the flashlight because we were afraid to light the lantern to beckon any sordid strangers that might be lurking. Carol loved the excitement. She made a party out of it. She'd tell spooky stories and get everyone all jittery, then make us laugh. It was especially spooky going to the outhouse with only the moon lighting our way. A six-pack of beer kept us company after the kids had climbed into bed, still making light of the situation by being mighty silly. We were all huddled together in the little cabin waiting for some word. What seemed like hours later we heard a car out in front. "It's all right," Auntie hollered making the rounds as the town crier. "They found those two buggers just a short ways from our house! Relax, kids," she waved a swift goodbye.

As peaceful as the next three days were, I had much difficulty in forgetting about my wonderfully important, deep feelings for Ron. I wondered if I was just obsessed with him. I couldn't help it. I missed him. I went through the motions during the following vacation days, experiences that become an ever-flowing memory. There was a fishing expedition, or rather a fish-less expedition. No pole, just a stick and string, but a real fish hook with a worm wiggling on the end of it. The skinny winding trail along the river became very real as I slipped out of sight. I was tumbling down the bank. The boys' giggled. "Do it again, mommy". Mood swings took over as I watched the huge waves roll in. I sat in front of the picture window in the little cabin to watch the kids playing in the waves. Carol was sitting on the rock. The boys started to laugh, loud shrieking laughter. Carol was stuck on the rock, the tide had come in all around her. Her sopping body sloshes through the waves to shore, her clothes wet through and through. She chuckled heartily, "time to sit by the fire!" She waved the boys on. "Come on, kids, gather the wood." I was so thankful for my friend's laughter and nonsense. We cooked chicken on our little barbecue, l left it there to sop up the wonderful zesty flavors of outdoor cooking. We went back to turn it. There were only remnants left . . . bones strewn all around the yard. The dog had eaten it . . . every last morsel. We drowned our sorrows with the wine that was left from the wonderful wine sauce we had bathed the chicken in. Then we turned to beer, too much beer. The garbage cans were getting fuller and fuller. I became embarrassed because Auntie emptied the garbage cans. We sneaked around at night depositing the evidence in other people's cans, evenly distributing them.

I began to get anxious to go home. There was one last errand, though, that I had to make. I left off a little gold knife on a key chain for the old man who had helped us. I had purchased it with my last $5.00 after I had gassed up for the trip. He wasn't home. I was glad because I hated to face him, but happy to have been able to show my appreciation.

All the way home I hung on to my fears. *Will Ron ever call me again? Is he mad at me?* We hit a terrible thunderstorm putt putting over the mountains. I could hardly see the road. The old windshield wipers were thudding, straining with each thud. I just wanted to get home safe and sound. Just the word "home" sounded good. My heart pounded as I drove up in front of the big old house. The phone was ringing. Frantically I tried to unlock the door. I made it! It was still ringing as I picked it up. "Hello?"

It was his voice. "You're there, huh?"

"I just walked in the door," I chuckled with a deep relief. I was again safe.

His voice was so deep, so warm. "I knew you'd be getting home just now."

We GLORY In Tribulation

Knowing That:

Tribulation Works PATIENCE
Patience—EXPERIENCE
Experience—HOPE
And Hope Makes Us NOT ASHAMED

Rom 5:3-4 (KJ)

Chapter 7

"I'm No Ghost"

My kitchen had become more of a hiding place than a homey one. Again I was into the beer remembering of those days of the "hope-line", my red telephone. There it hung on the wall in front of me reminding me of my cleverness in making what might've been a disaster into an interesting color scheme. The kitchen floor and drain-boards were a dull deep red when we moved in. My stove and refrigerator were pink, so I had ordered a red telephone to put on the wall and painted my kitchen pink to make it appear "on purpose". A cheerful kitchen it was even though the big old house had somehow become my fortress away from the world.

The little pink flowers, which hung down from a copper hanging basket, were floating back and forth, it seemed, in front of the window which I gazed out at from my kitchen table. That little basket of flowers triggered memories of my little ghost tale. I chuckled whenever I thought about how funny Ron was that day . . . a painful day, a disastrous day, yet a fun day to remember. It was a day that culminated all of the pain and heartache of two people who were in a dilemma. We knew that there was no way out of it without a lot of heartache. I suspect we had known it from the start. The original shock of discovering that we were taking a trip into an unknown world hadn't stopped us.

Ron had become anxious to meet Clarabelle even though he thought it was complete silliness to name a car as one would name

142

a person. It didn't set well with his practical nature. "Yeah. Just about what I expected, even worse," he had shaken his head in disgust.

"I don't care what you think," I patted the dull, colorless tank-like automobile. "She's dependable and cheap."

"Cripes! That thing isn't a horse, you know." I just grinned a "let's not be so practical" look.

On this particular visit Carol had taken a night out. About the time that Ron usually started looking at the clock to fit in his bus schedule, calling it a night, Carol came waltzing in feeling no pain. She had evidently had a good time. She looked very cute in her icy-brown pleated skirt with top to match. Her black eyes were especially sparkly this night, and her naturally wavy black hair was especially lovely. She sat in the chair across the room from me and Ron striking up some kind of conversation that had no reason or rhyme to it. Ron seemed to like her sense of humor. She seemed to bring the lighter side out in him for some reason. He had told me of how he was a clown, too, back home even though he hadn't shown me that side of himself. Well, maybe the burping session might've been a clue. Carol began making eyes at him. Ron began making eyes back at her. I began to squirm. *She's going to get even with me because of Jim,* I warned myself. Fuming embers began to overtake me.

"Don't you think it's time you went home?" I asked Ron.

"Oh, yeah! Gee! Time has gotten away from me. I'll never be able to make the last bus, now." He still had time to make another goo-goo eye at Carol, though. "If I could get a lift downtown, I'll bet I can hitch a ride out to the Fort from down there."

"I'll run you to town," I offered.

"In that heap of junk you've got out there?" he teased.

"Yes. That heap of junk . . . . " I began to see that he was giving me a bad time on purpose, sort of like a test. His flirty eyes connected with Carol's again.

"Come on . . . " I grabbed him by his arm and headed him out the door. I got even with him, though, by taking him down the waterfront route, through a tunnel, along a very dark road that he had absolutely no knowledge of.

"Where are you taking me?" he whined.

"Downtown."

"Uh-uh . . . Oh, yeah . . . ", he swung his head back in disgust. Then suddenly the dark road was turning into the well-lit downtown section. "Look, we're downtown!" he gasped in disbelief. "How did you do that?

"I know a lot of things you don't know", I winked.

He nodded, sharing a profound smile as he pointed out his usual bus stop. Just the spot to hitch a ride.

Fate had its own way of getting even with us. Early in the morning Ron called me. "Guess where I've been all night?" he bragged.

"Didn't you make it back to the barracks?"

"Nope. I've been in jail all night." He thought it was funny! "A guy picked me up to take me to the Fort, but then he started acting weird. First he drove through a gas station, I didn't think too much of that, but then when he sideswiped a car, the cops started chasing us and we got in a bad wreck. In fact, the guy that picked me up was hurt pretty badly. I put my sweater over him to keep him warm, and then they put me in the paddy wagon and took me to jail. I've been answering questions all night long. I told them that I had been to see my girl." With that statement his voice became soft and tender. I gleamed inside knowing that he had called me "his girl". "Looks like they're going to let me go now. Sgt. Smith is getting me out."

Getting back and forth from the Fort to town was evidently a problem for most of the service guys unless they had wheels. Wes, Carol's friend, was over at the house more and more often. He loved Carol's nonsense, too. Laughter was important these days before he was to be sent to Viet Nam. One afternoon he asked us if we would give him a lift to the Fort. "Yeah." I jumped on the opportunity. "In fact, I'll call Ron and see if he'd like to go for a ride. That's still being friends, isn't it?"

"Sounds good to me," the couple agreed, for to us it had made good sense. I got a hold of him.

"Hi! Guess what? We're going for a ride right out in your area. I thought maybe you'd like to come with us."

"No . . . I don't think so." Ron yawned. "I'm sitting here reading a *Reader's Digest*. I'd just as soon be by myself."

"Well, I'm sorry I bothered you," I snapped.

"Don't feel bad," he tried to explain. "That's just the way I am. I like to be alone and think sometimes."

"Have fun," I hung up fast as if the phone had suddenly become very hot.

I dutifully brought Wes home with Carol along this time, as I didn't want anything else to happen. I didn't fully trust Wes, yet. I was still mad as a wet hen when we returned back home. The phone broke into my private tantrum with Ron asking, "Did you have a nice ride?"

"Real nice." I attempted to rub it in. "We drove all around the Fort. We drove by a real interesting building." I had fun describing his quarters slowly, precisely.

"That's where I live," he whined.

"I know."

"Why didn't you stop?"

"What? And bother you?"

"Bother who?"

"Why in the hell don't you make up your mind what you want?" I swore as I hung up haughtily. Feelings of resentment were welling up inside of me. *This has got to stop,* I warned myself. *He told me he loved me that first evening he came to see me. Either he admits how he feels or I'll just call the whole thing off!*

I like to think of it as spontaneity, but in actual fact my compulsive behavior again reared its ugly head. The next thing I knew I was on the freeway hurriedly on my way out to the Fort, as in a trance, and pulling up in front of the barracks. A couple of guys were walking down the street. Beckoning them to talk to me I hollered, "How could I get a hold of Ron Passardi?"

"Oh, Ron?" They looked at each other secretively. One said, "He took his car and went to some dame's house." Then cupped his hand around his mouth and whispered to the other. "Do you think she's the one?"

"Where's that at?" I searched for answers.

"Some dame that lives up around here," they snickered.

"Whose car has he got?"

"His."

"He told me he doesn't have a car." Anger showed red in my face, my skin felt very hot . . . or was it just hurt?

"Does the car make you mad?" They looked at each other in puzzlement. "What about the girl?"

"If he wants to see some girl, that's his business," I snapped, "but it's my business if he's lied to me."

I slammed back into the car. Then something began to astonish me. *Why aren't I jealous of the girl?* I swung Old Clarabelle out onto the freeway. *Still, he lied,* I reasoned. I tried to calm down my feelings. Then I reminded myself. *The car. Why did he lie about that?* I felt sick inside.

I dragged through the next day. The phone rang at its usual time. It was, guess who? I was very offish.

"What are you doing?" he asked.

"Packing. I'm going somewhere this weekend over the Fourth of July. My folks invited us to go with them."

"Oh, you are? Where at?"

"Back up at my aunt's farm."

"There again? How far is it?"

"Quite a ways," I answered coldly.

"What's the matter, Pat? You sound funny. Tell me what's wrong. Something isn't right here."

"If you don't know, I'm not going to tell you," I blared it out. "Go ask your friends."

"What friends?"

"You know what friends," I blabbered.

"Pat, you aren't making any sense," his voice quivered.

I drew him a picture by telling him what had happened the day before. "They thought it was a good joke on me," I cried.

"Please don't believe everything you hear. Those guys were just trying to be funny. You know, for kicks. I don't have no car and I wasn't seeing no girl. I was here at the barracks all the time."

"It made me darn mad," I swore. "I felt like a fool, or something."

"I can see why," his voice was quiet in deep thought. "I'll take care of them. Can I come over and straighten this thing out?"

"Yeah, if you want to, I guess."

"Oh, no! Now you'll really think I've been lying," he moaned.

"Now what?"

"I just rented a car for over the holiday. Honestly, I just rented it."

"Oh, come on. I know you don't have a car," I gave in with a ticklish laughter.

My wait wasn't very long. He pulled up at the house backing into the driveway like a madman, like maybe something was getting away from him. Leaping out of the car he dashed up the walk. "Hi," I greeted him calmly as he poked his head in the door. Clothes were neatly folded on the table as I busily packed up the gear for the trip.

"How long does it take to get there?" he looked over the situation.

"A couple of hours."

"Oh. It'd be easy to make it in a day, there and back, huh?" he hinted.

I became independently stubborn. *I'm not going to ask him again and get turned down,*

I swore under my breath, *if he can't come right out with it and ask to go, I'll just go without him.* I carefully planned my strategy as I went about my business.

"Come on. Let's go for a ride," he said changing the subject.

"The kids and all? Won't they get attached?" I rubbed his own words back into his wounds.

"It'll be all right, I want them to come." He looked deep into my eyes wanting so badly for me to know how much it meant to him. The boys flew down the steps after we announced our intentions. "Yea! We're going for a ride, with Ron!" Their faces were beaming with happiness.

He followed behind them chuckling heartily as he lovingly watched little Betsy toddling out the door. She was so cute wearing her little red plaid pleated skirt with a white sweater. Her little chubby baby legs were going a mile a minute. The car was parked to the side of the house in the driveway. "Wow!" Blake's eyes were big. Robert took a trip around the car to examine it more fully. It was a pale lavender car with soft black upholstery. "It's a limo!" They shouted.

A peacefulness followed us as we cruised off to the park. Even the children were silent. Every little movement was precious as in slow motion. The intensity of the peace brought forth a beauty in the most ordinary of things: the trees swaying in the breeze, the vibrant colors of the flowers, the smell of freshness in the air, the silence of the water and the grace of the boats skimming along the waves. Such a serene peace.

Once in the park we pulled up to a roadside look-off. The kids piled out of the car. We just gazed out over the water and breathed in the fresh air as the boys took to the woods. Ron was holding little Betsy by the hand. It brought such delight to my heart that I had to fight back tears of joy. The boys came running back to the car, then up a tree. Ron became frustrated waving his arms helplessly in the air. "Boys, boys, you'd better come down out of that tree. You'll fall or get hurt, or something."

"Oh, they're OK," I laughed.

"I don't know about this. I'm not used to it." Just then he caught one of them sitting on the hood of the car. "Get down from there. You'll scratch the paint!"

I took care of that grievous situation immediately. "Get in the car!" I halfway pushed them in. "You sit still for a few minutes."

"I think it's time to go." Ron took his keys out of his pocket. "Where's Betsy?" We looked around. She was gone! "She must've gone down this path . . . " we searched through the wooded area coming to a fence. Possible disaster was just below the fence. It lurked in front of us like a big monster. It was a big hole about the size of a child that looked down over a huge cliff. "Oh, God!" Our frightened eyes met, "it can't be . . . but maybe it is!" Our horror was just brief, though, probably through God's mercy. Just then we heard the rustling of leaves.

"Mommy," the little girl came running up to us. "I found you, huh?" I picked her up in my arms, giving her a big hug holding her close for a minute with thanksgiving on my lips.

"Whew! That was a close one." Actual sweat was rolling off Ron's forehead. He made sure that we went straight to the car. "No more emergencies, please!" He looked upwards, probably in prayer.

Home safely, the boys took off to play some more. Betsy went down for her nap and I attempted to busy myself around the kitchen. He spun me around attacking me with a kiss. Such a kiss! It was all so fast. Our souls united as his body turned to gray mist before me. Misty bodies, lifted from the ground for a fleeting instant. I could see my arms around him, transparent arms. It was sudden. Brief. As we separated my knees wobbled beneath me in shock. In my weakness I leaned over the drain-board to hold myself up. I had seen his soul! Ron gazed out the window in deep disbelief over the happening. We both tried to gather ourselves together in sheer silence, never to dare talk about it, ever.

Getting on with the task of getting ready for our trip I announced to Ron that I needed to borrow some sleeping bags from my sister. He offered to drive me over there. My sister's home had the flavor of a country home: animals, kids and the usual clutter that's involved in raising them. He seemed very much at home there as he sat down to chat. He talked of his hometown, how he was the eligible bachelor in town. "The whole town knew it if I drove down the street on a Saturday night wondering who I was going to see", he bragged. His visit was short and sweetly expounded the virtues of home. Slowly we readied ourselves to leave as Jeanne walked us out to the car waving us on.

As the evening wore on I kept waiting for the invitation for us to spend the holiday together. It never came. We were in the front room relaxing when the hurt, mixed with fear, caused the words to come blurting out of my mouth. "Ron," I stammered, "I really think we'd better not see each other anymore."

He was shocked.

"Do you really mean that, Pat?" He was now the one in a helpless situation pacing the floor back and forth, back and forth.

"Yes, I do. I can't take anymore of this."

"Have I done something wrong?" he was wringing his hands together.

"No, I just think it's best."

By this time his pacing had taken on a new dimension . . . into the dining room and back out into the living room. "Pat, before I leave here there's something I want to say." He paced the floor faster. "Being with you is the most right thing I've done, at least since I've been in the service."

"All I know is," I answered . . . "this is all she wrote for me, Ron."

"What?"

"This is probably it for me. I guess God figured it was all I deserve, or something."

"You'll find it again, Pat."

I shook my head, "No. I don't think so. I'll just have to pretend that you're dead, or something." I began walking him to the back door.

His eyes expressed shock as they opened wide. "Dead?"

"Yeah! Dead."

"What'll you do if I come back?"

"Then you'd probably scare me half to death cause then you'd be a ghost!" I waved my hands in frenzy. "I don't want no ghosts around here."

"I'm no ghost," he sputtered. "See?" He pulled at his clothes. "Here I am, Pat. I'm no ghost."

"Good-bye, Ron," I opened the door.

"Bye," he walked away slowly shaking his head not able to believe what had just taken place. I watched him drive away. Tears came streaming down my face. Immediately I tried to lose myself in the tasks at hand. I attempted to finish the potato salad I had started, tears rolling down my cheeks the whole time as I stirred in the Miracle Whip. I wept as I boxed up the picnic food. The tears wouldn't subside. Once more my heart was so sure . . . *this is it, this is the end.*

The tears were still flowing the next day. Everything was as in a fog. I didn't even stop to acknowledge what was going on, just going through the motions. My folks picked us up, including Carol. I began to come back to the land of the living as I sat quietly, not able to say much, just watching the country scenes rolling past me on the way to my aunt's farm. Even Carol was quiet. She knew of my pain.

Even though my family was all around me, sort of like a reunion, Carol immediately busied herself. In her dignified mode, she tried to get acquainted, learning who was who. I longed to be alone as I experienced the peace of nature. Oh, the sweetness of the mountain air. I found just the private spot to be alone, away from the cheerful chatterings of the relatives as they enjoyed their visit. Looking out over the water I recalled every moment that I had spent with Ron. *It had been such a precious romance,* I reminisced. *God, thank you for Ron. I know I was fortunate to have his love even for a short time.* But the pangs of longing took over. Suddenly the deepness of the sky seemed so vast. The waters so deep. The love I felt was so consuming. I rose to my feet. "No!" I cried. "No, dear God." The universe was closing in around me. *Is it over? Really over? Ron, please come back to us . . . we need you so . . . "* The sobs came loud and hard, cleansing the pain in my heart.

The peaceful, yet painful weekend was finished. I was back home to kids and housework. They were the main focus of my life, now. My job became only a means. It no longer held joy as it once had. I went through the motions of each day as if the day before was just the same as the present. One day my sister, Jeanne, stopped in to see how I was doing. I was feeling physically ill from the pressures of a broken heart. "You need to get your mind on something else," Jeanne advised me. "He sounds mighty homesick to me. He's probably the worse thing that could've happened to you."

At that I fell into a tearful rage. "He's the best thing that ever happened to me." I had to excuse myself as I ran upstairs to my room flinging myself on my bed and sobbing. As painful as the day was, though, it seemed to bring with it a strength.

The need to feel a sense of accomplishment became very important. The house needed to be fixed up. *I'll show him,* I moaned to myself over and over. I had forgotten that this whole breakup had been my fault. I seemed to need the anger, it gave me an added strength. I rummaged around in the basement to find some of the left over paint I knew that I had hidden there, somewhere. *Ah, yes. I'll mix these colors together and paint the ugly red bathroom upstairs.*

I had brightened the kitchen up with that little basket of pink phoney flowers, which were now hanging above me, reminding me of the incident. I had added a little bright touch of contact paper on the table and behind the sink . . . voila! It had been a wonderful transformation. It had only cost me a couple of bucks.

The hard part was yet to come, that day. I had felt an obsession to contact Ron. I wondered, *What could I say? Would he even speak to me again? Something light,* I had told myself . . . *a silly card,* something light and funny . . . it might bring him back. I found just the card. It said, "I was walking by the card rack and noticed this card." Then I added, "I had to have time to get my head on straight." Prayers and kisses were placed on the card as I mailed it off. There was hope again, maybe.

Two days went by surprisingly quick. The phone rang. "Hello," the familiar low voice grumped on the other end.

"Oh, hi," I answered shyly.

"Did you want something?" he asked.

"I wanted to thank you," I made up something fast. "I wanted to tell you how much I enjoyed our ride in the park. That was a beautiful car you rented."

"I know. I went horseback riding on July Fourth. I figured I might as well do something as long as I had the car."

"Oh!" I felt a spark of anger deep inside. *Darn you. You did rent that car to spend the Fourth with us. Why didn't you ask me, you fool?*

"Pat?" He felt his words carefully. "You know that dinner you fixed that day? It was the best dinner I ever had. It was so beautiful."

"It was just chicken and spaghetti," I giggled.

"That part was good, too. But I'm talking about the other part, you know, the kids and all."

"Oh, yeah! I know what you mean," my heart raced.

He's really trying hard to express himself. I felt a deep warm glow.

"Is there anything else you wanted to tell me?" he asked.

"No. That's all."

"Oh." Silence. "If you need me for anything, I'll come running," he said quietly.

"I'm OK," I replied. "I just wanted to thank you." That was it. We hung up. "Why did I say that?" I threw the spoon at the wall with a wild frustration. Finally I lay my cheek on the table sobbing, which was the only sound that broke through the quiet loneliness.

A day came when I could no longer function. It may have been two days or two weeks. Time no longer had any meaning. A house being unattended can become emergency status after awhile. The floor needed mopping. The dishes needed washing. I grabbed the mop following the dirt and clutter into the front room. *I need to get the vacuum cleaner,* I ran into the kitchen to see the dirty dishes in the sink. Nothing was done. Everything had to be done all at once. *I can't do anything right!* I paced the floor mopping, wiping fingerprints, washing dishes seemingly all at once. It was frightening. *I need to talk to Ron,* all pretenses of being OK, of being independent vanished. I madly dialed the phone. I reached him. It was his voice. I sobbed. He chuckled. I laughed in hysteria. "Will I ever see you again?" I begged.

"Sometime . . . maybe," he said firmly.

"Oh," I stammered. I found myself still mopping the floor all the while holding the phone to my ear.

"What are you doing?" There was puzzlement in his voice.

"Mopping the floor."

"Can't you wait until you hang up?"

"I can do it better right now," I retorted. He laughed. "Ron. Oh, Ron . . . I feel sick. Please help me," I became hysterical again.

"Pat, I'm coming. I'll get there as soon as I can, one way or another."

"Thank you. I'll be waiting." I sat at the dining room table feeling refreshed and exhausted all at the same time. *He's coming. I need him so . . . .* Deep fear was mounting. How was I going to make it when he had to go home for good?

Within the second hour his body came flying through the door. He didn't bother to knock. He just walked gingerly through the door and grabbed a chair beside me. All of a sudden there was no hurry. I had been sitting there playing solitaire to while a way the time until he got there. We calmly looked at one another trying to read which expression was there. No words were necessary. Comforting warm feelings completely took away the fears and heartache. "You aren't no ghost, are you?" I smiled.

"Nope."

"I see you've done some fixing up."

"Yeah, I painted the bathroom, too."

"Oh. Now that you mentioned it, I could use a trip upstairs." He came back down looking rather stunned. "That's quite an experience up there," he grinned.

In my zeal to paint the bathroom with a very low pocket book, I didn't realize the effect I had created. The colors I had mixed had turned to a depressing blue gray. Like a battleship.

It had seemed so much better at the time than the ugly loud red. I had put touches of cerise which I had carried out to match the "Book in the John" book that Carol had given to me. It was quite a trip in there all right.

The next hours were a special time of togetherness. Ron had even allowed me to make a fire. It was a scene that he usually didn't care for because he didn't want any more romance than there already was. What a cozy fire it was. As we lay there on the floor in front of the fire nothing mattered except that we were together again. There were no pretenses. Love poured out. All guards were down. Suddenly he rolled over away from me. "I think maybe we should cool it."

"Do you like to suffer or something?" I snapped.

"I couldn't do it anyway. Remember? Maybe it's because I was never circumcised."

"I don't think there's anything wrong with you." I was
beginning to feel that if I could prove to him that there was nothing
wrong with him, that maybe he could relax more in this
relationship. I think it's your conscience stopping you and you
know it. *What if there is something wrong with him?* I had secret
fears not because of not being able to have sex, but maybe he
had a problem different from Bob's only just as serious. He had
mentioned to me that he didn't think he could please a woman
because he wasn't very "well endowed". I didn't care about that.
I just needed to be near him. He started to grin. I had to admit
that there had been times during my marriage that I had feared
that maybe there was something wrong with my own self. I shook
my head remembering how my conscience had taken hold of me
the night I had run into the kitchen so as not to make any
"mistakes". I couldn't help but grin back at him as he lay there
watching my mind race. Sighing resignedly I sat up continuing
my statement, " . . . but I love you for your strength."

He turned away. "Boy, you sure take the cake," he rolled on
the floor holding his head. The evening was over quickly after
that. As he left he had one more thing to say. "Pat, there's nothing
wrong with you, either."

I had nodded, "I know."

I peeked through a tiny slot in the curtains to watch him as
he stood there for the bus after he had kissed me good-bye. His
face showed bewilderment as if to say, "What have I gone and
done now?" My heart beat a warning. *Oh-oh, he's upset.*

The next phone call was evidently an attempt to alleviate
some of that puzzlement I had seen that night. "Pat, I've been
doing an awful lot of thinking." His voice sounded tired over the
phone. "I'm awfully mixed up."

"What about?"

"Everything. Just everything. I'm so dumb."

"You're not dumb, Ron . . . in fact, you're very intelligent," I
reassured him. "You're just mixed up because you're finding out
that nothing is all black or all white. Isn't that right?"

"I'm sure finding that out, that's for sure."

"Now, what are you talking about?"

"Well, you're divorced, right?"

"You know that for heaven's sake."

"Well, I've gone out with a lot of divorced girls since I was in the service. They were always trying to take me to bed. But not you."

"So?"

"I figure that I won't get too fresh or do nothin' wrong, you know, sort of help out a little, but they always end up going out on me . . ."

"All I know is what we have is a beautiful thing, Ron."

"I know that, Pat."

"Well, you don't sound like it. I appreciate the fact that you have a strong backbone and all, but I can be strong, too. Why do you think I don't care about going out on you? I want to keep it right just as much as you do." There was a great pause. I then started expounding about all the gory details of my marriage.

"Pat, Pat. I don't want to hear anymore. I don't want to hear it. It makes me sick."

"You think it makes you sick. You ought to try living it once."

"I don't blame you for getting a divorce," he cried. "I don't know what to do."

"Who's asking you to do anything?" I retorted. "You'll know what to do when the time comes."

"What do you mean by that?"

"I guess I still believe that what God wants us to do, He'll show us."

"Yeah, I see what you mean. Cripes! I'm so dumb. That has worked so far, hasn't it?"

"Remember that time I got mad at you right at first? I still don't know what made me say those things." I tried to hint to him that I had suspected that God had His hand in this predicament.

"You know, Pat, I'm glad you said that. Sometimes I don't even know what I'm saying when I'm with you. It's weird!"

"We rattled on trying to clear the air concerning many of our past experiences. Hours went by, three and a half-hours.

"Guess what? They're closing up this place, Pat. I haven't said half of the things I was going to say. I'll tell you what . . . I'll go outside and call you from a booth. OK? I'll call you right back. Now wait."

"OK," I giggled. "You know, we've already talked half of a work day."

"I want to get some things settled." He hung up. A couple of seconds, the phone rang. "Here I am again," he chuckled. "I've never been much of a talker. I never talk this long."

"Neither do I. What was it you didn't get said?"

"I've got to get up my nerve to tell you," he whined. "It's about a crazy dream I had. I just feel like I have to tell you about it. You know, like you get a feeling about what you're supposed to do, like what we were talking about before?"

"I know. Go on."

"Pat, it's embarrassing, it's so silly."

"Come on," I coaxed. "Don't start something, then not finish it."

"Here goes. I was sitting on my bed, see, shining my shoes. I shined away at them, polishing them, then reshining them. All the while I saw myself go up and I was flying all around the room. I could even look down and see myself shining my shoes."

"That was strange," I shivered a little.

"That ain't all," he interrupted. "There's more," he hemmed and hawed around.

"What is it", I asked impatiently.

"It's awful silly." He was so embarrassed that his voice became a little sneaky whisper. "It was about your little boy . . . I had his pajamas."

"You what? What did they have to do with it?"

"I just did something with the pajamas, Pat. I told you it was embarrassing. Just never mind. I'm not going to tell you anymore."

I was silent. *Maybe he is nuts,* I feared.

"Pat," he asked intently. "Do you think I need a psychiatrist or something?"

"I don't think it would do you any harm," I muttered.

That phone call really did it. The usual fill-up and tune-out-pain tactics brought Carol and me on one of our more and more frequent beer runs. One particular evening I had left Carol in the car while I ran into the store to pick up a six-pack. I opened my purse. *No money. I know I had a twenty-dollar bill,* I gasped secretly. *Oh-oh. Carol must have taken it.* My eyes met Carol's as she glanced at me through the window. *"I've got to put a stop to this right away,* I determined. I had a little money stashed away for emergencies in my makeup bag. Another problem called for more tune-out, so I bought two six-packs instead of just one. Climbing back into the car, Carol greeted me with "Two six-packs?" Underneath that question was a fear, a fear of what I might be up to.

"One for you and one for me." I retorted harshly.

"I'll pay for mine," Carol hurriedly reached into her purse.

"Forget it. They're on me." I shoved it down her throat.

When we arrived home I bee-lined directly to my bedroom. I threw myself on the bed thinking, trying to get a grasp on the situation. *Maybe she's paying me back for breaking her and Jim up, or . . . maybe she just can't help it.* Carol knew that she must face the problem immediately. She walked quietly to the edge of the bed and knelt beside me. "Pat, I don't deserve a friend like you." There were big tears rolling down her face. "My grandfather once told me that I had a silver heart. But some day I'd meet someone with a golden heart." Carol was good at saying flowery things at just the right times. She was a poet at heart.

"Golden heart, my foot!" I started to laugh through my own tears. "Look at the mess I made between you and Jim."

"You know, my mother told me," Carol continued to try to lighten things up. " . . . 'Carol, you'll fly all over the pretty birds, and land smack in the cow pile!' Jim is just a big cow pile. I'm better off."

That conversation was a relief, but on top of everything else, the next day I had an even worse workday. I came dragging into the house thinking of nothing but taking off my shoes, relaxing and drinking a cool beer to soothe my nerves even more. I threw my purse on the dining table when all of a sudden there was a huge, "Surprise! Surprise!" Friends were peering at me from all corners of the room. There was my mom and dad, a few neighbors and soldiers: lots of servicemen grouped around the room giving the celebration extra joy. They were friends of Wes'. Now they were Carol's and mine, too. Carol came rushing out of the kitchen with a cakefull of lit candles. "Happy birthday to you," everyone chimed in. Immediately I knew what had happened to the money. Carol had needed it to throw a party that, quite frankly, neither one of us could afford. I gave Carol a big hug, anyhow, letting her know that all was forgiven and that I now understood.

The evening became serious, though. It was the soldier's last fling before they were sent off to Viet Nam. Carol had asked my father, the most quiet introverted man I had ever known, to be the bartender. It would take someone like Carol to think that one up. He took the job very seriously and became the most outgoing I had ever seen him. I knew that he had seen the pain in these young men who were scared to death. I sat on the floor next to a couple of the guys who had squatted down against the wall. "You ought to taste the bugs we've been eating." He mentioned to me. "It's part of the jungle warfare and survival training. Ugh! This beer tastes so good, like its washing it all down."

"Yeah, buddy," his pal retorted. "Maybe we'll be glad we learned all that stuff. I want to come back, I have a girl back home that I promised to marry. I have to come back."

Wes was his usual obnoxious self trying to get the dog to bark and be mean. "Wes," I hollered at him. "That dog is a part Doberman. I don't appreciate you riling him up. I've got kids here, you know."

"Oh, he needs to be toughened up. He's no good til he's toughened up."

"I said, don't rile him up, or you can get out!" I screamed. At that he knew I meant business.

Jim, my blind-date friend from the macaroni fight night, came over to calm my nerves. "Come on over here. He's got your message."

We proceeded to sit apart from the others as I began to confess something that was bothering me. "It's Ron. He didn't come to my party. I don't know about that deal. I'm going to be hurt . . . and one of the first things he ever said to me was, "Pat, I'd never hurt you. Huh!" I popped open another beer.

"Yeah! I don't mind telling you that I'm scared to death. I know that half of these guys probably won't be coming back. It's bad over there. I wish I could see my girl before I go. But all I'll be able to do is call her." The two of us just sat there sharing our innermost feelings: I was feeling very rejected and Jim was full of fear. Soon the neighbors left. Then my folks were saying good-bye through the hub-bub. "Behave yourself, now, dear. It was a good party."

"Thanks Daddy," I kissed them both good-bye. "I really appreciate you guys coming to my party. It was special."

Afterwards the beer flowed like water. The guys had gone up to the store for more cases of beer. I was crying in my beer. Jim was crying in his beer. Carol was crying in her beer thinking of all the pain everyone was in. Jim and I snuck off out to his car. One thing led to another. Jim was deflowered. I felt cheap. We left the car and joined the others both feeling rotten over what had happened. Jim had never had sex before, he had been saving himself for his girl. *I never thought I'd do a thing like that."* I just sat there on the floor. Sullen. Sad. Guilty. Drunk.

It was just a couple of days later, I fell apart. I couldn't calm down, *I need some kind of help!* I was getting scared. My heart was racing, sweat pouring from my brow. It was the weekend. I couldn't get hold of my doctor. I couldn't manage anymore. I was dizzy. "I'm going to the emergency room!" I bounded out the door. Carol was worried about me driving in that condition. She called my mom.

I found myself at the end of a very long line of an assortment of people with bleeding fingers, fevers, broken legs, arms in slings, etc. A little nun was coming up the line trying to cheer them up hoping that her conversation would lighten their load a little. When sister got to me she asked me softly, "What's your name, dear?"

At that I became hysterical. "I can't tell you. I can't tell you . . . !" I didn't want anyone to know who I had been married to. *Everyone knows about the bowling alley, and the queers . . . and now I'm a whore . . .*, secrets I couldn't divulge to anyone. "I can't tell you, sister."

Sister went to the nurse at the front of the line. "We have an extremely nervous lady down here," she told the nurse. "Do you think you can get her in? All I did was ask her what her name was." By this time I was crying in hysteria!

Evidently, they had received a phone call from my mother. "Will you be well enough to make it to your mother's house?" the nurse asked me. "I'll give you something to calm you down a little and give you something a little stronger to take after you get there."

Just knowing that someone was there to help, that someone cared, that I had someone to lean on was all I needed to feel calmer. When I got to my mother's, though, I began getting new symptoms. I was hungry. My mother gave me a bowl of soup. I was still hungry. She made me a cheese sandwich. Then a large can of chili, another sandwich of leftover hamburger . . . "My gosh, where are you putting it all?" Mom was flabbergasted. "I don't care how much you eat, I just can't imagine anyone being so hungry! I guess it's just nerves". She handed me a dish of ice cream.

"I'm beginning to feel better," I smiled. Ice cream was my favorite. It seemed to do the trick.

The fact that I hadn't heard from Ron may have been at the bottom of my problem, but the guilt over what I had done with Jim was probably a more accurate diagnosis. I hadn't mentioned my disappointment of Ron not showing up at the party. *I'm sure Carol would've invited him,* I reasoned. *Oh, well, I should probably forget about him. He's driving me nuts.* Miraculously, or at least it seemed that way, Ron called.

"How are you feeling?" he asked.

"Oh, I'm OK." I lied.

"That's not what I heard," Ron sputtered.

"What did you hear?" I was shocked.

"Carol called me. Told me you were in the hospital."

Darn her, I swore under my breath.

"I'm sorry I upset you . . . " he said.

"Ron, don't blame yourself. It's just everything all put together . . . it just caught up with me."

"Oh, yeah . . . "

"Well, I guess I was upset that you didn't come to my party."

"I didn't know about no party."

"Carol didn't invite you?"

"No, she didn't".

"She probably figured you wouldn't come, anyhow," I socked it to him, reminding him of the time he turned me down. "You know the way you are, and all." I could see that he still blamed himself.

The minute we got off the phone I questioned Carol. "Why didn't you invite Ron to my party?"

"Oh. I didn't think he'd fit in with the rest of them."

"Oh, he would too." Then I thought about it. "No, maybe he wouldn't. Maybe you're right."

Ron came over soon after. He was so upset that he had upset me. "I've hurt you," he cried as he smothered me with more of his affections.

Another phone call, and still another puzzle. "I'm doing my laundry and I thought I'd call."

"Oh, that's nice." I didn't know what else to say. "I talked to Carol. I was upset that she didn't invite you to my party, being as how she knows I'm in love with you." I decided to just say it the way it was. Let the truth hang out. "To tell you the truth, Ron, I think you love me, too."

Quickly he answered, "I like you, Pat, but I don't love you." There was a slamming of the telephone booth door. "Get out of here. Go on. Get out of here." There was a banging sound . . . and another bang.

"Ron?" My voice was a little shaky with concern. "What are you doing?"

"Oh, I'm having a little trouble here," he muttered. "Go on. Get out of here," he yelled again. *Bam. Bam.*

Maybe he's nuts, I warned myself.

"It's OK, now," he sighed, pausing. "Did you think that maybe I had another girl in here or something because of what I said?"

"No, Ron." My voice reflected my disgust. "I just don't think you'd have another girl on a date to do your laundry."

"Oh, yeah. I forgot I told you that," he grumbled. "There really wasn't anyone here, you know."

"Sure." I couldn't help but be sarcastic.

"Pat, I told you I can't express my feelings very good."

A ticklish little glow began beaming inside of me. I knew. It was special knowing the way he felt even though he couldn't say it.

The more I thought about that silly phone call, the more I felt that I needed to write him a letter. The words poured out of my head onto the paper, the best letter I had ever written.

"I feel you do love me, Ron. You tell me you can get along by yourself and . . . 'the words gushed forth from the most secret places in my heart.' . . . if you can, all the more power to you, but to do so would make you more than human. Everyone needs love. Come down to earth, Ron." *I kissed the letter before I shoved it into the mailbox.*

The next day embarrassment took over. What had seemed to be a good idea the night before was now becoming a nightmare. A phone call to straighten out my seeming error in judgement became a strong need. "Ron, I did something terribly foolish."

"What now?"

"I wrote you a letter. You haven't received it yet, have you?"

"No, I haven't gotten no mail all week. What do you want me to do with it once I get it?"

"I thought maybe when you get it, you'd just tear it up as a favor to me." He was snickering gloriously on the other end of the phone enjoying my uncomfortable situation. "Ron, I'm so embarrassed," I confessed coyly. "Will you?"

"I'll probably read it then tear it up. I'll give you a call when I get it."

Oh, darn! I swore as I hung up the empty phone. *A lot of good that did me.*

The hours dragged until the dreaded phone call came promptly the next day.

"I got it," his voice was teasing.

"Oh, you did?" My knees started to shake. "Did you read it?"

For a while he was silent. But then suddenly he blurted out, "Pat, there wasn't nothin' wrong with that letter. Not one thing."

"Nothing?" My nerves suddenly were calmed to the point of a careful ecstasy. I giggled in relief.

His voice continued in a sweet and tender tone. "It was beautiful! It flowed, like a book or something. I always wished I could write like that, then I'd write a book, but I think you should be the one to write it."

"I wouldn't know how to begin writing a book," I ridiculed.

"Well, I think you could write a darn good book."

In the last days, God says:

"I will pour MY SPIRIT upon all people
Your sons and daughters shall PROPHESY
Your young men shall see VISIONS
Your older men shall dream DREAMS."

Acts 2:17 (NIV)

Chapter 8

The Mountain

It couldn't have been a more beautiful morning, especially for Labor Day. The phone was ringing unusually early. I was surprised to hear the grand invite from his warm low voice, "Do you wanna go for a ride?" Ron had just bought an older used car that was about five years newer than Clarabelle. It was adorned with a rather new paint job, a cream color. He was tired of taking the long bus ride into town, and besides, he was planning on driving back home after he got out of the service. I tried not to allow myself to even think about that day. He had already sent for license plates back home so that he'd be all set for his journey that would take place in October. "I thought I'd show off my new car and try it out, you know, get all the little quirks out of it. How about it?"

"I'd love to! But, what about the kids?"

"I suppose we c-o-u-l-d bring them," he hesitated.

"I'll try to make some kind of arrangements," I suggested, remembering the nerve-wracking time he had with them the last time. It was our first real date since the night that we had met. I knew that it was in response to my complaint the night that we had talked on and on. I had confided in him maybe he was ashamed of me, or something, because he never asked me out, and told him so. *Now that he has the car, maybe it would be easier to go places together,* the hope sung in my heart. I was thrilled that he'd heeded my request. The day was fitting together in a grand way. My folks were doing nothing and were willing to watch the kids.

Ron arrived at my front door very quickly, hardly giving me a chance to get my act together. I had nothing to wear for I hadn't been functioning very well under all the stress and depression. I wanted to wear something feminine for the special occasion. "Come on, let's go", he was already to go and didn't want to wait. "I have a real trip planned for us. We need to get ahead of the traffic!" I threw on a little housedress type thing and off we went.

We brought the kids over to my folks and then, whew! We were alone! After we got all comfy in the car he pulled out a map. "I figured we'd go down the freeway here," his finger pointed to a perfectly laid out plan, " . . . then turn off up here . . . " His plan was to go up to the area near my aunt's farm.

The ride was very relaxing. In fact, the two of us didn't say much for we were absolutely content. I'd make a little comment from time to time. Ron was his normal quiet self. Words weren't needed between us for we were perfectly at ease with one another. We were just together watching the green Washington scenery. I knew that the scenery was reminding him of his own home town, especially since all the towns we passed through were very small as he'd described his home. We would barely enter a town and then quickly find ourselves back on the highway enjoying beautiful scenery til the next town, time and time again along the highway. As we drove over a little bridge bearing a sign, "Liliwaup River", the word Waup made me think of the slang for Italians. I began thinking how it was such a coincidence that Ron's mother and father had come from the old country (Italy) just as Bob's mom and dad had come from Yugoslavia. There must be something about people from the old country that interested me.

"Are you a "lili-waup?" I teased him.

His face was shocked, at first, until he realized I was just having fun. He caught on to my little joke. "I may be a waup, but I'm no lili," he retorted quickly. *Oh, my gosh!* I caught myself. *He probably thinks I'm referring to Bob's problem. What a stupid pun!* I kept silent after that for fear I would say something wrong again.

As we arrived in the town of my birth, which was near our destination, he acted as though he knew where he was going. "Have you been here before?" I asked.

"No," he answered calmly.

He kept driving with a strange determination. He drove up an old dusty road that led to a mill, stopped the car, grabbed his camera and got out. He began taking pictures very firmly and decisively.

"What did you stop here for?" I was puzzled. My aunt's strange words, 'I think there's something for you at the mill', came to me once more. They had brought back to my memory that horrible weekend when my folks had taken the kids and I to a place of safety; my aunt's wooded farm area, which was only about 20 miles down the road.

"You'll see, sometime," he said slowly, strangely, assuredly.

I shivered. He was sort of eerie.

"I heard there was a big mountain here somewhere, the town is famous for it or something. Do you know what I mean?"

"Oh, yes. It's Hurricane Ridge. We passed the road that goes up to the mountain, though", I filled him in with the little knowledge I had of the area.

"We'll go back to it," he swung the car around in a determined fashion, as though he knew where he was going and what he was supposed to do. The highway was narrow and winding. The day was beautifully clear so that we could see valleys below stretching out far, far away. Little blue streams could be seen as one's eyes followed the slender snake like waters clear across the state to the next mountain range. The crisp air made everything seem fresh and new. As we continued up the mountain there was a feeling of flirting with destiny, as though we were going to drive right off into the clouds. Then the road would suddenly turn, making our stomachs turn somersaults like when you take a ride on a "roller coaster".

The scene would then change so that we could view mountain

peaks below lifting their snow-capped heads up pointing towards us. The sight became more and more astounding as we wound up around and around until the mountain peaks were far below peeking at us through little white billowy clouds. We pulled off the side of the road to take a better look. Ron stood there on the very edge, his foot resting on a huge rock as his eyes scanned the panorama that reached so far across the horizon and so fearfully below. His hair was blowing softly in the gentle breeze. It was a special a moment that remained in my heart. It symbolized to me strength and masculinity. I felt that I could actually see the love in his heart for the beauty of creation. It was as though he could fly off into the blue sky and sit on a feathery cloud. God's spirit seemed to fill his heart with longing and love of all life. "Oh, I love this fresh air," his voice was bursting with delight as he stretched out his arms to the wonderment of it all. "Isn't it beautiful? So very beautiful?" In his eyes there were stars and in his face there was peace. *He is the King of the mountains,* my heart sang in a whisper.

As we stood there in awe a woman came up to us seemingly from nowhere. She was shaking her finger at him. "You know, you aren't leaving here, or if you do you'll turn around and come right back." Apparently embarrassed over her outburst she backed off. "I . . . I mean . . . I noticed the Massachusetts license plate, I mean . . . " He looked her straight in the eye in a frozen stance. She turned and walked off as abruptly as she had come. I laughed a shaky little laugh feeling fearful that those words would bring me some hope of his return after he had gone home. That fateful day was going to be on us in just one month or so.

That incident was not the end of hearing about Massachusetts that day. Everyone we ran into was from his home state: the waitress, the gas station man and several tourists. There was a strangeness around us all day long, as if we were walking on air.

I so wanted to take him to see my aunt's farm, but he never mentioned about wanting to go there. I just let him do the leading. The time was getting late after we had stopped for a hamburger at the mountain cafe. He was looking at his watch as if to say, "We'd better be getting back." It had been such a beautiful day. I was afraid to ask for more.

I showed him a short cut back home across the floating bridge. "Why didn't you tell me about that on the way up?" he asked in a rather perturbed voice.

"You seemed to have it all planned out what you wanted to do. I thought it was a nice ride. This way you get to see two sets of scenery."

"Oh, yeah. That's good," he grinned. "You're right." With that we quietly rode along exchanging a kiss here, a little fondling there considering that this was our day. We didn't care about any rights or wrongs, just that we had this time together.

We arrived back to town earlier than he had suspected. I was surprised when he decided to extend the perfect day and drive to the park where we had taken the kids in his limo. We found a private spot taking a stroll hand in hand down a path that led into a little clearing looking over the water. As we neared the clearing up ahead I became almost fearfully stunned by a sudden outburst of loud breathing, loud excited breathing from behind. His arms grabbed at me. He was all hands. He clung to me, his hands roaming everywhere. They attacked my breasts, then down all over my body. It was such a change! A scary lustful change. *Oh, my gosh!* I shivered. *Maybe he is nuts . . . or maybe he's a lunatic!* I shied away for a moment. He stopped. As our eyes made contact, all was well, the fear was gone. He grabbed me in his arms for dear life showering me with gentle soft kisses. I then knew that he had a deep yearning for physical closeness mixed with the inability to make a lasting commitment. It was as if our situation had suddenly become unmanageable. I had only care and concern for his predicament for that moment. I attempted to help him release the life giving substance.

"I don't know if I should be letting you do this or not." He arched his back. I could feel his deep breathing in my ear. "Oh, Pat . . . Pat," he moaned. I watched the stream of fluid fall onto the ground. *There goes the baby we could have had,* my heart secretly ached. It almost seemed like a loss. I was beginning to see that this thing was a win-lose situation.

I insisted that Ron come into the house to meet my folks when we drove up to pick up the kids. He was reluctant as I led him through the front door. I then found out why he was reluctant. Evidently, he had expected that there would be a coldness. After all, didn't we both come from the same belief system, of no marriage after a divorce, which our folks had handed down to us? I had never seen my mother so cold to any of my friends. But this was so special! Couldn't they see that? Ron stood by the front door being as how he wasn't only treated with an icy politeness, he wasn't even asked to sit down. I stared at him from the kitchen door across the room to say, "that's the way it is." He nodded in understanding. Just then the awkwardness was replaced by Dan, my brother Bill's best friend, who came bounding out of the hallway. Ron's eyes brightened up for he had met Dan on one of his visits to my house. Dan had become my confidant and I had become Dan's. Ron held his hand out to Dan as if to say, "Boy am I glad to see a familiar face!"

After we piled the kids into the car and were on the way home, I couldn't help but think about Dan who had fallen in love with a young high school girl the past year, and had recently gotten her pregnant. Seeing Dan reminded me what they had gone through so that I was relieved over the fact that Ron and I hadn't consummated our relationship this day. I knew that if we had, I would surely have gotten pregnant. I didn't want him that way. I didn't want him to feel forced into anything. Dan had been going through terrible pain trying to talk his girl and her father and mother into the fact that he loved her and could take care of her. He was fresh out of school and, as yet, hadn't found employment. He was willing to make the sun move to have her for his wife. But the pain, pure pain of not knowing whether or not she really loved him back, all the while wanting her so badly. *No, I'm glad we used our heads,* my good sense overcame me once more.

As we drove up in front of my house, I smiled over at Ron wondering if this was the end of the day, a day that he had planned alone. The drapes were drawn. All was quiet there. I was wondering, *Where was Carol?* The kids had piled out of the car and into the house. "Do you want to come in?" I reached to kiss his lips as he puckered them out the door window at me.

"No. I think I'd better be going back."

"Thanks for a beautiful day," I slowly turned to go into the ominously quiet house.

Once inside I was in for a shock. There was a front room full of guys, soldiers. Carol was entertaining them with her usual silly yarns and games, etc. "Hi, guys," I waved. "You're all so quiet! I thought the house was empty. It's like a morgue in here."

"Might as well be," one of the guys piped up. "We just got our papers. We're leaving in a couple of weeks. We're headed for Viet Nam."

"Oh."

Beer was flowing faster than usual. I found myself cuddling up to Jim, my special army friend, sipping on a beer thinking . . . *what a different world than the one I was just in.* I was sort of glad, though, to have the opportunity to come down off of the high that I had experienced that day. The little party slowly brought me back to the earthlings. I began to realize, *these poor guys are in genuine pain . . . scared to death!* Carol and I were trying to remove it with silliness, ridiculousness or just downright tears. It was pitiful! The evening ended with lots and lots of hugs and kisses.

Tuesday, workday, came much too quickly. The weekend over, I was back on the job rather jubilant over the beautiful memories of the eventful weekend. Of course, when things seem to go well something always has to spring up from nowhere. I was informed of a phone call from home. "Pat. We have a terrible mess here on our hands," Carol was using her very best business-like manner. "You need to come home, right away! It's the boys. There's a policewoman here . . . now, everything's all right . . . "

"What in the world is going on?" My voice burst throughout the whole office. "What did they do?"

"You mean, what did Bob do?"

"What's Bob got to do with it?" My heart pulsated.

"Plenty. Come on home and we'll talk about it. Not over the phone, Pat."

I rushed into my front room after having driven like a maniac through town. There the boys were safely sitting on the davenport with a very attractive policewoman. She looked sharp in her uniform. In spite of the authority that it symbolized she shared a warmth and understanding as she extended her hand to me introducing herself. It seemed awkward for another woman to be greeting me in my own home as though I were the stranger. "Mrs. Surina? Could I talk to you in private?"

"Yes. Let's go out to the kitchen," I made the invite, feeling very baffled. It seemed that Bob had met the boys at the small park about a block away from the house. It sloped down into a gulch that contained small streams and lots of woods. It was a place where my "adopted" grandfather had taken me to hunt salamanders when I was a little girl. I was so happy that they had a place to enjoy nature. The boys played there often rushing home to tell of the imaginary lions, and elephants, etc. This time it was no imagination. They told of an incident, an unforgivable incident! It seems that Bob had taken them down into the gully and tried to seduce them. The younger boy had related how he had plugged his ears and screamed, "You're not my father . . . " as Bob had tried to show him some of his nasty tricks.

"I was always scared of the possibility," I told the policewoman about my ex-husband's problem. "In fact, I saw him just a couple of Sundays ago laying out there on the grass visiting with them there."

"Will you be willing to press charges?" the officer asked.

"I don't see that I have a choice," I threw up my hands. "Do you?"

Papers were served on him. He was picked up. It was just enough legal business to stir him up, but good. They couldn't keep him in jail very long because of the legal system, or so I was told. In the back of my mind I wondered if it wasn't because he knew people in high places due to his experience he had had in politics.

The afternoon after Bob was freed, my mom and dad had stopped by to see how things were going. They had been aghast at the news about the boys. They wanted to help if they could. "That front porch is a sight!" Mom busied herself by grabbing a broom from the kitchen. "I'll sweep it off. My gosh, anything would be an improvement." She drove away the dried up old leaves and stickers from the sticker bush. The broom came swooping down the cobwebs that were up in the eaves. Just then Bob's car pulled up in front of the house. Slamming on the brakes he stopped in the middle of the street.

"Patti, Patti. If you ever loved me. Please talk to me!" He was kneeling there in the middle of the busy avenue like an idiot, his hands held together as in prayer. "Please talk to me at least! They threw me in jail!"

My mother ran into the house attempting to close the door. Daddy grabbed the door out of her hands and out he flew toward the street. "I've had it with that bastard!" He jumped onto the driver's side of Bob's car. Bob had already fled into it and started the motor.

"Dee! Dee!" My mother called after him. "Dee . . . my God! You'll be killed!" She was feeling pure horror at the sight of Dee hanging onto the car, the two of them barreling down the street together, with Daddy hanging on for dear life. Jumping off the car as it screeched around the corner, he brushed the dust from his pants as he walked back to the house swearing, "Anyway, I broke his damn glasses. Serves him right!" He threw them down on the table with great pride.

Mom threw herself back on a chair, weak from fright. She held her head in her hands shaking it back and forth. "Now I see why you don't sweep your front porch!"

A few days went by, just enough time to get over the idea of the whole sordid incident. I was summoned to appear at the prosecuting attorney's office. I felt shaky in the knees and as I opened the door to the large plush-leather furniture I felt even weaker. The P.A. was sitting at his desk "feverishly, or more likely phoneyly busy". It was no wonder I felt that way since this was the very man, a friend of Bob's, who had so drunkingly and stupidly tried to seduce me last Christmas Eve. Just to the right of him stood a smartly dressed man, his back to me, gazing out the window onto the boulevard below. He didn't have his jacket on, obviously so that I could see a gun which was strapped under his arm and around his chest. *They're trying to frighten me*, I alerted myself. I fumbled around for a chair knowing that I had better be on my toes. "I thought it important to have a small chat with you," the P.A. addressed me. He leaned back in his chair smugly . . . "Well, let's see now . . . those ridiculous charges against Bob. Don't you think it's a bit of a strong action to take?"

"No, I don't. It was bad enough what he was doing to other boys . . . but his own?"

"Now, we must look at this in the proper light," the fat well-dressed politician folded his hands. "We must think of what this would do to your sons. Why, they could be marred for life. Made to testify against their own father? Now you don't want to put them through all of that, the court proceedings would be terribly painful for them."

I knew that he was soft-soaping me for his friend, my ex-husband. *A favor, I think they call it*, I warned myself. *It's probably more like blackmail. I'll bet Bob has something on him.*

"What guarantee do I have that he won't try something like this again?" I asked.

"We're not taking this lightly," the P.A. explained, even though it almost seemed like a turn around of attitude. "We're closing up the business . . . *and* he's been asked to leave town. If he comes into the city limits, *bam* . . . in the slammer he goes." I was never too sure if the whole deal made sense to me or if the gunman made more sense, but I did drop the charges.

Now, you would think that would be enough. For Bob, enough was never enough. There was a knock on my front door a few evenings later. A stranger excitedly screamed at me as I opened the door, "A guy just slashed the tires on your car . . . I'll see if I can head him off . . . " The Good Samaritan dashed back towards his car.

"No, don't bother," I hollered after him. "I know who it is," I waved him on with thanks on my lips.

I snuck out to the car with Carol close behind as we quickly checked out the damage done. Poor old Clarabelle was acutely crippled with all four tires completely flattened. Big knife gashes gaped up at us. I didn't even bother to call the police knowing that they wouldn't do anything. I just waited until the next day when I could call my lawyer.

This was one of the times that charges, which were brought against him, stuck. Except they plea-bargained and he was fined and told that he had to make restitution for the tires. I was surprised, as only Bob could surprise me, a night or two later, by an unexpected sight as I entered my front room after a day at work. There was brazen Bob and the boys sharing big wide smiles with me. Evidently they had been having a long chat. "I hope you don't mind, I let him in," Carol confessed. "I figured it would be better not to have any more trouble."

"What are you doing here?" I glared at him. I thought you weren't supposed to come around here anymore!

"I just came here to set things straight with the boys."

"Mom," one of the boys piped up, " . . . we were just making up a story about down at the gulch." They both shook their heads. The other boy said, "Dad didn't really do those things, anyway, he's going to fix the tires on the car."

"Bull shit!" I screamed. "He's got to fix them, anyhow." *Damn! He's done it to them. He can make anybody believe anything.* I stood there with my arms folded wishing that I could wave a magic wand and just make this whole nightmare go away.

Bob spoke up. "Boys, I'd like to talk to your mother."

I wasn't in the mood to talk at this point, but decided to see what he had to say. He sat there in the rose colored chair, one of a set that we had bought for our first home eight years ago. It seemed like 100 years ago. There appeared to be a silvery shimmery shaky light all around him.

"Patti, I really didn't mean for things to end up like this. It's just that I figured that no matter what I did you would take it because I knew how strong you felt about your beliefs. I never thought you'd divorce me!"

"You told me they were your beliefs, too. Remember? There comes a limit!" I tried to say it nicely, but it came out firmly snotty.

"I see." He walked out the door quietly without any further discussion.

When Ron had made his usual phone call earlier in the week, I had been full of still more stories about poor Clarabelle and her dilemma. Now, I had more stories to relate, this time about Bob and his further deviousness. I could tell from Ron's voice that he was beginning to think that I was a storyteller. "Oh, yeah. What kind of holes were they? Thumbtacks?"

"They were big gashes with a knife!" I reported feeling insulted.

"I've got to come over there and see this for myself!"

"Hmmm . . . " I sighed. *He doesn't believe me. I'll show him.*

He stopped over on the pretense that he was just passing through. *Just being nosey*, I chortled. On inspection Ron's eyes became wide open, probably disappointed that I was not a storyteller. I felt he was still looking for any excuse to lessen his deep feelings for me and our situation.

Saturday morning brought with it a knock on the front door from that "other man" in my life. It was Bob. "Give me your keys. I'm going to get the car fixed." I figured that he probably needed to get into the trunk for the jack. Suddenly I caught sight of the car going down in front of the house on all four flat tires! Bumping, bumping along like a Flintstone car. It looked so ridiculous watching the rubber on those four flat tires flop and plop along the street. *My God, he'll ruin those tires!*

An hour or two later he brought the car back, all four tires, plump and full of air. "I had the station guy put boots on the old tires. I don't have enough money to buy new tires after what you did to me."

I just let it go. I wanted to forget about the whole thing. *What's the use?*

I went to bed that night still humming my "What's the use?" song. I found myself in a very deep slumber escaping from all of the happenings. Suddenly, for no apparent reason I sat up in bed. I caught myself praying, *Reach out! Reach out! Lift yourself . . . open your heart to God! Please open your heart! Be honest with yourself, feel for others, feel, feel . . . .*Sweat seeped from my pores . . . all over my body. My eyes slowly became adjusted to the room, back to reality. *It was just a dream!* I heaved a sigh of relief. *What was it about?* My mind scanned my senses to give me a clue. *Oh, yeah. I dreamt that Bob had a heart attack! For sure that was a dream. That would be too good to be true.* I fluffed up my pillow, then tried to go back to sleep murmuring to myself, *I must be nuts praying for him. Dear God, wipe that out.*

In the morning Carol and I were having our usual cup of coffee. "I sure had a crazy dream last night," I attempted to share with Carol what was on my mind and what was making my hands shake. "It was awfully real. In fact, it gave me shivers to think of it. I dreamt that Bob had a heart attack."

"That sounds great to me!" Carol laughed. "It couldn't ever happen, though, with your luck."

Just at that moment the phone rang. It was my lawyer. "Well, our boy went and did it. Get this," the man was chuckling aloud. "Bob had a heart attack last night. He's in the hospital. May not pull through."

We were dumbfounded. "I can't believe it, Pat! I just can't believe it!" Carol danced around the kitchen in shock. "It's so weird! We were just saying . . . "

"I know. It's weird all right."

There was an aura of celebration that day. It was made perfect by a phone call from Ron . . . as usual. He didn't expect to hear this next piece of unbelievable news, though.

"Bob had a heart attack last night," I announced.

"Oh, no! Everythin's happenin'! My car just broke down. Now my camera doesn't work. You know, I planned on driving back home and take some pictures along the way. It sounds like maybe I shouldn't make that trip." He sighed. "Boy, now I am confused."

It was just a day or two later when I had still another surprise from my least favorite person on earth. The telephone rang with the operator on the other end saying, "Is this Mrs. Surina? I have an emergency call for you. Being as how you have an unlisted number the party cannot get through."

"Can you tell me who it is?"

"He says he's your ex-husband. He's in the hospital with a heart attack. You may reach him at this number."

I didn't know what to do. Should I, or shouldn't I? *Maybe he's trying to get something off of his chest. Maybe he's dying. Maybe I'd better call.* I dialed the number.

"Hello?" a cheerful peppy voice answered.

"Where's the emergency?" I flat-out swore at him.

"No emergency. I just wanted to get in touch with you. You know, with the kids making their first holy communion this year, I thought I'd better warn you to remind them to rid their consciences of what they did to me."

I hung up the phone.

Ron called again that evening. He was concerned about what was happening. "I worry about you driving around in that car with those tires so unsafe."

It made my heart leap with joy that he was concerned. "I don't plan on taking any long trips," I assured him. "I just need it to get the groceries home in."

"How's Bob?" His voice was cautious and even a little scared sounding.

"You wouldn't believe me if I told you. He's OK now. Too darn stubborn to kick the bucket. I just keep telling myself he'll get whatever he deserves someday, somehow."

"I think dying is too good for him. Let him suffer a little." *If he only knew what he did this morning. I'd better not get into all that.* I kept it to myself for I was getting tired of trying to explain Bob's stupid escapades. People at work were also beginning to raise their eyebrows everytime I tried to tell them about the latest happening.

"I got my car running again," Ron continued to share his news. "My camera is in the shop getting fixed. It looks like I'll be making my trip after all. Pat? . . . " he hesitated. "Time is running out for us." There was stone silence. "I'm going home, Pat." He needed to make it very clear. "I am."

"I know," I had already resigned myself. "I know you are."

Bob was not at all through with his surprises. Another workday and still another phone call at the office. Bob's familiar aggressive voice was just an annoyance. "I had to call you and explain."

"What could you possibly explain?" I felt like strangling him.

"I'm getting married."

"Married?" *The gall of that man!* I cringed. "Wasn't one marriage a nightmare enough?"

"I got this girl pregnant. I have to do the honorable thing. You know, man cannot live on bread alone."

"Oh, Bob! When that was written that's not what was meant. Talking about twisting things. The most honorable thing you could do is drop dead."

"I need kids in my life, Patti. I can't live without kids. I just want you to know that you'll always be my wife."

"I've never been your wife." I hung up on him.

Enough was enough. These pressures and drinking were good companions. I was ready to let my hair down and *really* relax. One beer, then another went down the hatch. Carol had taken the evening off, the kids were in bed for it was rather late in the evening. I turned on the radio for company, dancing around the kitchen, twisting, romping through the house, watching myself in the mirrored effect in the windows against the darkness of the night. "Forget all your troubles," I sang aloud all by myself. The phone rang.

"What are you doing?" It was that deep tender voice that I loved so much.

"I'm having a party!" I giggled.

"Who with?" he sounded amused.

"Me, myself and I".

"Pat, are you drunk or something?"

"I guess you'd say that. I decided to have some fun. Carol's out for the evening. I decided to have some fun!" I repeated again.

"Oh! I guess I'd better change my plans then," he socked it to me. "I figured on taking a shower and getting cleaned up and all, then I was going to come to see you."

"Oh?" *Darn it all*, I scolded myself. "Do you have to change your plans?" I gulped, hoping that I could keep him from changing his mind.

"I don't think you're up to it, the way you sound."

"I'm uptoit" I slurred. "I'll straighten up. Come on. I want to see you."

"OK. I'll be there in about an hour. Are you OK?"

"Yep."

The coffeepot went on almost as fast as the phone was hung up. I sipped cup after cup trying to sober up. I had just started to relax in the dimmed room feeling better than I had in days. I was suddenly soothed by soft footsteps slowly tapping their way up the back stairs that led to the kitchen. I didn't need to turn to look. I knew who it was. It was a comfort. It was a special knowing, a special revealing of his presence before I ever set eyes on him. He hesitated in the doorway. I turned to greet him. My eyes met with his. His eyes were bright. They seemed to light up the darkened room. There appeared to be a soft steady glow all around him against the deep blue of evening. He stood there smiling with his arms outstretched to me. "Hi," he whispered. I cuddled into his arms holding him near. *Please don't leave me.* My heart trembled. We stood there for a moment in the closeness.

After we had filled one another's yearning we walked together into the front room. Ron wrinkled up his nose. Phew! You smell of booze!"

"I know. I tried to fix it up."

"Well, anyway, I'm here."

"You don't sound very happy about it."

"Well, to tell you the truth, I think you should lay off of that stuff." Ron sat himself down in the overstuffed chair.

"Mr. Perfect," I grabbed on to the mantle, hanging on it to balance myself. "To tell you the truth . . . " I brazenly began to expound, " . . . this whole thing is sick. Sick, sick, sick. It's too much! . . . not practical at all." I threw myself on his lap. "Now, *I* think we should just be friends."

He closed his eyes and threw his head back. "This is Friday the 13th, you know. It sure has been Friday the 13th for me, all day. Nothin's gone right today," he shook his head over and over again. "I tried not to come here. Then I do come here and you say that!"

"What do you expect?" I grabbed a cigarette from his pocket. "Maybe you should just leave, now that we're just friends again. I just want to make one thing clear. There ain't one damn thing wrong with you."

He walked over to the door. "Friends?"

"Friends." I nodded. He hesitated, leaning back against the doorjamb for a moment, then sauntered out to the porch where he sat on the ledge. "Boy is this Friday the 13th, for sure!" He lingered there for a few moments shaking his head back and forth some more, not knowing what to do. "Pat, you do know me." He turned to slip off of the porch onto the ground.

"I know I do, Ron."

"I'll see you . . . sometime." He trotted to his car.

A couple of days went by and Ron made his usual phone call, except it was an hour early. I was relieved to find out that there were no consequences to my escapade that night. In fact, he was in the neighborhood. "I've been driving in this part of town quite a bit, lately. I don't have to stop by just because I'm in this part of town, you know."

"Oh, of course not," I agreed, wondering what he was up to now.

"Yeah. That's what I say . . . " he fidgeted around.

"What are you going to do now?" I asked.

"Are you busy?"

"Nope."

"Can I come over, Pat?" His voice was shaky as he heaved a deep sigh.

"Sure. Come on."

It was a very few short minutes. A knock came at the door. I opened it to find the young man appearing to have a heavy weight on his shoulders for they were stooped. *He looks so sickly,* I worried to myself. There was a paleness in his cheeks. His eyes were sad and wet, and he was shaking. "I'm glad you're home," his voice quivered as his arms enfolded her. "Let me hold you," he begged. His arms were strong as they clung to me squeezing me tightly. "I'm so confused!" Grabbing me by the arm he pulled me down to the floor squatting in Indian fashion very intent on what he was saying. "I've been doing a lot of thinking. I've been thinking about re-enlisting. Oh, gees," he threw his head back in exasperation. "Oh-h, I think I'd better call my folks. Boy, do I ever think I'd better call my folks!" I smiled hoping against hope . . . hating the fact that he was giving me hope, yet loving the hope . . . the excitement almost made me dizzy. *He's climbing the mountain . . . our mountain! He's almost to the top!* my heart whispered.

"I gotta go now." He stumbled out the door. I felt ecstatic. *Maybe, just maybe it'll be OK.*

A couple of days later came the usual phone call. "Pat, I called my folks last night." The words blared into my ears. "I figured I'd better call you and let you know. I'm going home." He heaved a deep sigh. "I can't go against my folks' advice," he paused . . . "You know, they're the ones who taught me right from wrong. They have never steered me wrong, Pat."

"I know," I nodded sadly. "They're the ones who made you into what you are."

"Maybe it's got something to do with what my brother did."

Right away I began to wonder if his brother was a deviant of some kind. This kind of thinking was prevalent after my experience with Bob and now with this mess. "What's the matter. "Is he queer or something?" I blurted it out.

"No, Pat." He sounded firmly annoyed. "It's just that he married a woman with a couple of kids, and my mom and dad were very upset about it. They didn't even speak for awhile. It's

OK now," he explained, " . . . but I don't want to do that to them again. Can I still come to see you?" he asked.

"When?"

"Right now."

That night the two of us found ourselves, face to face, in the middle of a battle of wits as Ron sat in the fireside chair and this time I paced the floor. "I guess I'm just a rock," he grinned in a far-off way. *Hm-m-m . . . he seems so smug about it,* I stared him down.

"There's something you're forgetting," I shook my finger at him. "I'm a rock, too." His mouth dropped.

" . . . but I'm from waaay back . . . " He grinned.

I stared him down.

"Oh, brother! What have I gotten myself into?" He fidgeted.

"You're a fool," I said softly.

"A fool?" His head bounced as though it had been hit with a rock. Then he gathered his senses. "Yeah, I guess maybe I am . . . maybe."

"Ron, do you love me?" I came out with it point blank, as I meandered into the kitchen.

"I don't know what love is," he confessed skillfully dodging the remark.

"I have a feeling you know, now," I shouted from the pantry as I poured us a cup of coffee.

"Know what now, Pat?"

"What love is, you dummy," I slammed the cup down on the table next to him. "You know, just because you tell a girl you love her doesn't mean you have to marry her."

"I know, Pat," he slurped. "I like you. I like you a lot. But I don't love you," he wrinkled up his nose.

"Oh, then you don't love me, huh?" I cornered him.

"I didn't say that. You're putting words in my mouth," he squirmed in his chair. I threw myself on his lap kissing him hard. It was a strong and demanding kiss, almost like a kiss of death!

"Oh, Pat, Pat," he cried.

I slowly and firmly drew away. My eyes were mean. Their glare was piercing through him. He stared up at me and gulped.

"What are you looking at me like that for?" he cringed.

"I love you," I said hastily. "I can say it."

"Pat . . . " he sat there dazed. "I have a terrible time expressing my feelings. I don't know what love is!" he screamed. "I just don't!"

"What about that first night you came to see me?" I demanded him to explain.

"What about it?"

"You know what about it. You told me you loved me."

"I did?" He tried to think. "I don't remember. I keep telling you. I've never told anyone I love them."

"You told me," I screamed.

"I don't remember it. I don't!" He slammed his fist on the table spilling his coffee.

"That's convenient," I snapped at him, "evidently you didn't mean it." I went into the kitchen to get a dishtowel to wipe it up with.

"You saying I lied to you?" he asked in a mad voice allowing it to carry with me as I did my thing.

"It looks that way."

"Pat, I never lied to you. I just don't remember it."

"What does that mean?"

"I guess it means, I really don't know what I'm saying when I'm with you."

"You stupid poop," I threw the kitchen towel at him.

"I'd better leave now," he changed the subject. "I'll see you one time or maybe two more times before I go home." At the door he put his arms around me to kiss me goodnight.

"Ron!" I clung to him. "I'm frightened."

"What are you frightened about?" he grabbed my shoulders to hold me there square in front of him. He looked deep into my eyes.

"Please hold me," I begged. Hysterical feelings welled up inside of me as short sobs gushed from my mouth. Suddenly, I pushed away from him much like a ballerina will do when dancing a farewell to her lover. I wasn't myself. I could see myself going through motions, pacing up and down the room waving my arms and babbling. Around and around the room I circled, even stepping up on the couch. Yes, walking on the couch, babbling, wringing my hands. He stood there watching, quietly scared. I slowly gathered myself together standing there before him like a limp rag.

"Don't cry, now. Don't start crying," he held me close. The panic subsided. "Are you all right now?" he asked.

"I'm OK."

"I'll see you. Chin up," he kissed my cheek.

"Ron, could I ask you just one more small favor?"

"Yeah, what?"

"Could I have a cigarette? I'm all out."

"Here. Have two, three. How many do you need . . . ?" He poured them into my palm from the pack. Slowly he made his way to the car. I shakily lit up a cigarette sitting on the couch trying to calm my shivering body. I suddenly realized that I hadn't heard Ron's car pull away. Carefully, I parted the curtains so that he wouldn't see me peeking out at him. I could see his lit cigarette moving as he sat there so quietly, gazing at the house, thinking. Long minutes later he drove off still peeking over his shoulder at the house.

Why am I so scared? I was puzzled. *He said he'd see me again.*

The phone rang at its usual assigned time a couple of days later.

"Hello," I sang into the receiver. *Play it cool, girl,* I warned myself.

"Hi." His voice was it's usual low quality, but with an unusual coldness to it. He sounded strange. Actually, he sounded tired. "It was raining out and I ducked into this phone booth to keep dry. I figured I might as well call you as long as I don't have nothin' else to do."

"Is that right?" My heart pounded from trying to control my temper, no, my hurt. My temper, my hurt. *Am I mad?* I asked myself . . . *or am I going to cry?* "Thanks a lot," I stuttered. There was a deafening silence. The sound of traffic going by his phone booth was the only noise. I could her him tapping his fingers.

"Well?" he finally said stupidly. I didn't answer. "Why don't you say something?"

"Why in the hell don't you for a change?"

"What's the matter, Pat?" he feigned innocence.

"I hate to be wasting your time talking to you," I retorted.

"It's not a waste of time. I wanted to call you."

"You sure needed a stupid excuse."

"What excuse?"

"You know what you said. I'm sick and tired of explaining everything to you. That hurt."

"I wouldn't hurt you," he assured me.

"Well, you sure do a pretty good job of it. Anyhow, I appreciate your truthfulness about not loving me."

"When did I say that?" he asked.

"The last time we were together. I suppose you don't remember that now."

"I never said I didn't love you," he denied, "I never said I did, but I never said I didn't, either."

"Oh yes you did! What the heck are you trying to do to me?" I screamed. "What's more, I don't think you'd ever better come over here anymore."

"I won't, if that's what you want," he retorted. "It'd probably be better, anyhow." Suddenly, I could hear him sobbing. He was crying hard. Real hard . . . gasping for air, sobbing.

"What are you crying about?" I asked in an impatient bored tone.

"I've hurt you. I didn't mean to hurt you. Oh, God! I'll never have anythin' to do with another girl as long as I live!"

"Ron, don't get so melodramatic."

"I mean it, Pat. I really mean it," he started to sob some more."I don't know what it is, but I just can't seem to control myself." I was silent, listening. It was upsetting. "Pat, Pat! Are you still there?"

"Yes, I'm here."

"Promise me. I realize I don't deserve no promises, the way I've been acting and all, but please promise me this one thing."

"What?"

"Don't ever let Bob get his hands on those kids. No matter what happens. Please don't let him get near those kids!"

"I promise."

He was in better control now.

"I never cry," he blew his nose. "I'm sorry."

"It's OK, Ron. This whole mess is getting us both down, I guess."

"I just wish I hadn't done what I done some time ago," he started, in a shaky voice.

"What was that?" I asked, trembling at the sound of his ominous voice.

Now the whole truth is going to come out. I knew he was too good to be true, I warned myself.

"It happened some time ago, back home," he went on.

"Were you in jail or something?"

"No, nothing like that," he sounded disgusted, "It's just something that happened one night. I was a nervous wreck. My folks were pushing at me to do what they wanted, and my sister was on my neck about something she wanted, and I got in my car and took a drive up the mountain. Man, I was driving crazy! How in the hell I got there I don't know 'cause I was all over the road. Anyhow, at the very top of the mountain there's this restaurant. I walked to the coffee bar and ordered a cup of coffee. I was shaking. I was such a wreck! Then the waitress came up to me and asked me what was the matter. She was really nice."

Oh-oh, I surmised . . . *I knew it, I knew it. He tried to rape her or something, I'll bet.* I tried to hide my suspicions by carrying on with the conversation. "What did you do then?"

"Nothin".

"What do you mean, nothin?"

"Just what I said. Nothin," he retorted.

"I don't get it," I pried for an explanation. "What point are you trying to make with that story?"

"Don't you see, Pat? She was really nice to me. A perfect stranger, yet she was so interested in my troubles and talked to me . . . " He let out a huge sigh in the difficulty of trying to make me understand. "If it hadn't been for her I know I would've killed myself on the way back home. I would've driven right off of the mountain. I know I would have."

"I don't get it, Ron. I still don't get it. If that's all there is to it, then why were you so sorry about what you did that night?"

"I was sorry I stopped at that restaurant and met that waitress."

"Why? What did you do? Rape her?" I blurted it out.

"No, Pat, no. I was sorry I stopped there because if I hadn't, I'd be dead right now. That's it. I wish I was dead! I wish I had driven right off that cliff! I wish . . . " he started crying again. "I hurt you. I didn't mean to, but . . . but I hurt you. I'm so mixed up." He hesitated a minute. "Can I still call you Pat?"

"You can call me if you want, Ron, but after this, I wouldn't let you near me with a ten foot pole . . . even if you crawled on your hands and knees. Well, then maybe, I'd start listening."

"I wish I was dead," he kept harping. "Really I do. I wish I was dead. I wish I never had anythin' to do with you."

"OK", I retorted in cool calmness. I hung up the receiver. That was that. It was over. As I walked up to bed I felt weak with relief. It was finally over.

My flesh and
My heart may fail
but my God is the ROCK
of my heart
and my portion FOREVER.

Psalm 73:26 (NJ)

Chapter 9

Hanging In Limbo

In the state that I was in this morning, thinking back to my precious tender, yet, painful romance, I was amazed at the strength that I had mustered up those months after Ron had gone from my life. I was now the frazzled product of those days sitting there day after day sipping on coffee, to create a dignity about myself. Later on I would change over to beer, as soon as it seemed acceptable. I remembered how placid I had become in those days just performing motions: going to and coming from work. No tears. That in itself should've been a clue that my pain had become so unbearable that I was beginning to hide from my emotions. It had only appeared that I was coping well. However, little interludes of true peace had been flittering through my life, now and then, such as the day when a young soldier friend of ours decided to stop by on his motorcycle, just to say "hi". His name was Lonnie. He was a lanky six-foot-six, an awkward young man reminding me of teen-age years for he was still suffering from his youthful acne complexion. His home was in Tennessee where he had given birth to his southern accent, which was one of his cutest attributes. His nonchalant manner during the visit put me at complete ease for he had been content just sitting at the dining table sipping on a beer while I went through the motions of doing my housework, even washing the windows. There was a simple peacefulness between us there that day.

Carol had taken the boys to a ballgame so we decided to take little Betsy to the zoo. As we strolled together so comfortably in the park, each of us holding on to one of Betsy's little hands, I even had a fleeting wish that, perhaps, we could be a couple instead of my heart being with Ron. Back at the house after the kids were in bed Lonnie and I began to get better acquainted, both of us silently surprised how comfortably close we had become. "I have five brothers," he had informed me . . . "not a one of them is over five seven."

"Oh, I can't believe that," I shook my head.

"No, it's true. I'm the opposite of the runt, or something like that." We both laughed. "Yeah, I was lucky. When us guys would get ready for church we'd all have to get in front of the mirror all at the same time to comb our hair. All I had to do was just stand there and comb mine 'cause I could see over the whole bunch of them."

I loved his back-home humor.

Being a loyal person to things of the heart, my pangs still zeroed in on my feelings for Ron, though. I knew that the last thing I needed was to get involved in another affair.

It was drawing very close to the time of Ron's discharge. It seemed such a shame to end it with bitterness. I took steps to set my mind at ease. I was looking for anything positive I could do to make me feel better. I wrote to him finalizing my feelings by writing a letter of thanksgiving. . . . *your love and patience were not wasted.* A few days went by, I heard no word from Ron. The timing was extremely painful because Bob was getting married this very month.

The gall that man had displayed was still unbelievable. One day, a few weeks previous, he had brought Anne to meet me. There they were hand in hand coming to the door. I met them using all my strength to hide the rage that I was feeling inside, rather well I might add, until Bob said, "I wanted you to meet Anne so that you could approve of her." My heart pittered a few too many patters. *Who in the hell does he think I am, his mother?* I tried hard to choke back the anger. *She must be a doozie, herself,*

I further felt, . . . *for her to go along with this ridiculous protocol that Bob had dreamed up.* I finally told them both to leave saying, "I don't care what you two do, just leave us alone."

It had all hurt so much! Bob getting married and here Ron was leaving. I was aching inside so badly! *Why, Oh God? Why does he always get what he wants and I'm always left behind? Don't you love me? Oh, if Ron could only have said he loved me . . . much of this pain would have been taken away. Oh God, Oh God, why?* It was at this moment that little Blake interrupted my deep thoughts hollering, "Mom, the phone. I think it's Ronnie!"

It's Ron! My heart skipped as I leaped to my feet and to the phone . . . "Hello?"

"Hi!" the familiar voice exclaimed. It was familiar, but not Ron's voice, it was Lonnie. "Oh, hi," I tried hard not to let on about the disappointment, especially after I found out why he had called.

"You'll never guess where I am," he snickered. "I was taking off on my motorcycle last night to come and see you. I fell and broke my leg. I'm in the hospital. Won't be able to ship out with my company. They're leaving the day after tomorrow."

"Wow, that's a lucky break!" I was happy for him, but the tone in my voice was flat. I had no more room for any emotional ties, not even one more emotional experience. I didn't want to encourage his affections, especially another soldier who was going to leave, anyhow. All I could think of was to cut the conversation short and not get involved. Deep down, though, I felt, *I'm probably flying over a "pretty bird".*

A letter was smiling up at me in my hand just a few days later. It was from Ron! I was so excited that my hands fumbled as I opened it. *I didn't expect no mail so I hadn't checked my mailbox,* his wonderful bad grammar sounded like music. He explained why he hadn't answered my letter sooner. *A friend told me it was there. Was I surprised!* he confided. *I hope I'll always be your dear friend.*

The day of his discharge came and went lodging in my gut much like a lump in one's throat will lodge there causing much discomfort. I tried not to think about it. In just a couple of days, though I was soothed. A post card came. *Hi, I'm in Disneyland. It's the only thing I've enjoyed so far. Your friend, Ronnie.* Another week, another postcard. *Had car trouble. Will be glad when the trip is over. So far all I enjoyed was Disneyland.* Then another one came. I rushed to take off my coat to read it. I placed the card on the mantle for a moment. *Oops!* The post card fell behind the fireplace facing. *Oh, no! I've got to get it out of there.* I was so frantic I couldn't even stop to cry. *A coat hanger, that's it. That should work* . . . My hands tried to form a hook out of it so that I could fit it into the crack and pull it up. I fished up bills from 1924. A postcard from 1946, a matchbook, more trivia, but no post card from Ron. *Maybe if I put some honey on it it'll stick to the wire.* I tried that. No luck. *All that did was probably feed the ants,* I feared. I wanted to cry as I stood there staring at the dilemma in disgust. It was defeat. I had to face it.

Another week, another letter, only this one was different. Carol couldn't wait to show it to me. "Oh, no," my face turned pale. "Darn him. Darn him!" I stamped my feet.

"What's the matter?" Carol was stunned by my reaction. "I thought you'd be so happy!"

"He makes me so mad! It has his return address on it! I didn't want to know it." I was helplessly pacing around the room again. "Oh, no! What am I going to do? Now I'll probably make a fool of myself. I don't want to write to him. I didn't want to know how to reach him. Oh, God, I feel so helpless . . . . " I finally calmed down enough to read the letter. *I'll be milking cows and chopping wood all winter,* was the message.

Hopes mounted in my heart. Hopes that I wanted nothing to do with, yet everything to do with. I had had moments of feeling that I would crawl across the country on my hands and knees, then moments of not ever wanting to hear from him again. Mixed feelings. Weak moments.

Against my better judgment I wrote a letter. I made the big mistake of expounding on my daily life: going to work, raising kids and car troubles. I tried to keep it light, but let's face it . . . that was my life. There was no answer. *He's just dangled himself in front of me like a piece of bait. He's probably thinking he's real cool . . .* I got very huffy after not hearing from him. It was getting on near Christmas.

I relied on my good old friend, the booze. I decided to forget about the whole thing and go out to drink, leaving Carol home to babysit. I just wanted to get out of the house and find someone to talk to so that I could get my pain and agony off of my mind, even if for just a few hours. I had just had an experience at the laundromat that week, listening to a woman there going on and on about how much pain she was in since she had lost her husband. This was a rather young lady, far too young to be a widow . . . but it upset me. With a death, people sympathize. I had lost a deep love which no one really understood about, making light of it like, "You're not the only one who's lost a boyfriend, you know." I knew it. It still hurt terribly.

I piped up, "At least you had a chance to be with him and build a life with him . . . " The woman got very upset and slammed out the door. *Oh, my God, I hurt her. I didn't mean to. I've got to handle this better.*

Anyway, on this particular night out I came waltzing in about midnight. Carol had become very protective of me. She was worrying about me as I sauntered up the steps teetering. "Boy, did I ever have a good time, tonight," I swung my purse into the air not even watching to see where it landed. "I went for a ride with a new father", I droned on with my thick speech. "Oh, hi." I had barely noticed a friendly new face sitting in my big old armchair. "He wanted to do it right there in the car." I continued. "His wife was in the hospital having a baby, and he wanted to screw me, right there in the back seat of his car. I threw up all over his car." I sat down in the middle of the floor.

Al, the new fellow, was holding his stomach and wiping away tears from laughter. "Who is she?" he asked Carol. "That's the funniest thing I've heard in ages. It's great!"

"Maybe we'd better wind up the evening," said Al's friend, Stuie. Both Carol and Stuie were laughing at my antics, too, which of course spurred me on.

"Hey, guy, what more do you want?" Al said. "We've got the gal with the sexy voice over the phone sitting over there, and a floor show over here. This is great!"

"You know what he cleaned it up with?" I crawled over to Al. He leaned down to hear what I was saying in almost a whisper. "Pampers. Yes, it was a present for his wife. Pampers!"

Al nearly fell off the chair from laughter. I proceeded to entertain. I was on! Jokes and laughter went on for several hours.

"What's this letter here?" Al picked up Ron's letter that was laying on the end table. "Who in the hell is this creep?" His eyes scanned the letter. *I'll be milking cows and chopping wood all winter.* Al read it aloud with a mimicking snicker.

"What's the matter with that?" I glared back at him. "Makes sense to me. He lives on a farm, you know."

"A farmer. What a creep . . . " Al sat there sipping his beer, making farmer jokes until somehow the evening finally ended.

Al and Stuie became fixtures around there for awhile. The phone call that Carol had made was to a tavern, this time. Carol, too, had decided that dealing with soldiers was too painful. Her boyfriend, Wes, was gone to Viet Nam, and she was hurting, also. She never did receive a letter from him, at least none that I knew about. It seemed that Carol could always reach out and find another group of guys. Deep inside I wondered if, perhaps, I should've objected, but they were always nice guys. This new crowd was a little older than the soldiers had been and had been around a little more. In the next few weeks to come they would just come around with a couple of more guys (one of them was named Snake), have a beer or two and then take off.

Weeks in the same time frame went by and still no word from Ron. The creep! I was beginning to take Al's opinion to heart. *That was the cruelest thing he ever did, to write me and give me his return address and then leave me dangling! I'll fix him . . .* I got on my high-horse one night. Feeling a little mischievous I found out his phone number from the operator. *This'll frost him . . .* I smiled thinking about how shocked he would be. His sister answered. "He's not here. He went down the road to look at a trailer . . . " Her voice was cheerful and friendly. I liked her right away. *She's got it too, whatever it is.* I smiled just thinking of the warmth even in his sister's voice. But somehow I knew. I knew Ron was there and was squirming. I could picture him standing there behind his sister begging her to tell me that he wasn't there. I took the chance. I persisted and called again. I had been right. He was there. He was caught.

"Why did you send me your address?" I prodded him with resentment. "I didn't want to know it, Ron".

"You knew it."

"I did not," I retorted. "I purposely didn't ask you for your address because I didn't want to know it!"

"You knew it, Pat. You knew it all the time." His voice became strangely sneaky. "Did you get it?"

"Get what?"

"My letter. I just wrote you a letter" he whispered. "Oh, I just mailed it yesterday. No, you couldn't have gotten it".

"No, I didn't get it, yet. Is everything OK?"

"I guess," his voice became cold. I didn't dare say anymore. The conversation was getting a little awkward. "We'll see you, OK?" His voice had that sneaky strangeness about it again.

"Good-bye, Ron." I answered flatly, in a finality mode. It was a finality that I couldn't accept even though it was a finality that deep down I knew was inevitable. I grasped on to straws the next day or two telling myself, *Maybe he'll come back. He said, "We'll see you". I wonder what he meant by that?* I knew deep down that the comment was a generic sign off. Yet, that sneaky tone in his voice. *There's something he was trying to say.*

It was the very next day that I received the much yearned for letter. It was not only a letter and a Christmas card but a check for $15 for a present. The words were somewhat stabbing, yet a comfort to understand his thoughts. *I'm ashamed for the way I behaved. I'm sorry if I hurt you. I know, now, that I did.* The words blurred in front of me through my tears. *I don't want nothin' to do with no girls. The girl I used to go with has been pestering me. I told her to leave me alone or I'll kill myself. I will, Pat . . . I want to be left alone.* The rest of it didn't seem to matter. It was perfectly clear: there was no hope. Yet, it was not completely hopeless. The oneness of our hearts was still complete, our hearts were still together.

There were also some other changes going on in my life during these painful days. I had been feeling the crunch of expenses, getting more and more behind with the bills. I was earning far less money than my male counterparts, the reasoning of the company being that men had to support their families. I had to support my family, too. I had received no support payments from Bob and no one could tell me how I could go about getting him to pay without me going into the expense of getting a lawyer. It was a catch 22. Here Bob was getting married again, had filed bankruptcy keeping his new car by turning it over to his father for one dollar. He hadn't even incorporated our bills into his bankruptcy that he had been ordered to pay by the court so that the bill collectors would be off my back. There seemed to be nothing I could do about it. He had been ordered to pay through the court, but the court knew nothing about it. In fact, they acted as if they could care less. It was all getting me down.

Dan, Bill's friend and still my confidant, had advised me to go to public assistance. They at least had listened to my story. However, the only hope that they could give me was that if I quit my job I would be able to clear fifty dollars more a month on welfare and still be able to stay home with my kids. Of course, this meant that Carol would have to go, which might be good since our drinking was getting out of hand. *Maybe I could get back to a more normal home-life,* my new thoughts became my ambition.

I managed to make it through to the first day of the year. The people in my office were rather rude to me when I left. I guess they'd gotten tired of all of the escapades I was enduring, to the point that I believe they thought I was cracking up. They had cold fear on their face that last day. Their coldness was almost like a conspiracy to make sure I didn't want to come back to work there again.

The New Year started out all crazy. Bob decided to pay me a visit and wish us a happy New Year. I was quietly sitting in the kitchen when the visit took me by surprise. "Can I come in?" he grinned. *He's got the greatest gall in the world!* I had to laugh inside. I was in no mood for trouble. Depression set in on me from the first day I was imprisoned at home. There was too much time to think. I was feeling so low that nothing really mattered, anyhow. Not anymore.

"Come on in," I felt a relief in laughing at his ridiculous audacity.

"Do you have a cup of coffee?" He was his most charming.

"Yeah. I guess so. You should be buying me a cup," I purposely poured it over the sides of the cup giving myself a feeling of retaliation, as small as it was.

"I just wanted to wish you a happy New Year. Where are the kids?"

"Carol took them to the movies. It's her last fling with them. I quit my job. I'm staying home with the kids now. Can't make it with no support. By the way, I thought you weren't supposed to be in town."

"Oh, they figure that now that I'm married again I won't be a threat." I didn't even bother to ask who "they" were. I was so tired of trouble I just went with the flow. He hesitated for a moment. "Do you think that there might be a chance that we could get back together in about five years or so?"

I nearly spit the coffee from my mouth in pure shock. "No." I said softly, but firmly.

"I guess I don't blame you. It's just that I don't think that this thing I've gotten myself into is going to work out. I'm going to school, Anne is a beautician, you know. I have to start all over."

"What's the problem?"

"They're kind of funny. Her folks are sort of different . . . I don't know, it's just not the same . . . " *Yeah. I'll bet . . . she's probably not a fool like I was . . .* I scolded myself for even listening. "Remember when you told me that I acted like I didn't want anything to do with, you know . . . your body? I don't have any trouble with her. I guess I respected you too much."

"Oh, Bob." I sighed out loud with exasperation. "That wasn't respect, it was hurtful disrespect . . . on purpose! You've got things so screwed up!"

"Live and learn." he tried to change the subject.

"Do you change light bulbs?" I took the hint with gusto. "Remember? I'm scared of height. These ceilings are so high!"

"What'll I get for it?" he kidded.

"I'll knock ten dollars off of your support for each light bulb. Three in all. Thirty bucks!"

"It's a deal!"

We good-naturedly played our little game both knowing that the support payments were a joke. With the job done he left as quickly as he had come. He didn't even ask to see the kids. *I suppose that was supposed to make me feel better about things,* I said to my God whoever or whatever He was these days. I wasn't very sure about that anymore, either.

Now that I was no longer working during the week, I was no longer in contact with the outside world except through the activities of my children . . and of course, Carol's escapades now and then. The kids would be in the front room watching TV perfectly happy as long as they had the cinnamon rolls or whatever treat I showered them with to keep them appeased.

My love is deeper than the ocean, higher than the sky . . . the love songs floated out onto the airwaves filling my heart full of memories of Ron as I sat there reliving each moment. *Why? Oh, why did he have to go? My love for him was so beautiful . . . it was his purity that I loved. Oh, God. I tried so hard to keep things right. Did we sin? We tried to listen to our consciences . . . but sometimes that's not enough. Only You know that I trust my own conscience better than those hypocrites who call themselves God-fearing . . .* I felt so helpless. I tried to remind myself that no one is perfect and we all have weaknesses. *But, here I am expected not to ever have any tenderness, no one to hold me, ever again? God, I can't do that. I know you gave Ron to me to help me. Knowing such tenderness and then losing it is so painful! He just wanted to help heal the hurts from my past, that's all. All I wanted to do was to help him, and love him. How is he going to find out if he can function with a woman? I just wanted to help him . . . Oh, God, I'm so mixed up.* I started thinking back to any words of wisdom that might help me. "Better to have loved and lost then never to have loved at all . . . " came the words which I now had a greater understanding of. Through my thoughts the music from the radio soared into my being. *I need your love, God speed your love to me.* These love songs would keep me company until my little tribe would go to bed, with my own self-following close behind.

My weekends, though, were still quite full. Carol stuck close by to me especially on weekends. She had found another babysitting job in the same part of the city, but not within walking distance. As usual, she had a plan. She had brought an idea with her that a girlfriend of hers should meet Al. "Let's have a little party and let them two get acquainted!" I agreed to it . . . anything to get her out of her deep misery. Deep down, though, I was a little jealous of this new girl matching up with Al. I had enjoyed the visits with him and his friends, and of course, the beer. They would usually leave a near case of beer after they left on one of their night-out-on-the-town escapades. I liked having friends around for it helped me not to think so much.

Carol's girlfriend was a very nice, dignified girl. She had brought her knitting with her to impress Al with her homemaking qualities. *That's the last thing that Al is looking for these days,* I chuckled to myself. Al was just newly divorced from his wife. All he wanted these days was fun and games. As the evening wore on, the rest of us retired into the kitchen to let the two of them get acquainted. Al was politely listening to his blind date trying to be attentive to her.

Stuie and I were getting curious as to how they were getting along. We were tipsy. What seems normal to drunks seems very weird to others. It even seemed weird to Carol who was shocked at our indignant behavior. In fact, I still can't believe we did this. We snuck into the dining room, hiding under the table of all things, trying to listen. Al knew we were there. We knew that Al knew we were there. It was all very crazy. Suddenly Al got up saying, "I think I'll go home." He stretched his arms.

"Yes, I think it's getting late," the young woman picked up her knitting soon thereafter leaving. *They didn't hit it off too well,* I grinned to Stuie. Stuie wasn't surprised. But then Al pointed at a picture of me that had been up on the TV ever since Ron's last couple of dates. I had hoped that he would hint for me to give it to him, but he never did. It was a picture of freshness and innocent trust. It had been my engagement picture . . . before all of the trouble.

"I want her." He was very point blank about it. I was stunned. Al picked up the edge of the tablecloth to peek under the table at the two of us, laughing all the while. I guessed that he liked my silliness more than anything. We certainly did look silly, two adults hunched over under the table. Al pulled me up to my feet and started dancing with me. Stuie disappeared into the kitchen with Carol who was talking to a third party that they had brought with them, someone I didn't even know.

It all happened so fast! Suddenly we weren't dancing any more. Within a quick minute we had found ourselves thrashing on the couch and over with it before we even knew what had happened. "Wow! What happened?" Al jumped up from the couch, scratching his head.

"It must be what they call physical attraction, or something." I straightened out my skirt. "Damn. This is the worst time of the month for me, too."

Al grabbed me by the arm pulling me through the front door all the way outside to his car. "They all have too big of ears in there, we need to talk about this. You don't take no pills or nothing?" he rounded the corner as they drove around slowly.

"Nope. I try not to do this sort of thing."

"Unsuccessful, huh? Are you Catholic, or something?"

"Yeah, I guess. At least I was."

"Me too," he grinned.

"You are? I mean were?" I smiled. "How come every guy I meet and like is Catholic?"

"I guess we just have things in common. I'm not divorced yet, just separated. We're trying to figure out what to do. We have five kids."

"Oh, I see. I hope there isn't going to be another one."

"Me too! We'd better pray about this."

A few days later I found myself very angry about my dilemma. It never even dawned on me that my drinking might have something to do with these terrible sinful goofs. I was feeling mighty helpless in my heart that ached so much. *If Ron hadn't just left me hanging here in mid-air, I wouldn't be so weak. If only he could have just told me he loved me . . . at least I'd have something to be true to.* I stormed up into my bedroom expounding my exasperation in a letter: my fears, but mostly, my anger. *I'm going to settle things one way or another!* I swore to myself as I licked the envelope and the stamp. Very busily I ran out of the house and across the street to the mailbox and slammed it in. My heart was racing. There. I brushed my hands together in good-riddance style. I went up to bed and cried. Morning time came and I hadn't slept. *What a terrible thing to do!* I had come to my senses. *I have to write an apology to him.*

At least good news came within a few weeks. The big fright was over. Al stopped by one evening about a month later for the last time. He had come over to find out if everything was OK. Thank God, it was.

Beloved, think it not strange concerning
The fiery trial which is to try you,
As though some strange thing happened to you:
But rejoice, inasmuch as you are partakers
Of Christ's sufferings,
That, when His glory shall be revealed
You may be glad with exceeding JOY.

1 Peter 4:12-13 (KJ)

Chapter 10

Wishful Thinking?

Another day passed, and still another one. They were all alike. Again I was listening to the music . . . *more than the deepest love I have for you alone.* The radio was playing beautiful words of ecstasy and agony . . . there seemed to be little difference. I sang along with the music, tears rolling down my cheeks. *Now, I've really done it!* I had so regretted mailing those stupid letters to Ron. I lay with my head on the table sobbing. *What am I going to do? I can't go on like this the rest of my life. I wish I had a Bible, or something.* Suddenly that idea struck some interesting new thoughts. *I wouldn't know what to do with one if I had it. Cripes! Here I went to school all through Catholic schools and I don't know the first thing about the Bible . . . just that stupid catechism they pushed down our throats year after year. Somebody sure goofed there!* My body shook with these thoughts which were rather shocking.

The clanging of the mailbox interrupted the shock. *There's the mailman. I might as well see the bad news he's bringing: bills, bills, bills!* As I pulled them from the mailbox my hands sorted through them. *Sure enough, there's the electric bill.* I opened it to find it wasn't so bad after all. The telephone bill was there, and a letter. *Is it from Ron?* My eyes scanned the envelope with excitement. *No, it's postmarked here in Tacoma. Darn it! I wonder who it's from?* I tore open the envelope. It was a chain letter of all things. I read it over. *That's a bunch of garbage,* walking back to my chair in the kitchen I threw the mail on the table. *On top of everything else it tells me I'll have bad luck if I don't follow the instructions. Damn, damn, damn. That's all I need is more bad luck!* I reached out for the letter once more. *Wait a minute,* I choked as my eyes hit on something. *It says here to look up Matt 17:20-21 in the Bible. Hmmm. I was just wishing I had a Bible. Gee! I really do wish I did now. Maybe I can go borrow mom's Bible.* On second thought. *I don't think mom has one.* I tried to think back if I had ever even seen one in my parent's home. *Better yet, I have that money that Ron sent me for Christmas. I wanted to buy something special with it. I think I'll go out and buy one.*

The minute Betsy and I got home from my little shopping spree at the Catholic bookstore, which was just up the avenue about six blocks away, I opened the Bible all excited about looking up the passage. I just guessed. The first number must be the chapter, and the second number, the verse? Sure enough. There it was. "Faith can move mountains. But this can only be done through prayer and fasting." I thought it over. *I'm sort of sunk,* I slumped back down into my chair. *I don't even know how to pray anymore.* Then I began to mull over the second tool. Fasting. All I knew about fasting was that we used to give up something every Lent. It was called fasting. *What could I give up? It's got to be something important! I know what, I'll quit smoking and drinking. That's a good idea. I can't afford the darn things anyhow.* I still had to think over the prayer bit. The only way I had learned to really pray was memorizing prayers of repetition. I didn't just want to say those same old prayers that I had learned year after year. They didn't even mean anything to me anymore. I remembered about some little saint that sister had taught us about in school who used to say her rosary while she was mopping the floor. *I know what! I'll use my housework as my prayers! I'll pretend that it's praying. If nothing else, it's constructive.* Just thinking about it pepped up my spirits. *Now let's see here,* I re-read the letter. *I'm supposed to mail copies of this stupid thing to four friends.*

I'd better get that done first. I don't want no more bad luck. I'll mail it to out-of-town friends. I cleverly decided. *That way I won't be so liable to get another copy sent to me. I sure don't want this thing sent back to me again. Once is enough. I'm not taking any chances.*

It took me quite awhile to write four letters for the letter was quite lengthy. Finally, they were written and mailed out. *Now, getting back to business.* I was actually anxious to get started on my prayerful housework. I picked up my broom. *Brother, I didn't realize this place was such a mess. That sure was a crazy letter.* The letter had also gone on to say that it had been around the world 3 times. *That's strange. How would the writer know that it had gone around the world three times? Who but God, Himself? Well anyhow, whoever wrote that thing was awfully smart. It seems like if you do one thing that it said to do, you just naturally end up doing the next thing. It's really silly, though. It said, 'If you burn up the letter at midnight tonight, you'll get something good in the mail in four days'.* I shoved the dirt into the garbage bag all the while trying to figure out the mystery of the letter. *I wonder if maybe I'd get a letter from Ron? Wouldn't that be funny? I think I'll do it, for kicks. What the heck?*

That night I planned to stay up until midnight making a fire in the fireplace so that I could burn the letter when the magic hour arrived, but I had fallen asleep. Through my sleep I was awakened very suddenly by a voice saying "The Lady of Fatima!" I got up on my feet as in shock. My whole body trembled. I stood in front of the heat register to warm up. *What's going on?* I felt a chill as I rubbed my arms while my mind twirled around with many questions. *What's the Lady of Fatima got to do with it? The letter! The one the Lady of Fatima gave to the children and it was supposed to be opened in 1960? Maybe this was that letter! Oh, I must be cracking up.* I walked into the kitchen to see what time it was. *It's almost midnight. I'll burn that thing for sure. In fact, I'm going to burn up these damn cigarettes, too, so I don't get tempted.* I lit the fire in the fireplace as I silently sat there watching the flames gobble up my sacrifices.

Once upstairs I tucked myself into bed. I was exhausted from my experience just an hour previous. The job done, I was somewhat troubled over the strangeness of the day. I tried very hard to sleep. Just when I had almost dropped off to sleep I heard a little teasing voice. "Who do you want to see?"

"I just want to be with him!" I sat up in bed crying out. Suddenly I saw furniture come flying into the room. It was so real that I felt as though I had to dodge them. A sofa arranged itself around the room then a little table . *What's this?* I rubbed my eyes. I felt Ron's presence. *Maybe that was his bedroom furniture.* I panicked. *No, no! I don't want to see him like this!"* I was trembling from fright.

Then I saw a field of grass: acres of grass. There he was way far away, walking in the grass. He was searching for something. He was so lonely. *Who is he? He's so far away* . . . I tried hard to see his face but it was blurred. *Who is it? I can't make out who it is,* I worried. I was so scared my heart pounded. I lay back trying to calm down.

Then a deep serious voice asked me, "Who was here in the beginning?"

I was already so shocked I just listened, thinking. *Adam and Eve?* I felt so stupid.

"No, before that, before the earth."

God?

"Who else?" the voice asked.

The Blessed Trinity? I don't know. Then the voice was gone. *I think things have gone too far. There was nobody but God.* I fell asleep wanting to forget the whole ordeal. I tried not to even think of it again, thinking that it had been a demonic experience or something.

The following days I kept myself busy throwing myself into my housework with great fervor, as in a prayer, in answer to my resolution. Problems began lurking at every bend. The very first day I went to the welfare office to see if I could get some help from them to make Bob pay support. Bob had been up to his usual weight-slinging to the law officials, or something. He had contacted the kids telling them that he wanted them to meet their new stepmother. The kids were all excited about it. I didn't know what to do. *After all, they did take back their accusations about him. But what about my promise to Ron? Oh, so what? He didn't do much to help me do anything about it. He was right. He didn't have any right to ask me to keep the kids from their father. I don't see how I can as long as I have no proof of him mistreating them.* Bob contacted me telling me that he was told by "them" (whoever that was) that "it would be OK as long as Anne is with me on our visitations?" I searched my heart trying to figure out if maybe I just wanted to use the kids as pawns to get back at Bob. I also knew that I couldn't handle one more problem, keeping in mind how I was apparently cracking up and all. *I can't fight city hall."*I suppose that would be OK," I had agreed, trying to keep peace.

After mulling it over, though, I began pondering, *Yeah, along with the court order for visitation for him was also my right to child support.* I couldn't afford a lawyer, so I decided to go and see the people at welfare. By now my errand was more the principle of the thing because since I was no longer working, it wouldn't matter much to me, anyhow. The welfare people would get the money. I went ahead, though, hoping to get some advice on how to handle this visitation thing. You might know it: my car broke down right in the middle of the main street during the noon time rush. *Be patient, Patricia. Remember that when something is important it doesn't always come easy.* Fortunately a kind soul gave me a push. There was more bad news at the welfare office . . . "you know we can't get blood out of a turnip . . . "

"It's so unfair," I was so upset I couldn't even cry. "Here he gets a girl pregnant, and gets married, his business has been closed down by the moral squad, and he never has to pay for anything. It's not fair."

"I know dear, it does seem awful unfair, doesn't it?" The woman was very kind and evidently felt very helpless from her standpoint, also. "We can go after him now that you're here for help, though. Here are the papers. We *will* go after him. I'll make an appointment for you to see our legal representative in a couple of weeks. That'll give him a chance to look into the situation. "That was good news, maybe. If I could start to get support, then maybe it would pay me to go back to work. Things just might be looking up.

But then, when I got home, just in time for the boys to get home from school, I wished I had still been stuck in traffic. I had picked up Betsy from a neighbor making it home just in time for the boys to get home from school. One of the neighbor kids came home with them. As they frolicked around the front room, this kid got his earlobe bit off by our precious doggie, Duke. He had taken his job of protector a little too seriously. Of course, this took days of quarantine and eventually he was put to sleep.

The kids began to misbehave terribly. It was as if all hell had broken loose all around me. *It seems that something is trying to make me a nervous wreck so that I'll smoke a cigarette or drink a beer or something,* I reminded myself as I stumbled through the week keeping my hands busy more and more: housework, braiding Betsy's hair, mending. *I'm not going to give in.*

The fourth day after I had burned the letter I waited by the mailbox anxiously full of hope that miraculously there would be a letter from Ron. *It would be a miracle!* I dreamed. *Oh, mailman, please get here. You're a little late.* I paced from window to window. *Here he comes. Yep, he's bringing some mail!* I ran to the door. One envelope. A brown envelope. *It's just my welfare check,* my heart sank. I opened it. *Well, at least I got a raise. A substantial raise at that! That is good news,* I reminded myself, feeling guilty for not having been thankful for my welfare check. It was just that I was so disappointed.

I dug back into my housework. I was now feverishly going about my duties trying to keep my mind off of smoking. *I'll pick the chicken bones for soup, I'll wash out the garbage can. Keep busy,* I pleaded with myself. Ten days went by. Finally. *What's the use? I can't keep this up. I'm going to light up just one cigarette.* Immediately, I was off the housework merry-go-round and back on the cigarette one.

I followed through with my appointment with the welfare man.

"I'm sorry, ma'am," the receptionist informed me. "Mr. McMurray has transferred to another department."

"What do I do now?" I asked the young woman for some direction.

"I think you should go to the prosecuting attorney's office."

"I've had dealings with that creepy guy," I remembered back to last summer when he got Bob off the hook.

"There are a half-dozen assistant attorney's there. One of them should be able to help you."

I gathered up all of my strength and high-tailed it down to the County-City Building immediately. A very nice man invited me into his office after a brief wait. I let loose on him . . . all of the happenings of my divorce, from the closing of the bowling alley to Bob's vandalism, having to run away from town to my aunt's farm, how Bob had even followed my lawyers around and had thrown the hammer through the window and the boys' accusations which were then taken back . . .

The man got on the phone quickly and ordered a copy of Bob's police record. A few minutes later a messenger brought a very large file. It was Bob's file! It was as thick as several encyclopedias. The attorney scanned the pages quickly mumbling to the messenger. "Not so surprising, though, after you hear this lady's story." The two of them had their noses in the file. Then the young attorney slowly raised his eyes searching for mine so as to make a very clear and definite statement. "Ma'am, you were lucky to get out of this mess as easy as you did." He instructed me to call him in a couple of days. "We're going to shoot the works on this boy," he promised.

A few days went by. I made the phone call. The answer, "I'm sorry, ma'am, but Mr.Latimer has resigned his position." I was stunned. More than that I became frightened. I dropped the matter. I was afraid. I remembered the attorney's warning.

When I told my folks about it, they just pooh-poohed it all saying, "I think your imagination is getting away from you, dear."

Then one afternoon I had a surprise to beat all surprises. Fortunately, Carol happened to be there for moral support. The surprise started with a knock on the door. It was one of the women from the bowling team that my sister had offered to pay for me to join. In return I had done her ironing. "Hi!" I greeted this near stranger wondering what the purpose of the call was . . . *perhaps she wanted help with the end-of-the-season plans.*

"Hi." I'm Al's wife," she smirked a glare at me.

"Al's wife?" I put my hand to my mouth in shock.

"Can I come in to talk?"

"Sure." I motioned her over to a chair. Carol just sat there in her chair totally speechless, which was a wondrous thing for her to experience. "Al told us he was divorced." I nodded my head to Carol to back up my story.

"He lied. He's been with me and the kids all the time. I found your phone number in his pocket with your name on it. Never had the nerve to call you. When you joined the team I couldn't believe it when I saw your name on the roster."

"Darn him, he lied to us," I slowly slithered down into my chair.

"Did you guys go to bed?"

"Not to bed." I tried to explain. "It did happen once, though. We were both pretty upset about it. Just one time." I tried to reassure the woman realizing that one time was enough to give this woman much pain.

"We've got five kids. That's all he needs is another one to support. That's the problem. He's just running away from our problems."

"Hey, I'm sorry. We agreed we won't see each other anymore, anyhow. Honest. Especially now!"

"What would you do if he was to come over here? Would you refuse to talk to him?"

"No. I'd talk to him," I answered as truthfully as I could. " . . . but on the front porch just long enough to straighten things out. I think he needs to hear it."

"Well, I hope so." The woman left peacefully having handled the situation with much dignity even though she left with the words. "If you don't, you might find five kids on your doorstep some morning."

After the she left Carol and I had a long talk. We were both shaking. Carol had noticed how immaculate the house was so I had told her all about the strange happenings with the letter and all. She told me about the beautiful home she was now working in. All in all we had a very pleasant evening chatting, trying to forget the strange visit earlier in the day. The hours were creeping into the late evening. The time had gotten away from us. The kids were in bed asleep. "Gosh, how am I going to get home? The last bus has already gone by." Carol asked.

"I'll take you home," I offered.

"Do you think you should leave the kids?" Carol checked out the wisdom of that decision.

"It'll be OK. They never wake up after they go to sleep, they play so hard. A friend of the family told me how in their neighborhood they always leave the kids home in bed after they're asleep and go down the block a couple of houses over to play cards. You don't live so far. The kids will be OK."

We got just about two blocks away. Old Clarabelle, bless her little engine, was clunking on down the street . . . feeling old age or something, then stopped. It just stopped. We just sat there in the middle of the street in the middle of the night stunned. "I feel so foolish. I wonder what happened? It won't do a cotton-picking thing, no noise, no nothing. Now what am I going to do? I've never seen a car do this. No warning or anything!"

Just then a man appeared, walking over to the old Chevy with the two nervous women in it. "You need some help?" He was a pleasant looking fellow, a rather young man with black hair slicked back, bright brown eyes and a friendly smile. "What happened?"

"I don't know," I threw up my hands. " . . . it just stopped."

"Just like that?" He scratched his head. "Didn't you have a chance to pull over or something?"

"Nope. It just stopped. All of a sudden."

"Well, I'll push you over to the side," he offered. "Can I take you anywhere?"

"Gee! I'd appreciate it," I sighed in relief. "I was taking Carol home, but she lives about a mile or two away."

"I'll take you," he smiled. "I'm not doing anything special, anyhow."

"Thanks," we sang.

He took Carol home and then promptly took me to my door.

"Would you like to come in for a beer?" I asked. " . . . it's the least I can do. I sure appreciate you helping us out like that."

"Yeah. I'll come in for a few minutes." We sat on the couch rather cozily enjoying a beer. "Do you have a radio or something?" I motioned to a little old thing that was sitting over in the corner. We got acquainted enough to start joking, then the next step was, "Do you want to dance?" Suddenly things were more serious and quiet. It was a slow, polite, peaceful dance, very little was said. "You're kind of mysterious," I flirted.

"Who? Me?" he sounded shocked.

"Yeah," I giggled, "you!"

"What's *your* story?" he held my head in his hands in a loving way. "Look into my eyes," he ordered. "You're upset. Real upset about something."

"I am," I sniffled. "I'm in such a mess."

"Come on. Tell me about it," he pulled me down to sit on the couch. I poured it all out. "You know, you never forget your first love," he informed me. "Do you feel better now?"

I nodded.

"I have to leave now, but I want you to make me one promise before I go."

"What's that?"

"You make an appointment with Father and tell him every little thing. Don't leave nothing out. Even if it takes several sessions."

"I will," I promised. "Thanks for everything." I kissed him on the cheek as he left.

The very next day I went to see Father as I had promised. *Boy, that was an ordeal,* I took my coat off and threw it on the chair once I was back home. *Father was sure nice to sit there and listen to me.* I went to the refrigerator and made myself a glass of iced water. That part of my fasting was still sticking. *I didn't get very far,* in fact, I was feeling embarrassed. *For crying out loud, I only got as far as telling him about my mother-in-law. One whole hour! It would take me forever to tell him everything,* I mumbled. *He can't be wasting his time listening to me belly-aching hour after hour. What if I had to go through the whole story again? I'd never be able to go through that. Never.* I sat down at the dining room table. *Hey! I wonder if I just wrote it all down. Yeah. It's fresh in my mind, I'll bet I can remember exactly what I told him.* I started to write it down on paper. I recalled with amazing clarity what I had told Father as I started talking about the night before my marriage . . .

> *My feet were even bleeding as I trudged along toward the church, that stormy night, to make my confession before I received the Sacrament of Matrimony. My soggy, wet shoes had ripped the skin right off of my heels.*

Father had asked me, "What does that have to do with anything?"

"Nothing," I had tried to explain, "except it made me remember just how painful that walk to the church was that night, that's all."

I went on writing:

> *"The wind was blowing against me. I felt so alone! The tree limbs were slashing in front of me almost daring me to go on. My foot slammed into a mud puddle, the gooey wet splashing all around me. "Darn him for making me walk in this soggy mess", I swore, "tonight, of all nights!" I had managed to remain a virgin all the way through my romance with Eddie, my high school sweetheart. But things were never the same after he had joined the air force. In fact, I had written him a Dear John after Bob had asked me to marry him. I compared*

them: Eddie being just a boy, but Bob, a man . . .
ambitious and knowledgeable about the world, and all.
But now I had to confess how Bob had talked me into
making love to him, that one night when we were fixing
up our new home by painting the furniture.

"You know, you're not a kid anymore," Bob snickered as he has led me to the bed, "You're in the adult world now." I guess that's what had happened to Eddie, I thought it over. I know he'd been cheating on me after he went into the service. Oh well, so Bob and I didn't wait. So what? We were engaged, weren't we? It had not even been a pleasant experience. I had felt so cheap. I thought I didn't enjoy it because it was a sin.

My memory brought me back to the last words that Bob had spoken to me when he had called to break our date to go to confession together. "I just want to go out with the boys," he had told me, "just a little bachelor party!" I couldn't help it. It made me darn mad for some reason. Am I going to be one of those wives that gets upset every time her husband wants to go out with the boys? I figured I'd just better get over it and go on with my mission. He said he would see Father about confession in the morning.

I wrote on . . . *The lights of the church glowed*
through the streets as I rounded the corner. It looked so
warm and welcoming on such an evil dreary night. I
gathered myself together. "Tell it all, Patricia" I ordered
myself as I walked up the steps to the church.

"You know, Father," I had added to our conversation, "I wondered why none of these so-called friends had come to our wedding, or had been introduced to me." This was the only proof that I had had of Bob's homosexuality before our marriage. I then had gone on telling of my first experiences with my mother-in-law and our relationship.

Now, I had to get that all down. I hadn't the foggiest notion of how to write a book. But, when I got started it was as if there was a silent voice telling me what to do. As I continued writing down my thoughts, I was guided. "First, write down one thought and follow through with that. Then you can explain another one after you complete the first one. You can always drop back into a past mode and bring up something else later on." Word after word was carefully planted on the paper. I found that I even had a larger vocabulary than I thought I had. I came up with a word that I wasn't at all familiar with. I looked it up in the dictionary. Sure enough, it was the right word. *I must've heard it somewhere before*, I felt spurred on in great encouragement. *This is great!*

That first evening I had thrust myself into my writing, Mom stopped over on one of her rare visits. "What are you doing?" she noticed the paper strewn out all over the table.

"I don't know," I answered. "Maybe I'm writing a book, or something."

"A book?" my Mom retorted in a shocked voice.

"I guess," I shrugged my shoulders. I knew that she already thought I was nuts. "It's funny the way it all started, but it's constructive. It keeps my head from spinning. I just started dumping everything down on paper. It makes me feel better. Anyhow, it has all the ingredients of a best-seller!" I threw my hands up in jest.

"Well, if it makes you feel better," my mother gave in to the inevitability of it all, " . . . it looks like you've done quite a bit."

"Yeah, but I have a long ways to go yet."

"Do you know what happened to me last night?" my mother changed the subject. "After thirty-five years I finally did it!"

"What did you do?" I asked in a worried voice.

"I told your father I loved him for the first time."

"You what?" I raised my voice in a desperate tone.

"Yes. I did."

"You mean you never told him that before?"

"I couldn't," she blurted. "I just didn't know for sure. I didn't want to lie to him."

"Mother, how could you?" I slammed my hands on the table.

"He understood . . . all these years." she said.

I thought to myself, *Yeah, that's probably why he never went anywhere with you, and everyone thought you were a widow.* I kept my thoughts to myself, though, for I didn't want to make any waves.

"Daddy has a lot of patience, doesn't he?" I remarked instead.

"A lot," mom smiled. "A lot."

Seeing that she had disturbed me from my project she started to leave. "Mom," I started to weep. "I need Ron so much. I know God gave him to me for a reason. I don't think he's going to come back."

"I don't either," she held my hand. "You're strong, dear."

"I'm trying to be. I think that if God doesn't send him back, He'll send someone just like him." I stood at the door leaning my head on its edge as my eyes followed that unusual woman to the car and watched her drive away.

I discovered how weary I really was after my mother left. I closed up shop for the night. I rose early the next morning ready for another day of writing. I finished the part about Bob and the queer stuff. Then the fun part came when I began to write about Ron. The words flowed out of me like a river. Beautiful words of the simplicity of love. The tendernesses. The pain. The cute little things and the misunderstandings. I kept writing, forgetting to eat. I had been living on iced water into the second day now finding only minutes to feed the kids sandwiches. Reality stepped in. I was running out of groceries so I trudged on down to the grocery store. I needed a break anyhow, and I needed to get something to heat up for the kids to give them a hot meal for a change. It was a refreshing walk to the store two blocks away. My head agonized back to all of the happenings of the past few months, though. It was as if a curtain was being lifted. I could think so much more clearly now that I had emptied my mind of all the far-out, emotional happenings. As I neared my house with my hands full of groceries I started to hear some words coming from deep inside of my breast. They were very precise words. "You'll have a hard time of it. You will experience all the things that young women of your generation are experiencing. Write it down. Don't worry, though. Everything will be all right."

The news didn't make me happy. My knees were trembling as I entered the house. *Oh, no . . . . God. Why me? . . . Oh, no.* My whole body shook as the full realization of my future took hold. *"It can't be that bad. No, it can't be that bad,"* I tried to console myself. I shifted into a daze. In that daze I had a dream, a dream with my eyes open. I was lying on the floor next to the dining table. The globe of the world was my head. I lay there on the floor trying to get up, but the globe was too heavy. I couldn't lift my head! Mama . . . Maama . . . " I cried in agony. Then I snapped out of it. Shaking my head to rid it of any ridiculousness, I decided to get back to my book and get my mind off of things. I just wanted to finish it so that I could rest. I began writing about the final days with Ron. "I just want to be with him." I wrote. "I love Him" . . . *oops! That's not supposed to be capitalized.* I erased the capitol "H". "I need Him", I wrote. *Darn, I did it again.* Again I erased the "H" replacing it with an "h". *Who do I think he is anyway, God or something?* I asked myself in disgust. The words came to my mind . . . *God is love . . . God is love.* I stopped. *I know I heard that before, somewhere. Yes, I remember. It was in the movie Elmer Gantry. It was written on a big banner . . . "God is Love".* I just sat there for awhile, thinking. *I love Ron so much because he's so good, no, our relationship was good . . . quite pure and beautiful. That's why! I love the beauty . . . the likeness to God that's in him,* I smiled. My thoughts continued . . . *Gee! The first part that I wrote was about Bob. The happenings were like steps, one after another. It was a story of Bob taking and taking, step by step. But, the part about Ron just flowed together,* my brain seemed to be explaining my life to me. *Bob was like the devil, like communism, which takes country after country step by step. Materialism is taking over the world!* My brain was spinning. I thought back to how my sweet old friend, Robbie, an old man who had adopted me as his honorary grandchild when I was just a little girl. He had sat down with me one day back in the 1940's and shown me on his "globe of the world" how communism was going to take country after country. He had even known how far they were going to go. Those things didn't even happen until after the old man had died. *Hmmm. I wonder how he had known that*, I smiled thinking about those sweet innocent days. Then the words came to me, "Cancer is from the rot within". Again my thoughts went to Robbie. *That sweet old man*, I wanted to weep thinking of how I had missed him all these years. He used to gather up the kids from the neighborhood and take us into the mountains once a year to pick boxes of a small plant he called "sorrel". He used to prepare the green stuff and bottle it. The slimy green spinach-like substance, he claimed, cured cancer. He had distributed it to the many people he knew who were suffering from cancer, as he made his rounds from home to home, reading meters for the city. He had been kicked out of many a doctor's office as he had tried to share his findings with the medical world. He didn't like doctors much. Years later I had read in a *Reader's Digest* article that they had found that there were certain green leaf plants which were found helpful for the remission of cancer. *I wonder if he really did have a cure, or if his faith in the "cure" had just given these people hope, like Jesus gave us Hope when he died for us on the cross. He died to cure us from a spiritual cancer . . . the rot from within ourselves and our society.* I resumed my thoughts of the present. *Our country is supposed to be built on Love. God. "One country under God, indivisible"* . . . the words of the Pledge of Allegiance came to my mind. *Oh, God,* I shivered. *I just want to be with Him,* I whispered weakly. My whole body reeked of hunger. Not just physical hunger, hunger for the "Bread". *The Bread, the Bread . . .* I moaned in my weakness as I hovered over the table. I glanced at the picture of Jesus that hung on the wall near the table. A brightness came right directly to me hovering over the table. I felt His overwhelming Presence! *Jesus,* I trembled. I was frightened, yet comforted. *I can't look at the picture. Am I going to be with Him? Am I going to die?* I asked myself. *I feel so hungry! Jesus, I need you,* I began to sob. *Oh, Jesus,* I pleaded. *Help me. Please help me. Don't ever leave me!* The words came to me, "God can destroy the devil if He really wants to." *I know too much!* I lay my body on the table, from the waist up, prostrate over the table. I began murmuring sounds I knew nothing about. I began to see suffering faces in green and blue hues. They were Asiatic faces, women and children. *Oh, world, please love Jesus, I pleaded. He's so beautiful!*

We that are in this tabernacle
DO GROAN
Being Burdened.

2 Cor 5:4 (KJ)

Fortunately, during this time, the kids had pretty much taken care of themselves and gone up to bed. I had been completely unaware of the hours that had fled by. I checked on them thanking God that they were safely tucked in their beds. I was also feeling purely exhausted. I finally managed to get to sleep, or was I still awake? Suddenly the room was lit up! There was a light beaming down the center of the room towards my bed, like a heavenly slide or a ladder or something. There were little laughing spirits waving at me. They seemed to be riding on the beams of light. "Come on, come on," they goaded me. "It's beautiful up here. Come on, come on." I was frightened. I was afraid that I was going to die right then and there.

Oh, no!" I wiped my eyes trying to clear the scene that was before me. *I can't go now . . . my children. My children need me!*

"You won't have to do any more housework," they giggled.

I can't, I can't! I sat up in bed, my heart pounding so hard in my chest that I could feel it pulsating in my head. Then a soft voice calmed me down as I lay back in almost a trance.

"Shhh. Go to sleep. Go to sleep, now" . . . the soft melodic voice sang its lullaby. "Go to sleep, it'll be OK." A softness, a wisp of wind stroked my cheek. I went to sleep.

Morning came with the sun streaming into the bedroom. I turned on the radio next to my bed to see if I could hear what time it was. There was an excited voice on the news. "The bombs are falling!" the voice raised to a high, excited pitch. I became frantic! *The bombs are falling. Oh, no! They're being so stupid. God is Love, you dumbbells!* I threw my clothes on fast. *What am I going to do? What can I do?* My feet carried me swiftly down the stairs. *Ron has to come back! If he comes back then everyone will see how beautiful love can be!* I paced around the house wringing my hands. *How am I going to get him to come back? I've got to do something!* I grabbed my manuscript. On a piece of paper I scribbled a message to Ron. "I was half-way to Heaven last night," I wrote. "God is Love. God knows all things. Love knows all things. Heaven is where there are no apples, no temptation!" I then added a P.S. "Share this only with those whom you trust. They won't believe you anyway." I then placed the paper behind the last page in the book. On the title page I wrote, "This is my bomb." Swiftly, I gathered the kids together. I didn't have any stamps. I marched up to the post office with my little kids trailing behind, to mail it.

Later on, I chuckled to myself at the irony if it all. In my last letter to Ron I had told him, "Be careful if you should get a package, it'll probably be a bomb." I was thinking of sending him my picture that still sat there on the TV. That picture had already caused me enough problems. I took it down. It took a few days for me to begin functioning more normally. The more I entered the world's reality, I dismissed it as having cracked up. I tried to make a little sense of the whole incident. *I know that God is love, though. I wonder what Father would say? Maybe I'd better go talk to him. Yes, I'll call him today. Sounds like a good idea.*

The rectory had become a work of art. I walked around the room admiring it, waiting for Father to descend the stairs. It was decorated in wooden hues. "You're really fixing things up here," I complimented him as he entered the room.

"Yes, it's taking shape." He pointed out the antiques he had refinished. The plush wall-to-wall burnt orange carpet enhanced the deep dark wood of the desk behind which he sat. "It takes a lot of imagination and most of all love."

"I know Father," I nodded in elation.

"You do." He stated the words flatly, his arms folded in an arrogant and proud posture. His eyes searched into my being.

"God is love, Father," my voice had an air of mystery in it.

"I've never heard that before," Father blurted out his words, rather stunned.

"You haven't?" I questioned him.

"Well, I've heard of the Holy Spirit being called love before," he squirmed.

"Isn't the Holy Spirit, God?" I asked.

"Well, yes, but I've never heard it said like that. Say! Isn't that a beautiful view there over the water?" He pointed through a picture window that allowed us to take in the view of the waters of the sound. "The peace and the calmness and the beauty of God's creation. To me, that's God."

"Yes. Isn't that l-ove-ly?" I emphasized the "love" part. "Isn't it God-like though?"

Father looked confused. "I just remembered I have an appointment with the carpenter over at the school." Quickly, he gathered himself and started out the door. I picked up my purse and started out after him being careful to close the door behind me. As I was walking down the steps I watched him as he took off down the street. *By golly, I think he's scared of me,* I chuckled.

The following Saturday my mom called to invite the kids and I to go to church with her. "By the way," she added, "did you call out for me the other day? I heard someone call 'Mama, Mama . . . '."

"That was me," I smiled, though somewhat shocked. *She heard me . . . she heard me . . .* my heart sang, for it was telling me that there truly was something going on.

The kids and I went to church with my mother every so often. Mom played the organ at a different Catholic church than the one in our own parish. I had been a little uncomfortable each time I went to church for it seemed as though each time I had had a thought about my needs concerning the church, I would find that they were making that very change. For example, the time I had told Ron that he would be a good priest because he would speak in the people's tongue. It felt so eerie to me that very shortly after that the church changed their liturgy to English. Each time I went there, there were more and more changes. The Catholic Church was making new changes, and good ones, at least in my estimation. I could see that they were trying to reach the people and include them into the service more.

This particular Sunday, about a week after I had that talk with Father about love, I was handed a bulletin when I entered the church. On the back of the bulletin was the message for the week. There in front of me were the cherished words . . . "God is love." There was a whole excerpt on love taken from the First Epistle of St. John, Chapter 4 verse 8. I was dumbfounded. *I thought that the all the churches in the Catholic Church were supposed to believe in the same thing . . . Universal! That is what we were taught in school. Why, Father doesn't even know this, and he went to the seminary for how long? What in the world do they teach them there all that time? Latin? Yeah, that's probably right. They spend all their time learning Latin. They don't even learn the Bible!* Anger stirred up in me. *Why they've made Christ's beautiful church into a god instead of bringing God into the church. I think that priests should be getting married, too. It's a wonderful haven for homos to hide their problem and gain the respect that they yearn for.*

This new found strength I was finding, standing up for my beliefs inside of myself, began to bring me comfort, even though deep in my being I was weeping for Jesus' beautiful church. *He must be real upset seeing it all crumble into a mockery . . .*

Now that I had realized these things, I was now a freer person. I found that I was able to actually enjoy my home and able to play with my children. I had been feeling guilty about having been so far away from them in mind even though I was present in body. I had joined them around the TV this particular evening when the telephone rang. I popped up to answer it. "Hi," I sung into the phone.

"A call for Mrs. French," the operator announced.

"There's no Mrs. French here," I informed her.

"Sir? . . . no, sir . . . we cannot give a message . . . yes, sir. I'm sorry, no." The operator was talking to an unknown person on the other end. I tried to hear what was being said. "Thank you, ma'am," the operator was gone. *That was funny.* I mulled over the incident in my mind. *Mrs. French. Whoever it was still wanted to give me a message. Long distance.* Then it hit me. *It was Ron!* My heart raced. *He knows I'm French. It was Ron, I know it was Ron!* The more I thought about it the more positive I was. *That last letter I wrote him and sent with my book said, "Love knows all things!" I'll bet he maybe thinks I'm nuts. Or maybe he's worried if I'm OK. I'll bet he was worried, but he didn't want me to know it was him, or maybe he wanted to see if I would know it was him. I know, I'll call him back and play a trick on him. See if he can figure it out.* I called his home. His sister answered. "Is Ron there?" I asked.

"No, you just missed him. He went into town. Can I ask who's calling?"

"Just tell him Lili-waup called."

"Who? Lilli what?"

"Lilli-waup." I hung up fast. I chuckled to myself, *I feel mischievous, like Carol. It's so silly . . . Lili-waup!* My thoughts went back to that glorious day when Ron and I had driven to the mountain and had crossed over the Liliwaup River. *Now we'll see who knows what?*

However, in a few weeks the strange things were comfortably pushed aside once more. It was easiest for me to tell myself that I had just "lost it" from the strain I'd been under. Then one morning, and a very cheerful, bright morning it was, I had just finished cleaning up the kitchen. The radio was playing soft music. As I took a few last swipes to polish the stove, a newsbreak on the radio came to my attention. *This is the roving reporter up here on the mountain pass at the site of an accident! I'll ask this gentleman standing here what happened."*

"It was awful!" the man moaned, breathing heavy from the excitement. "I was driving along about 30 miles an hour over the pass when that damn fool pulled his car and trailer around me and lost control. His trailer jackknifed, and the driver . . . . and the whole works, went right off the cliff! He's down there so far that no one will ever find him."

"Those words were the words of an eyewitness here at the scene of a horrible, horrible accident," the news commentator babbled on. "Here, now, is someone who wants to say a word or two".

"You'll never guess who this is," the voice started. "I was driving along for miles and miles. I was stuck behind this car which was poking along. I was getting nervouser and nervouser. You know how it is after you've been driving for days, you get a little anxious to get where you're going. I kept behind this guy for at least twenty miles, curve after curve after curve. Finally, I got mad, real mad! You know what happens when I get mad!" the voice reminded me. "Well, I went over the side and here I am. I guess I'll be here until someone . . . one of my friends, or something, comes to find me." My shaking body found a chair to plop into. *Ron.* I gasped. *It was Ron!* I repeated over and over to myself. *Ron is dead! Wait a minute.* I tried to gather my senses. *That was really a strange broadcast. How could he be talking on the radio if he was dead? He must be dead. They said he went to the bottom.* I tried to figure out the problem. That was really strange, I mulled over the whole incident . . . *really strange! I wonder if he is dead?* I then made a decision. I chose to believe that he was. It was easier that way.

Everyone that Loves
Has been born of God
And Knows God.

1 John 4:7 (NIV)

PART 3

The Chastening

"Endure hardship as discipline . . . . "

Hebrews 12:7 (NIV)

Chapter 11

Money, Drinking And Sex

In order to heal my wounds from Ron's "suicide note", I found myself in a small cabaret that Carol had introduced me to a couple of times while Ron and I were dueling. It was in a little area close to the very park where Ron had taken me after our special trip to the mountain. The cabaret was a little drab, but the music was peppy. I was sitting alone quietly sipping on a beer watching the husband and wife drummer and organist team. They were playing their nightly assortment of oldies but goodies with a little rock thrown in. Even though the environment was different I still brought with me my same old ever-so-deep thoughts. *How did this all happen?* I was trying so hard to take the recent happenings of my life in stride. I was too numb to cry. It was all so unbelievable. The kids were with Bob. There wasn't much I could do about the visitation. *Now that he and Anne were married it's as if I am the naughty little "alki" and he's Mr. Prince or something.*

I was trying to bring my thoughts out of the past and into the now taking notice of several booths which bordered the large bar where a couple of fellows sat drinking their schooners. As I nursed my drink, minding my own business, I heard a loud voice screaming, "Money can buy happiness!" It got my attention immediately as I looked up to see this fellow throwing his money on the counter. "Buy the house!" he hollered. I remembered how cute I thought he was in an obnoxious sort of way. His eyes were different. They were dark brown and slightly bulging under very long black eyelashes. They sparkled with a zesty brightness. Aware that he got my attention, he nudged himself into a booth across from me moving the guy that was already sitting there further toward the wall. "Hey, Joe. Do you mind?"

"Sit down," Joe answered.

"Oh well, money can buy happiness," the loud guy laughed as he repeated his slogan for my ears.

I wrinkled up my nose at him as I started to match his remarks. "You think so, huh?"

"Yeah," he said. "Who are you, anyhow? I've never seen you in here before."

"I've been here a few times," I took a puff on my cigarette. "Who are you?"

"George." he snarled. "Hey, why don't you come over and sit with us?"

"Nah, I'll stay here." I stuck my nose in the air proclaiming independence. At that moment I knew I had met my match. He got real snotty. Popping out of his seat he grabbed a girl by the arm who was sitting in a booth up a ways. "Hey, Judy. Come on over and keep us company." He sat her down next to Joe and ordered another pitcher. "Now do you want to come over?" he looked over at me.

"Well, since you put it that way, OK." I grabbed my stuff and slid in the booth next to him. That was when the fun started! It was a battle of two stubborn, very stubborn, awfully stubborn people. In fact, I was in such rare form that I shocked even myself. The result was that he ended up with Judy and I ended up with Joe.

"I have three hobbies," George shook his finger at me. "Money, drinking and sex."

"Everyone to their own thing," I retorted.

"That's right!" Getting up from the table he announced to his friends, "I'll take you guys home."

We didn't go home, though. It was a unanimous decision to spend the rest of the evening doing a little bar hopping and serious beer guzzling. I won the duel when I put the pitcher of beer to my lips, tipping it as it freely flowed into my mouth. Amazingly, it didn't even phase me. The young evening turned in to the last song of the evening. It so happened that we ended up very near my house, and it was empty being as how the kids were with Bob! For once Bob had done me a favor. I invited the foursome to come over to finish the night off. It was a sneaky way for me to let him know where I lived. We were both into a situation with partners whom we didn't necessarily desire to be with. Actually, I already surmised that I would feel a pang of loss if we parted and he didn't know where I lived.

Once in my own little part of the world the four of us relaxed as we got acquainted over a half case of beer. "What did you say your name was again?" George wriggled up his nose in inquiry.

"Pat. Pat Surina."

"You're lying!" he promptly accused.

"I'm lying? I ought to know what my name is", I answered haughtily.

"I grew up with Pat Surina, and you're not her!"

"Oh." I surprised him with a little knowledge. "I'll bet you knew the Pat Surina that's a nurse. I used to get her phone calls by mistake."

"Yeah! She's a nurse all right." He calmed down. "It's a small world." He shook his head as if to say, "this is not real". He then decided to become practical. "How about fixing us some breakfast?"

"I'd love to. How about pancakes?"

"Pancakes? I want some eggs and bacon. The works!"

"Then you'll have to buy. I don't have any bacon and not enough eggs for everybody."

"We'll go to the store," he grabbed Judy by the arm. "Come on, Judy. I'll take you home." He had left Joe and me sitting there waiting.

Joe was mighty quiet. He was no dumbbell. He knew that something was going on and he was along for the ride. After waiting about an hour as we polished off the rest of the beer, Joe and I surmised that we had been stood up. Joe left. I went to bed.

About this time Carol came waltzing up to my front door and back into my life. "Are you managing OK, now?" she asked.

"Yeah, I'm doing OK. Mom and Dad are helping me out. I didn't want to tell her about my financial situation. I was trying to keep an arm's length away from her. One day I had gotten the nerve to visit my dad on his lunch hour. He spent it at home often very quietly so that he could read the paper and relax. I had gone to him with a heavy heart having accumulated one hundred and fifty dollars worth of bills that I couldn't pay. He had arranged for the money and told me that I didn't have to pay rent until I got on my feet. Mom and Daddy had bought the house after Bob and I were unable to take up our option on it. It had been a great investment for them and at the same time had helped us out.

"Pat, I'm having a little trouble," Carol blurted out the words. It was not easy for her. She had no place to stay. "My mom said she'd help me out a little financially if I could just find a place to stay." It seemed ironic to me that we had both hit the skids at the same time and had to go to our folks to bail us out. I wasn't too sure how involved I wanted to be with Carol. How could I say no? Anyway, I knew it would be fun having her around. I figured that maybe she could help me keep my mind off of the past.

It didn't take too long to exchange notes on what had been happening in our lives. Carol had lost her baby-sitting job. She never did say why. I hadn't told her about the strange dreams I'd been having, and especially not about meeting George. We were both keeping facts to ourselves. Facts that, perhaps, no one could understand. Facts that even we couldn't share.

Carol had no more than settled in when the doorbell rang. Guess who? It was George. "Hi," he grinned.

"Come on in," I invited him to sit down. "This is George," I explained to Carol, which explained to her absolutely nothing. There was an awkward silence, then . . . "I had the craziest dream the other night," he slowly confided. *Not him, too.* I pretended not to connect with what he was saying. "Yeah, my car was sitting right out in front of your house." He pointed out the window. "Right out there."

"Really?" I peeked at the empty curb in front of the house.

"Yeah. Besides that, the motor was running and the lights were on, but there was no one sitting in it. I don't know what the heck my car would be doing sitting out there like that, but it was."

I decided to start a "can you top this" scenario. "You think that's bad . . . " I retorted. "I wrote a book and mailed it off to my boyfriend. I ended it with a bunch of far-out stuff. I'm so embarrassed!" I waved my arms in the air. Just talking about it made me frantic. "It's probably for the best, though. Now he most likely thinks I'm nuts."

"You too, huh?"

Carol made herself scarce leaving the two of us alone realizing that we had some strangeness in common. We managed to maneuver ourselves over to the couch. Leaning my way he kissed me: a deep, comfortable kiss. We embraced. The embrace turned to frantic clinging to each other for dear life. "I'm so frightened," I laid my head back on his arm staring into his nearly tearful eyes.

"I know what you're going through." He stared down into mine forcefully, meaningfully. "I really do."

After George left, Carol and I sat in the front room sharing some more about the last few months. "Where did you meet that George?" her curiosity got the best of her.

"Oh, I just went out one night when Bob and Anne had the kids and ran into him."

"Why did you let Bob get visitation?" Carol said.

"Oh, I don't know. Nothing much I could do about it." I couldn't begin to explain things, it was all too painful. Suddenly huge, gulping sobs came out of me. *Ron, Ron,* I cried out helplessly. I could feel him right there with me. The sobbings wouldn't stop. Carol felt so helpless as I wrenched there holding my stomach from the pain of gasping for air between attempts to choke back the tears. Carol just sat there allowing me the freedom of accomplishing whatever it was I needed to accomplish, to wash away whatever emotion I needed to wash away. After about fifteen minutes later I gained control of myself. The crying ceased.

Carol shook her head. "God, you must've loved that guy."

"Carol, it felt like he was in this very room".

"You know what you were just doing don't you?" she coached me. "You were saying good-bye to Ron and hello to that George fellow".

"Yeah. I know what you mean," I shook my head. We sat in silence for some time just breathing it all in.

A few nights later after Carol and I had consumed our usual six-pack I finally got a night's sleep. Morning time came. As I opened my eyes after being in deep slumber, I saw Ron's face up on the ceiling gazing down on me. "Who are you thinking about?" he snickered. It made me real mad. There he was sitting there laughing at me wherever he was at. I didn't even know if he was dead or alive". *Who are you thinking about?* I mimicked him to myself, repeating the words in disgust. It did the trick, though. I climbed out of bed and started in tackling the day's problems out of pure anger.

The sparks really started to fly one night when Carol and I decided to go out on the town. I knew I should've stayed away from Carol, but I didn't". It all started when we decided to go the cabaret. There we were prancing on down the street late at night in our mischievous mode. We were no longer employer and employee, but two friends out on the town. "We're going to whoop it up tonight," Carol hollered. She had decided that I needed to get out of the house. I had agreed wholeheartedly.

"You bet," I followed after. We were passing that same little hole-in-the-wall heading for a place further on down the street. "Hey look!" I stopped as I stared through the window. "There's George!"

"You're kidding," Carol peeked over her shoulder.

"See? . . . oh, oh! He sees us!" I stammered.

"Let's go in," Carol said. I shyly followed in behind her.

George invited us to sit down. We were all in the same mood: full of fun, full of laughter. We bombarded the dance floor attempting the Charlston, the swing, the twist . . . you name it. As we finally returned to the booth George said, "Come on down the block, here." He pointed in the direction where we were headed to begin with. "They have some real music down there. The James Boys are in town!"

He was right. The James Boys were special! They were so handsome in their red blazer jackets. One was Frank, an Italian-type of fellow: medium height and build, with dark wavy hair. He crooned his songs like Frank Sinatra, and played the guitar. His side–kick, Steve, was a tall lanky blonde guy who sang harmony most of the time, playing a tune on his harmonica every so often between songs. He was even more handsome with his long blonde hair slicked back, sort of a blonde Elvis Presley. The third fellow, Billy, the piano player, was a comical little fellow, sort of the comedian of the group. The enjoyable evening was ending too fast. "Why don't you guys come over to my apartment?" George offered as the evening came to a close. "I'll make you some breakfast."

Entering the apartment George introduced his roommate. "This here is Bob," he gestured to a guy sitting there watching TV. "I brought some friends over for breakfast," he explained.

"Great!" Bob joined in. "I'll get you guys a beer," he made for the kitchenette. It was a nice apartment throughout. A big black leather chair faced the TV with a comfortable davenport across from it. The place was neat as a pin, and there was a swimming pool out front! We all chatted away while George was fixing the breakfast in between it all. He interrupted his chores just long enough to have a quick friendly dance with me, caressing me with great affection. Carol was getting giddy.

"I'm going for a swim!" She started out the front door.

"I dare you," Bob egged her on.

"Double dare me," she flirted.

"I double dare you," he retorted.

"All right." She walked out to the ladder, which provided an entry into the pool, and with all her clothes on she walked into the water.

"I don't believe she did that." Bob threw his hands up helplessly.

"Oh, no!" George held his head. "I never thought she'd do it!" he wailed as he peeked out the window. "What'll my landlady say? There's rules to the pool! Get her in here."

"Ho, haw, hee-hee" Carol came bouncing in the door.

"Bob, put something around her to dry her out before we get into trouble," George hurried them into the bedroom.

"What'll I put on her?" Bob bellowed.

"Anything you can find," George hollered as he went back to his cooking. A few minutes and Carol came marching into the room, a bedspread wrapped around her. She was laughing crazily.

"How did I get mixed up with you girls?" George tittered.

"I don't know." I plopped myself down on Bob's lap trying to go along with the silliness. It was much easier than getting serious about anything.

"Give me a kiss," Bob puckered. I gave him a little smack in jest. At that, George threw down the pancake turner and grabbed Carol. He backed her to the wall and kissed her, and he kissed her, and some more.

I was jealous. "Things are getting disgusting." I grabbed my coat. "Do you want to stay here or are you coming with me?" My stammering was aimed at Carol.

"I'll come with you," Carol gathered her stuff, getting dressed in the half way dried clothes, and followed me out to the car.

"Hey!" George ran out to the side of the car, "do you want to go and get a cup of coffee? Do you want a cup of coffee?" He danced there in the middle of the street in a frenzy.

"Get in the car. I'll get you a cup of coffee," I ordered. It seemed that the drive to my house took only seconds. As I parked the car I slammed out the car door, flew through my front door and into the kitchen grabbing the coffeepot. I poured water in it. I threw coffee grounds in it slamming on the lid and plugged it in. "There's your damn cup of coffee," I swore. "I'm going to bed." Up the stairs I went.

When I awoke next morning I knew that it was too beautiful a morning for me to be so angry. I greeted the new day with the previous evening's nightmare on my mind. *OK, George,* I threatened him under my breath, *you got me this upset, well, now you can just unupset me.* Carol and the kids weren't even up yet. I climbed aboard Clarabelle in a nervous fit. *Let's see. I think this was the way to his place.* I felt more confident after I began to recognize familiar places. *Oh, yes. Now I know where I'm at,* I smiled nervously. *I wonder if he's mad at me. I hope not,* I bit a big chunk out of my fingernail. *I don't care. I'm going over there, anyhow, and straighten it out.* I had made up my mind for the last time. Clarabelle began to slow down. There was something wrong. *Come on, baby,* I talked to the naughty old car, *we're almost there. Just a block or two more.* A terrible racket sounded: a loud scraping from behind. *Oh, no! I cried . . . the car's falling apart! Come on, Clarabelle, come on, girl,* I pleaded. *You always get me where I have to go. Come on, come on,* I cooed. The car barely moved down the street. Then it stopped. *Bam! Clunk! We made it,* I cheered, although my whole body was shaking. *Here we are right in front of his place. We made it.* I talked to the old buggy like it was human.

As I had walked up to the front door George was just opening his drapes to let in the bright sunshine of a new day. Our eyes met. His eyes were sparkly warm and friendly sparkles. *He's happy to see me,* I waved, silently giggling. "My car broke down," I rushed through the door grabbing a seat. "I'm shaking from head to foot!"

"Where is it?" he surmised it was just an excuse, a big joke.

"Right in front, here," I pointed out to the street.

"I'll go look at it," he laughed. "I'm sure there's not too much wrong. You knew I'd fix it. You don't need an excuse to come over." He grabbed the keys and walked out to the car. *I know he thinks this is a phony setup. Well, maybe it isn't as bad as I thought,* I hoped. Long minutes later George walked into the room. "Dump it," he grumbled as he threw the keys across the room. "That crate won't budge an inch. Bob and I even tried to push it. The damn thing won't even move." He dropped down in a chair. His face was pale as he slumped into deep thought, looking very strange. There was an eeriness about the moment. His nasty self took over. "Bob will take you home," he demanded.

"I don't want to go home with him," I whined.

"Go!" he shouted.

"OK", I agreed disheartened. *He is mad at me. Maybe he thinks I'm just a cheap floozie or something.* I thought over the situation as I followed Bob out the door. "I think I'll stop drinking," I stated looking back at George.

"Don't stop drinking now," he warned as we left him behind sulking.

Somehow I made it through the rest of that day. Carol left as soon as I was left off by bad news Bob. As night came into being, I was bothered by the fact that Carol hadn't come home. The turbulent night of tossing and turning turned into a bright sunshiny Mother's Day. I had taken care of first things first. "I just called up to wish you a happy Mother's Day, mom," I greeted my mother. "My car broke down yesterday so I won't be able to make it over to see you."

"That's just as well," she replied. "Your father is taking me out to dinner today, so we probably won't be here, anyway. What's wrong with your car?"

"I don't know. It just fell apart. I think."

"I'll have your dad look into it and help you out."

"Mom, I don't think it'll be worth it this time."

"We'll see," she assured me. "You have to have a car. We'll look into it, anyway."

"Thanks, Mom. Have a nice day." I said goodbye and hung up the phone. I had actually wanted to cry. I was so depressed.

I sat out on the front porch trying to allow the sun to warm the cold feelings of despair that I was feeling. *The kids don't know it's Mother's Day, nobody bothered to tell them,* I thought. *God, I'm so lonely,* I held my head in my hands, my elbows resting on my knees gazing into nothingness. The phone rang. It was Carol.

"Pat? I'm over at George's place. He wants to know if you and the kids want to come over for dinner."

"Really?" my face lit up. "I'd love to."

"Bob will pick you up."

"Great! Thanks," I said even though I had suspicions of some underlying problems lurking in the awkward situation. *I wonder what she's doing over there?"* My mind busied itself as I rounded up the kids. "Come on, kids . . . we're invited to dinner*!" Well, I guess I'll know pretty soon.* I tried to prepare myself for whatever was on the agenda.

My suspicions had begun taking shape when Carol pulled me aside as soon as the kids and I arrived, with Bob trailing behind. "I figured this was the way it would end up," she whispered.

"What do you mean?" I dared to ask.

"I stayed here last night and this morning. He asked me to call you."

"You spent the night here?" I was stunned all the time knowing that I already knew it.

"Yep.*" This was her way of getting even with my encounter with Jim.* I knew it in my heart. Carol had told me that she had forgiven me for that kiss that had rocked the boat of their love voyage, but this predicament had gone much farther, I suspected.

The dinner was served like clockwork. George fixed most of it by himself, every now and then ordering Carol to do some task to help. He seemed to be somewhat perturbed with her. However, the awkward situation of George being with Carol, and my being with Bob, made for a rather quiet dinner. The happiness of the kids being treated as honored guests was the highlight of the whole ordeal. They were all excited. "Look at the swimming pool!" their eyes had bugged out when they had walked into the apartment.

"You guys can come to swim whenever your mother wants. Of course, she'll have to wear a bathing cap. Pool rules, you know," he grinned a bratty grin. "Now, the girls can do the dishes," he ordered.

I dug into the dishes. There was very little drain-board space so I decided to put the large pots and pans in the oven and save them till last.

"Oh, no you don't!" George hollered from the front room.

"I'm saving them till last," I explained.

"Don't make up stories. I know you're hiding them."

I was furious as I finished up. Carol sat in the front room with the guys trying to regain some kind of closeness. After the dinette was cleaned up George bellowed, "Bob will run you home."

"What's the matter with you driving us?" I threw the dishrag at the sink.

"Come on, now. Don't be like that," he retorted.

"I'll be the way I feel."

"Come on. I'll run you guys home then," George smirked a smile of satisfaction.

Nothing was said all the way home. As Carol and the kids high-tailed it into the house, I was reluctant to get out of the car until I had finished what I had to say. "I hope you're proud of yourself," I stammered.

"What do you mean by that remark?" he responded in a snotty tone of voice.

"You know damn well. You invited us over there just so you could flaunt your little affair with Carol in front of me."

"Well, if that's what you think."

"That is what I think," I sputtered as I stammered into the house.

Carol and I never again mentioned what had happened that weekend. I just tried to rack it up to the fact that Carol had gotten even with me for Jim. Deep down, though, I felt that Carol had gone too far.

It seems the only way I could start tackling my housework and the kids was just to get so angry. The anger must have shot adrenaline into my veins, or something. I was just beginning to get my house back in order, and going about my chores. However,

I began noticing a strange fact. *What in the world?* The plate around the doorknob was loose, held by one little screw. *I've got to tend to this house a little better,* I thought. *The house is falling apart!* I went about my business, cleaning up and putting away dishes. I opened the cupboard door. It swung out at me on only one hinge. *My gosh! Everything's falling apart around here,* I swore. As I went down into the cellar to put a batch of wash in the machine, the doorknob came out in my hand. *Something's going on here.* There were too many things falling apart all at the same time. "Boys!" I hollered out the back door. They'd been playing out in back a lot these days. There was an old garage out there with old wood floors, an old workbench and some chairs. They'd been busy making it into their clubhouse.

"Yeah, Mom? Wait a minute. We're busy!"

"Right now!" My voice rose in anger. They knew that sound. They came running. "Do you know anything about my door knobs and cupboard hinges falling off?"

Little Robbie looked me straight in the eye. "I did it. Mom, it was important! We're making a clubhouse in the old garage and I needed some nails. So, I took the screws. I just took one or two from each place."

"Rob, I know we're poor." I didn't know whether to laugh or cry. " . . . but mommy can still afford a little sack of nails once in awhile. We'll walk up to the hardware store and get you some nails and some screws so *you* can replace them. OK?"

He smiled a big grin. "That's great, mom. That's great!"

It seemed that every time I started enjoying the kids, Carol came to the front and frenzied things up a bit. I couldn't believe what she did for an encore!" It was in the middle of the night. All was still. We were all asleep, except for Carol. Through the stillness a loud knock on the door came thundering through the house. I was quickly aroused into a numb state until I got my bearings. *What in the world is that racket on the porch?* I flew around the room throwing my denim dress over my body as I ran to answer the door. Cars were arriving from all directions, screeching to a halt in front of the houses up and down the block on both sides.

"We're having a party!" Carol greeted me. "I invited the whole tavern over to cheer you up!" she giggled mischievously. "Come on everybody!" she called to the chattering party seekers.

"Carol!" I argued, "do you know what time it is?"

"Sure. Closing time. That's why we decided to come over here. We were all having such a good time. The band is coming, too! We're going to have great music!"

Secretly, that was the wild card in my deck. I was wild about the band. They were so cute and so talented and so unpretentious and single. "Be my guest," I gave in. I had to admit it sounded like fun.

"Come on, gang," Carol beckoned them into the house with her arm out-stretched, much like a general hailing his army to attack. More than a couple of fellows came in carrying cases of beer. "Put the boxes right here by the fireplace." They took over the art of organizing this entourage. A couple of gals and a guy came in with more beer. "Pile it up on top of these," the self-appointed master sergeant gave orders. As more charmers came bouncing through the door, more cases piled up.

"Where's the music?" a young fellow shouted.

"They'll be here pretty soon," Carol's enthusiasm cast away all doubt that they were coming. "They had to pack their instruments and stuff. They'll be here."

"Let's open a beer and get the show on the road," the great organizer climbed up on top of the beer boxes quickly popping caps as he distributed the beers reaching through his legs as he sat on top of the pile of boxes.

"Look at that bartender!" Some voice came from the crew who had pulled up the floor as they sat around the room guzzling away.

"He's got the right idea," another voice trumpeted.

The old grey mare, she ain't what she used to be . . . someone started singing. Everyone joined in. "Who the hell needs music?" the laughter broke through the song.

"Here they come, guys, here they come," Carol announced the arrival of the music makers.

The band was its best and loving every minute of it. One

could tell they just loved what they were doing whether they were paid or not. Then a couple here and a couple of guys there had the sense to go home, saying, 'It's getting late. Tomorrow's another day. Thanks for the fun. Bye now'. The music was dying down. Finally, only the musicians were left except for a bum who was passed out on the window seat. A couple of girls were hanging around. A couple finished the final minutes of the party shooting pennies against the wall in the dining room.

Frank, the guitar player was tired out. He stretched his legs laying back in the overstuffed chair. "We must be nuts! Play all night at the tavern and then come over here and play for nothing. It was a lot of fun, though," he laughed. "What the hell, if you enjoy it, so what?"

I praised them. "I felt a little honored, you guys playing here at my house. You guys are really good!"

"It's a good way to get acquainted with the crowd. We don't get too much of a chance to mingle with the people stuck up there on the bandstand.

"Everyone sure enjoyed it," I continued my amorous compliments.

"Hey, Frankie," one of the girls called to him.

"Yeah?" Frank answered.

"Come here, Frankie," she teased.

"Don't pay no mind to her," he laughed. "You come here," he patted his hands on his lap motioning her to sit there.

She curled up on his lap, arms clasped, dangling around his neck. "Are you going to take me home with you?"

"If you're a good girl, maybe," he stated. "Why don't you quit chasing after me?"

"You're cute," she pinched his cheek.

"Baby, you turn me on," he slapped her on the butt.

"Hey, Frank," I interrupted. "Do you know a guy that hangs around down at the tavern? He's quite a fan of yours. Name is George."

"You mean that guy who has an apartment up there on the Avenue?"

"Yeah. That's the one."

"Don't mention that kook to me," he swore. "That guy is nuts."

"What do you mean?" I said. "I know he's stubborn as hell . . . "

"You know what nerve that guy had? He told me that I got some girl pregnant."

"Well?" I teased.

"Well, maybe I have. I don't know, but that's not all he said. You know what he said?" Frank stood up flailing his arms around nearly dropping his girlfriend on the floor. "He said I got her pregnant, and that she was living by herself but had to go live with her folks, or something like that, and I told her I wanted to marry her and then I ran out on her. Boy, it makes my blood boil every time I think of that guy."

"I wonder why he'd say that if it wasn't true?" I shivered.

"You know what I think? I think it's something that happened to him or is going to happen, or something."

"Oh!" I walked out of the room. The thought struck me . . . *I hope that isn't going to be me,* but then I pooh-poohed the whole thing as I walked away . . . *that's silly.*

Frank came running after me. "He started talking about grass. He said his apartment was all full of grass . . . miles and miles of grass that he was walking through . . . right there in his front room! He was scared! Scared stiff!" He waved his arms all in a frenzy. "He's nuts! He needs a head shrinker, that guy."

"Hey! What you guys talking so seriously in here for?" Steve, the harmonica player, came sauntering out of the kitchen.

"Oh, go play your harmonica," Frank laughed. "We're just talking about an old friend." He tried to explain quickly and off the subject, fast. "Some friend!" Frank mumbled in disgust as he walked into the front room.

"Boy, he's stirred up over something," Steve confided in me.

"It's nothing," I mumbled.

"You look like you've seen a ghost or something," he held my face between his hands.

"It's weird," I answered as if in a daze.

"What?"

I asked him if he'd ever heard about that grass story. My memory banks were turning to one of my strange dreams. *It was too much of a coincidence!* The memory of the grass I had seen with a guy walking through it began to haunt me. *It was George!* I was still shaking over the whole thing. *Hell, we were nuts before we even started seeing each other!*

Then Steve, the harmonica player, asked me if there was some place we could go and talk privately. I asked him "What for?'"

"I just want to talk to you," he explained.

"Well, there's the basement. I could take you on a little tour." I was being cutesy, cutesy.

"Yeah! Take me on the tour," he guided me down the steps.

After our eyes got adjusted to the dark we got so that we could see quite well from the light illuminating from the street. "This over here along this wall is where all the empty beer bottles are."

"There's a lot, isn't there?" he laughed. Quite frankly, I was surprised at how many there were, too. "Who's drinking all that, anyhow?" he prodded.

"Oh, me and Carol and whoever's around. I didn't realize it was that bad myself."

"Then this over here is the washing machine. That's where I wash clothes," I facetiously clued him in. "Then over here is the oil tank. That's to put oil in," I laughed at my own silliness.

"I'm glad you told me," he giggled. "What's that over there?" he pointed to the other end of the basement.

"That there's the furnace. You know, that machine that blows hot air?"

"Oh, yeah! That machine. But I mean over there."

"That's an old rotten couch."

"Let's go sit down and talk," he pulled me over to it by the hand. "Now, what's this about grass?"

"Not marijuana, if that's what you're thinking," I snapped.

"That's a relief. It looks like you've got enough of a problem with the booze."

"You're right! Have I got a problem! I think I'm going nuts, or something. I don't really drink as much as it looks, though. It's just been piling up there for a long time."

"You know, I meet all kinds of gals at the bar, but somehow you're different."

"I'm different, all right. I'm nuts. Period."

"Why do you say that?"

"One night I saw a lot of grass and this guy walking through it looking for something. It was in my bedroom that I saw it."

"It was a dream, right?"

"I don't know. My eyes were open and I was sitting up in bed. You ask your friend, Frankie, about the rest of it. It's sort of weird. It worries me."

"I will ask him. Sounds interesting. Is that when I interrupted?"

"Yeah."

"I'm glad I interrupted. I'm so sick of talking to them whores at the tavern. They never have anything to say, but they sure will do it. Any time. Any place."

"I hope I don't get like that," I started to weep.

"Hey! Don't start that. You're not like that, Pat. Sometimes I wish I had never started in this business."

"I guess everything has its good points and bad points," I shared my deepest thoughts. "I've been awful lonely. Ever since my boyfriend, an army guy, went back home. Then I wrote a stupid book and sent it to him. Now I'm too embarrassed to call him and so now I tell myself he's dead. Then, too, maybe he is. So many weird things have been happening. Ohhh!" I moaned. "It's just too much to explain."

"Boy! You've had quite a time of it, I guess." He pulled me over to him and kissed me . . . a sweet gentle kiss. "You make me feel like a teenager or something," he smiled. "It feels good." We were in each other's arms. The sweetness rolled over into passion and soon it was over. "Thank you," he kissed me on the nose. "Let's go back upstairs."

"OK," I followed behind him. *Gee, I hope I don't get pregnant,* I worried as I tagged along.

"Hey, guys!" Steve hollered as he entered the front room. "Time to roll on home. It's been terrific, but let's go!" Suddenly I felt so cheap*! I guess I was just another notch on his bedpost.* I felt dirty cheap.

Everyone packed up and left, all except for a drunk who had passed out on the window seat. "I'm going to bed." I announced. I was feeling mighty pissed-off at Carol. "The kids will wake-up soon. I don't see how they slept through the commotion as it is. You can sack out on the couch until that guy over there gets the heck out of here," I pointed to the passed out bum.

"I'm not staying down here with that geek laying there," Carol shivered. I'm coming with you."

"Oh, do what you have to do. All I know is I have to get some sleep," I made it up the stairs with Carol right behind. She was now sleeping on a cot in my bedroom. I had given little Betsy her bedroom when she had left. We just dozed off when the phone rang. I hurried down the steps in order to answer it, passing my two little boys who were already up helping themselves to a bowl of corn flakes.

"Is my husband over there?" a woman swore over the phone.

"No," I answered.

"I heard he was there at a party you had."

"He may have been," I informed her, "everyone's gone home." I knew that the guy downstairs wasn't him. "If he was here, he'll probably be home soon. Good-bye." I had just climbed back upstairs and returned to bed when there sounded an unusual clattering. Then there was a thump. A thud. It was coming from the boys' closet. Carol and I froze as we gazed at the doorway so frightened that we were unable to move. The sound of footsteps came shuffling down the hallway. All the while the odd clanging sound clattered over and over, sort of like teeth chattering very loudly. The door opened.

"It's OK. It's just me," a nice looking young man came staggering into the room. A coat hangar was hanging from his sleeve, another from his shoulder. They were clinking together as he walked. "I guess I fell asleep," he rubbed his face.

"I guess you passed out," I giggled. "I think your wife just called for you. Now, you'll have to sneak down the ladder off of the balcony because I don't want the kids to think you've been here all night. They're downstairs eating a bowl of cereal."

"Oh, no!" he held his head.

"Oh, yes!" Our mischievous ways took over as we escorted him, each of us had an arm forcing him down the hall to the balcony.

"Brother! I've never heard of such a thing," he oohed & ahhed holding onto the railing for dear life. "I think I'm going to throw up," he pulled his head back up from looking down. "Oh, gee-ee-s . . . here I go." Shakily balancing on the ladder he let himself down. The old ladder just happened to have been left there from when Bob had had the house painted.

"Bye now," we teased as he finally made it to the ground.

"That's enough partying for me." He laughed as he snuck around to the front of the house.

"Serves him right," I swore under my breath. "Carol, don't you ever do that again. Never again will I have a party like that. You hear?"

After that night I felt so messed up that I would never get back on the right track. That purity thing was like a big mirage. It's almost there to grasp, then *whop* . . . something knocks the rug out from under you. Anyhow, if we weren't expected to know more than one person like it says in the wedding vows, then why do we promise to stay with just one person? I decided, *if I'm not married, what's the big deal?* I tried that purity thing. Where did it get me? Just a bunch of stupid dreams. After that it seemed as though common sense went out the window. It was like I didn't even know what I was doing. It was like I was in a big fog! Of course, as usual Carol was in on it . . . "

Carol came home one night all aglow. "I bought one of the James' Boys records! They're a big hit!" she screamed in delight. "Even the bus driver on this route stays there until he has to turn around and go back. It's the end of the run for him! He says we can take the bus there at ten and he'll take us back on the last run!"

That was great! We still had no wheels. Thanks to Mom and Daddy, my car was in the garage. The mechanic had told them that he could give them a good deal on the cost of labor if he could work on it in between his other jobs. The axle was frozen, or something.

"Maybe we can sneak out about 10 o'clock and come back about midnight! The kids never wake up anyhow." So we snuck out in late hours of the evening, to get in on the excitement. The place was packed! Half of the time there was standing room only. Fortunately, about the time we arrived was when the early crowd was leaving. This went on several times a week for about two weeks. Then one night there was a terrible thunder-storm! *Oh, my God! What if the kids wake up? I've got to get home! Oh, God . . . how could I be so stupid?* I made a promise to God that very night. *Please, please let everything be all right when I get home. I promise I won't leave them again at night!* The others weren't ready to leave, yet. I can't even remember how I got home. Some kind soul brought me there, I guess. All was well. The kids had slept through the thunder storm. *Thank God.*

Everything after that became a little hazy. I was suffering either from shock or just from stupidity. I don't know which. I remember Carol bringing a really nice guy home one night. His name was Andy. He was about 10 to 15 years older than we were. He was a friendly fellow with a slight southern twang, sort of a dignified hick. He was a cross between Howdy Doody and Alan Ladd. I hit it off with him right away as well as did Carol. We became a threesome.

The following days seem to be going faster and faster, as happenings began to evolve. Carol got mad at me for nosing in on her friendship with Andy. He was even willing to pay for my babysitter! It was a Godsend! I wasn't too concerned about Carol's feelings after what she had done to mess things up between George and I. One night as we were all killing a bottle (Andy was in to hard liquor), Carol got mad and left. That was when Andy told me he had five kids. There was some problem with a custody battle. He didn't want to talk about it much.

I was beginning to wonder what had happened to George after our little episode. The next weekend of Bob's visitation I was out of the house. I went to the cabaret tavern hoping to run into him. I thought it was funny that I had never run into him there after that first night when he had introduced Carol and I to the James' Boys. My brief encounter with them had given me knowledge of how mad Frank had been at George's strange stories about the grass in his front room and his accusations. It was these stories that had really made me do some strong thinking and wanting to get in touch with him. There was something going on there. I felt driven to find out what it was. He didn't know what I had been through. I realized, *we are just alike . . . divorced Catholics!*"

I had gone to the "James Boys" place and was sitting alone listening to the music. The bar was on the right of me, which ran the length of the room on down to the bandstand. The couples were dancing all around me as I sipped my beer quietly, just people watching. Every now and then I'd catch Steve looking at me. I smiled slowly, trying not to show interest. Through the mild flirtations came a commotion. "A schooner!" a loud voice demanded. I knew who it was immediately. *There he is!* My heart flip-flopped as I looked over my shoulder. I could see George staggering along the bar, banging his fists. "Come on, bartender . . . a schooner here!"

"Haven't you had enough?" the bartender attempted to give him some sense.

"Not yet. It's not my time to go yet," he grumbled.

"Either straighten up, or get out." the bartender warned him.

"I'm OK," he picked up his glass. "I'm OK," he weaved over to a booth beside me. "Haven't we been here before?" he asked.

"Guess so," I snapped back at him sarcastically.

"Oh. Well, pardon me!" He got up and made a bow. Walking over to another booth he grabbed another girl to dance with. He was all over the floor. The music stopped and back he was with his big mouth. "Money, drinking and sex," he reminded me. "That's my hobby . . . money, drinking and sex."

"Oh, George. Quit feeling so darn sorry for yourself," I scolded.

"Can I sit with you?" he asked.

"You got anything to say?" I quipped.

"Plenty."

"Oh, come on over then," I scooted over for him to sit down.

"This is where I belong," he smiled. "I'm not as drunk as I look. I'm just disgusted."

"You and me both."

"Let's go for a ride. Honest. I'm not that drunk."

I thought it over for a minute. "Sounds good." I picked up my coat and out the door we escaped.

The night was warm. The sky was a blue black and the moon was especially white this night. We rode along saying very little. Finally he came out with it. "I'm awfully stubborn, you know," he confessed.

"Me too." I admitted. His arm pulled me close to his side.

"Let's start over," he suggested.

"Yeah. Let's."

He maneuvered the car around and parked it in a pleasant clearing. We clung to one another through the kisses, and yes, the tears. "Let's lay out on the grass." He opened the door to lead me to a patch of soft green grass. The kisses led to more. We were going for it all. "Move . . . " he shouted to me.

"You move," I swore back at him.

"OK." His body made the proper gestures a couple of times in an almost facetious manner. I forced myself to make a few sexy gestures then suddenly . . .

"Now what?" I asked him.

"This isn't going to work," he snapped.

"What's the matter?"

"This isn't a very good place for this."

"What's wrong with it?"

"Oh, shut up and move," he retorted.

"You just get off of me and leave me alone." I pulled myself out from under him. "Take me home."

That did it. I decided that I'd had enough nonsense. I had to get my act together and find a job. I needed to get on my feet and find some future for the kids. It looked like I'd have to do it alone. The big bug-a-boo problem as always was finding a babysitter while I went to work. My friend, Andy, had told me about his niece, Missie, who had just moved in with him along with her new baby. I got the bright idea to offer her a royal deal . . . free room and free babysitting for her if she would baby-sit for me when I go job hunting, and one evening on the week end. Andy had warned me, "Missie has a wild streak . . . I don't know . . . ", he shook his head. But he gave in and brought Missie over so I could get acquainted with her.

All was well for a few days. Then the weekend rolled around. Somehow or other I was talked into babysitting for Missie. She doesn't come home Friday night, nor Saturday night. I was running out of formula and getting very angry about it. Happenings become a blur after Missie popped in late Sunday night with friends. Somehow or other Lonnie, my soldier friend, walked in with them. Carol was there also. I went upstairs to lay down for I was feeling very tired and very angry and I hadn't slept well all weekend worrying about the baby. A strange fellow came into my room. "Hmmm. Yes, I could hire you. I think you'd probably bring in a few tricks."

"Who are you?" I asked.

"Missie thinks that maybe you'd like to work for me."

"Get out of here," I screamed. "Get him out of here! Get her out of this house . . . " I was uncontrollable. I went downstairs waving my hands around in the air in a completely helpless state. "Get out of here. Carol, please, get them out of here." Missie was rummaging around for all of her stuff. I went back upstairs to lie down. I never made it into my bedroom. I rushed to the bathroom. Blood was all over the place, splattered on the walls, the floor . . . "Carol, Carol. I need help!" I screamed over the banister.

Carol rushed upstairs looking in the bathroom. "Oh, my God!"

she screamed. "Quick, quick, get an ambulance! Pat is hemorrhaging!"

The ambulance man happens to be an old classmate of mine from junior high school. He stayed with me until I was brought to the emergency room.

The doctor looked at the papers I had filled out. "Welfare! It figures." He quickly examined me. "It looks like you've had a miscarriage. You welfare sluts! All you do is screw so you can make more babies for everyone else to feed. Or do you have a guy that's living with you?"

I was shocked at the diagnosis. I remembered back to that time with Steve, the harmonica player. "I was with one guy a little over a month ago. I guess I haven't had a period since then. That was so stupid of me." I was sighing a sigh of relief, though, that I didn't have to carry it full term.

The doctor was apologetic. "I'm sorry. I guess you're not the run of the mill."

After I got home and tucked into bed, Lonnie came upstairs by my bedside. "Everything is OK down stairs . . . Carol and I are watching the kids. I just wanted you to know that I'm going overseas next week. I'll be joining my company." Through his big grin I could see that he was plenty scared.

"Take care of yourself, huh?" I smiled giving him a big hug.

Things calmed down in my life after that. I had cleaned the house of everyone! One day Andy came over to let me know how bad he felt over what had happened. "Missie's gone back home . . . down south." The two of us sat out on the back steps just soaking up the sunshine. Andy thoughtfully gave me a manicure. Our relationship was strictly platonic. Our visits brought us together as drinking buddies. From time to time he would come over with a bottle of Vodka to escape the realities of life. It was the first real taste I had of the stronger stuff. In fact, one night I became comatose after a rather long siege of drinking with Andy. I had to cool it with his friendship, too.

I decided to tell Steve about what had happened one night when I went to listen to the guys. I was sort of in a nostalgic mood. I guess I just wanted to know about what his reaction would be if he knew that I had been pregnant with his child. "Oh, Pat! You lost our baby?" he feigned concern. He was so phony! I finally was managing to dislike him.

About that time Carol brazenly approached me with a project which she had started without my permission or my knowledge. She was all excited over the fact that she had invited the James' Boys over for dinner at my house. "I'm starting a fan club for them!"

I was somewhat annoyed over this particular event for I felt it was very nervy of her and I wanted no part of these guys since I was just coming to my senses. However, I went through the motions knowing that it meant a lot to her. We fixed a turkey and all the trimmings. The guys were hours late. Carol and I and the kids gave up waiting and ate without them. Wouldn't you know? Just then they showed up. "I didn't figure you'd show up," I explained. "We already ate. Go ahead, though, there's plenty left."

Carol went into her sales pitch on what she intended to do as president of their fan club. "What do you have to do with all this?" Steve asked me as he swallowed a large mouth full of turkey dressing.

"I'm just along for the ride," I calmly set him straight.

It was the last time we saw the James' Boys. They left town.

For I am persuaded that neither DEATH
Nor LIFE
Nor ANGELS
Nor PRINCIPALITIES
Nor things present
Nor things to come
Nor HEIGHT
Nor DEPTH
Nor any other CREATURE
Shall be able to separate us from
LOVE OF GOD
which is in Christ Jesus our Lord.

Rom 8:39 (KJ)

Chapter 12

"I Think I Caught It From You"

I was busy trying to start a new life, only the old one kept getting in the way. The awesome responsibility of raising my children alone had taken away the joy that I should've been having with them. By this time I was thinking more and more about God, faith, what I believed in, and what I was going to teach my children. I began to get a bit far-out in my thoughts.

I was watching TV one afternoon as I folded clothes trying to be more attentive to responsibilities. The newscaster broke in. Students were rioting in the streets! The signs that they were carrying conveyed the message, God is dead. My heart began to beat harder and harder. I feared it might burst. *No, No! You're wrong! God isn't dead. You just don't know who He is! God is Love, you dummies.* I stomped around the room feeling so helpless. My mind raced to the memory of an ad in the newspaper, which I had read recently, announcing a contest. It asked for contestants to explain what love was. It made me all the more positive that I was right. *People just don't know who God is, anymore. They don't know what love is . . . and they don't know who God is!* My thoughts stormed inside of me making me feel even a little frantic. *The priest didn't even know. For God sakes! Someone has to make them understand! The messages in the churches aren't reaching anybody anymore.*

I calmed down a bit then with great thought and anxiety about what is right and what is wrong? What God expects of us has got to be possible. *I should be able to follow the rules without messing up all the time. How do I do that? I need to understand.*

That very day my little boy, Blake, came walking into the room. "Mommy," he asked. "what's the Holy Spirit?"

It seemed a little curious to me that he would ask that question right at that particular day when the world was asking nearly the same question. I didn't especially know the answer, either. "Well, the Holy Spirit is God," I explained.

"I thought Jesus was God," he retorted.

"He is. You see, there's the Blessed Trinity: the Father, the Son . . . , which is Jesus, and the Holy Spirit."

"What's a spirit?" the boy continued, wanting to know more.

"Well, a spirit is something you can't see."

"Why can't you see it?"

"You feel it." I grasped for words to answer these surprisingly intelligent questions. "You know how when you feel that something is so, like if you feel you are sick. It means you *believe* you are sick. The Holy Spirit is a *holy* feeling. It's a *holy* belief."

The answer seemed to satisfy him, but it didn't satisfy me. I wondered if I was right. I had learned in school that faith, hope and love were the three most important virtues, and love is the greatest. Now, I figured this way . . . if love is the greatest, then God the Father would be love, perfection in Love. In school Sister taught us that God is perfection, but she didn't say anything about love. Now, if God the Holy Spirit is a holy belief, that would be the same as faith, perfection in faith." I was actually impressing myself with these interesting thoughts flowing through my head. *My brain went one step further. If God the Father is love and the Holy Spirit is Faith then Jesus would be perfection in Hope.* I summed it up like a math problem. *That's right, isn't it?* I asked myself, or wherever these thoughts were coming from. *Jesus died to open the gates of Heaven. He gave us hope of salvation! It sure makes sense to me. If it isn't right, it's sure a better explanation than the shamrock bit that St. Patrick used to explain it with.*

However, my thoughts finally came back to the reality of the times. I must confess that I was still wondering about George. I wondered what he had been doing? One day I was browsing around in the drug store. Snooping around was the only kind of shopping I was able to do these days. There in all its glory I saw it flagging my attention. It was lifted up among all the rest of the cards as if to say, "Here I am". It was perfection in silliness sitting on the card rack. Immediately I knew what to do with it. I used it to make up with George. This card had struck a vein of great hope in my heart. It was perfect! The card was all red on the front with the words, *The color red is supposed to make you think of sex.* Inside it said, *When I saw this card it made me think of you.* Then I had to figure out what I was going to write in it. I tried to get my mischievous self-working. "I've been working on your first two hobbies," I wrote, cackling aloud, " . . . but I'll be darned if I'll go for the last one . . . as a hobby." I was pleased with my imaginative stunt. But then the stunt turned on me bombarding me with more deep thoughts. *Money, drinking and sex! Some hobbies!" That's what's wrong with this world, anyhow. Money, drinking and sex! Money instead of love, drinking instead of hope.* That's pretty profound, isn't it?" Again I was impressing myself with these very interesting thoughts. There was more of the same mathematical reasoning . . . *and, sex instead of faith. It's true. Kind of far out, but true. That's why they're saying, "God is dead".*

Then one morning something happened! I found myself sitting at my kitchen table, savoring my morning cup of coffee. Suddenly, without any warning I saw myself leave my body and rise above it for a long second. Then down I slammed into my body again. It was such a shock! Right then and there I learned a lesson. Suddenly, I knew that material things are only here as tools for us to use. They mean nothing! Our true selves are in spirit form. Our bodies are really no different than the table, or the chair. Right then and there, I really felt like the sunlight had come into my life*! I don't care if I am crazy. I know it's true.* I settled it in my heart.

For some reason I felt closer to my children after that lesson from the great unknown. Rob even shared a great secret with me. He had a secret club! He even decided to share with me their secret club's secrets! He was so cute explaining it all to me. "We've got guys from down the block and we have dues. It costs a nickel to get in, but you're not a real member until you drink a gulp of Listerine."

"Listerine?" I couldn't believe my ears. "Where did you get the Listerine?"

"Oh, we went and bought it at the drug store with the money we collected from our dues," he explained in great detail. We saw on the commercial something about that Listerine was better than soda pop, so we got us a bottle of it. Mom! It tastes awful! Now we use it for instigation."

"Instigation? What's that?"

"You know, when a guy has to do something to get into the club? In our club a guy has to take a gulp of Listerine."

"That's initiation".

"Yeah. I guess. Anyhow most of the kids took a swig of it. It's terrible!"

Those kids were at such a cute stage, I shook my head. For some reason I wanted to cry. *I can't even enjoy them like I should. Oh, God.*

That card I sent did get some results. One afternoon I heard a knock at my door. "Hi," came that cheerful, zesty voice that I had grown to love. It was none other than George, only different. He seemed so at peace.

"Hey, I just got your card. That was cute. It was real cute." he chuckled. When George chuckled it made you a little giddy, clear from your toes. "I just wanted to thank you."

"Come in and sit down," I showed him a chair as I tried to explain why I did it. "I thought you might like it. I couldn't resist that card," I giggled. He nodded. A silence erupted. I walked to the window and fidgeted with the curtains.

"What shape are your teeth in?" he blurted.

"Awful. Say! Isn't that something you ask when you're going to buy a horse?" I smarted at him.

"Yup."

"Are you calling me a horse or something?" I giggled.

"Smartie."

"Why did I say that? I nervously paced into the dining room. I nonchalantly glanced at the table. I had to take a double look. I couldn't believe what was sitting on the dining room table. I picked it up. It was a rag with black stains all over it. I smelled the black goo and dropped it quickly. It was shoe polish! I was stunned. I took a closer look at the rag. It was the bottom part of a leg of my little boy's pajamas. It had been a good pair of pajamas, too. In fact he had just worn them the night before. I couldn't figure it out. Who would be polishing shoes there? I called for the kids. They came a-running. "Did you kids cut the leg off of your pajamas to shine your shoes with?" I asked them.

"No. Honest I didn't," they both shook their heads. *Well, I know Betsy didn't do it,* I assured myself.

"This is weird!" I showed it to George. He sat there smiling smugly. "Don't you think that's weird?" I asked him again.

"Yes, it is, isn't it?" he smiled again looking very strange. Then the memory came to me. Ron! I remembered his words, " . . . it has something to do with your little boys' pajamas. It's so silly I can't tell you." I looked over to George again. There was a soft strange glow around him. He just sat there smiling, his eyes sparkling brightly. The moment was so familiar. It was Ron's presence! I could feel him there. It really shook me up. George just nodded quietly, then excused himself, "I guess it's time for me to go."

I decided to go to church to see if I could get some help. I was getting scared. My mother offered to take the kids and I to church. There were great changes going on in the Catholic Church. I was especially delighted when I had found out that they were changing from Latin to English. I remembered how I had told Ron, "you'd make a good priest because you would speak in the peoples' tongue." I guess it was a need of the times. It was as if it had just come out of my mouth, and *zap!* . . . it was done.

Then it happened! A very special happening. A priest, whom

I had never seen before, climbed up to the pulpit to give a sermon. He was introduced as a guest speaker from New York. The message started out very abruptly. *There was a girl and a guy who lived in a town. She had three kids and he didn't have any.* It was a strange sermon. I listened especially hard for it certainly hit home.

I noticed that the people sitting around me were also a little stunned. "This is different," they had nodded to each other.

She told him she was pregnant, the priest continued.

'How did you get pregnant?' her boyfriend asked her.

'From the Holy Spirit,' she told him.

That's a likely story,' he retorted.

The people in the congregation twittered quiet laughter. It was a little funny. "He's made a modern story of Mary and Joseph," a little lady whispered to her husband.

The sermon continued on . . . *The boy was hurt. He went away, but then thought it over. 'I know she's not that kind of girl,' he told himself. 'I just don't know what to do.' But the merciful Lord sent an angel to him and told him, 'Don't be afraid. She is telling you the truth.'* Then the sermon went on talking about the journey of many nationalities and how they've tried to escape persecution in their countries and find haven in new lands.

Chatterings after Mass told me that they seemed to like the uniqueness of the sermon, but it hit me hard. I felt fidgety. It was so much like what happened between Ron and myself except I told him I was filled with the Holy Spirit. As I walked out of church I couldn't help but remember how he had told me, "I always felt I would write a sermon some day. I don't know why, but I always felt it."

Then a very quiet voice, so quiet it was like a mere breathing, said something to the effect, " . . . and there was a fire truck there." I shook my head thinking of the words as cobwebs, or something, and continued down the street to the car. I wondered, *is it just a coincidence . . . or my imagination?"*

I had a new awareness of what a terrible mess this world was in. I caught an afternoon session of the United Nations on TV the next week. I watched in amazement at the childishness of those world leaders. *My gosh, they're like a bunch of little kids playing with blocks. They pile one request upon another until the whole thing comes tumbling down around them. It's so damn stupid! They're more impressed with themselves, than anything. Don't they know that they have families' lives in your hands?* I turned the darned thing off. I couldn't hack any more of the nonsense. I had fun after that just sitting back in daydream fashion imagining what it might be like if Carol were there helping them to get along. *First, she'd probably have them all bring a dish that represented their country, beer or wine with the meal, only . . . no, I think she'd probably not be that conservative. It would be party time! . . . but everybody would be getting along, anyhow! They'd all have a good laugh and be friends!*

Sometimes I think she was good for me, then sometimes I know I wouldn't have gotten into so much trouble. To be fair, though, I met George all by myself. I couldn't blame her for everything.

All this deep thinking was taking its toll on me. I couldn't sleep from thinking too much. My head wouldn't turn off. I took up drinking, again. It usually took a six-pack to get me to sleep. One particular night I was having fun with my new thoughts. It seemed refreshing having some new ones. I finally turned the radio on to my regular station for music, even got up and did a little dance. Over the sound of the music I heard a knock on the door. It was pretty late. 10 o'clock! I carefully peeked around the doorframe slowly opening it.

"Hi. You sleeping?" It was George. He brushed past me at the door and tiptoed into the front room.

"Nope."

"I brought you a beer. Want one?"

"No, I have one going in the kitchen."

"You rat!" he chuckled. "Come on. Sit down here," he pulled me to the floor beside him. "I've missed you," he leaned over to give me a little peck on the cheek.

"I've missed you, too."

"What do you think about getting married?" he said abruptly.

"I don't know. I'd have to think about it," I answered. My heart was pitter-pattering like crazy. I wanted to say yes . . . yes! I just didn't. I just sat there in a daze.

"Oh, yeah. I guess that's understandable", he said. The subject was closed. Silence overwhelmed the room. Our thoughts were far away. "You know, money can buy happiness, Pat." He tenderly draped his arm around me.

"I don't think so."

"It can, Pat. Just think about it," he gazed earnestly into my eyes.

"Well maybe. It depends on how you use it," I replied thoughtfully.

"That's true," he leaned over to kiss me. We marked our agreement in each other's arms. Life was finally opening up for us. "Let's take our clothes off," he suggested. It seemed a natural thing to do.

I hesitated, thinking it over. Then I undressed.

"Isn't that a lot better?" he grinned.

"You bet," I smiled shyly as we caressed each other's bodies. Finally we were together enjoying each other fully. I looked up at him barely being able to make out his face in the dark room. But then slowly, very slowly, my head raised as though someone was lifting me up to see the united beauty of our bodies swaying together. Our bodies shown a warm crimson light: a radiance. I knew it was the beauty of the unity between a man and woman in the presence of God's Love. I looked up to watch George as he straightened his body and leaned back. Somewhere next to his face there was a face, in faint pink hues mixed with crimson and purples. The colors were as in a sunset. It was a faint resemblance of Jesus.

"Oh, my God!" George shouted as he fell to the floor. "Oh, my God!" He held his hands over his face. He lay on the floor as in a trance. It was beautifully scary. We lay there quiet for a time, then . . . .

"Do you ever dream with your eyes open?" I broke the silence.

"Dream?" he sneered with sarcasm. "I have movies. Two and three hours long! Do you make a lot of sandwiches or bread or something?"

"Yes," I replied . . . especially when I was writing. Why do you ask?"

"Because I see you making sandwiches or bread or something."

"You do? You mean you have . . . . "

"Yeah, something like that. I do see you."

This was all very peculiar. A warning surfaced as I tried to gather my wits about me. "I think you'd better go home before the kids wake up." I dressed myself.

"That's the way it always is," he sighed as he dressed.

"You dropped your comb," I handed it to him as we walked to the door.

"Good night," he kissed me. "See you."

The happenings of that evening were so surprising that my subconscious took over not allowing me to even think about it. It must've been a form of shock. All I knew was that there was a strange trust between George and myself, a secret trust. Every nerve in my body was squirming. I attempted to keep busy by baking some bread, probably at his suggestion without realizing it. Since I had been on welfare I had received many bags of flour. I had never baked bread except in school so I took this time to try to learn. I made three loaves. I was so excited when the little loaves came out of the oven. Their toasty brown crusts along with the smell of a bakery caused my mouth to water. The kids were right there to watch the unveiling. They each took a delectable warm slice barely giving the margarine a chance to melt on it.

The next day I went to the store. While there I noticed two rather mannish heavy bluish-green colored glasses. I thought they were the most beautiful glasses I had ever seen. I figured I'd buy them and serve beer in them when George came over. He always liked to pour his beer in a glass. I thought it was time for me to be a little more lady-like.

I was beginning to feel awkwardly at peace. It seemed as though someone was leading me around the house helping me to do my housework. A silent voice guided me. "Take this and put it there, and then pick that up and put it in the kitchen" . . . until the house was all picked up. I didn't even wince when the kids began complaining of having sore throats and stuffed-up noses. I know I flipped out a little then because I was thinking how the bread I had baked was holy bread . . . made out of love. I just gave the kids pieces of bread and knew they would be OK. I called them in for my little ritual. "Robert," I called. " . . . Blake . . . , Betsy . . . " They each got their bit of mommy's yummy bread which had a prayer accompanying it which they knew nothing about."

That batch of bread was already almost gone. I decided to bake another batch and bring a loaf to George. He said he'd been seeing me feeding bread to the kids. *This will surprise him.* That bread wasn't as good as the first batch. I brought it to him anyhow. I knew that I had to see him again, and soon . . . for I hadn't been quite right ever since his last visit.

I had finally gotten my car back from the mechanic who had given my folks a good deal on fixing it for me. It was running good. I knocked on the door to his apartment. It was early evening, but he didn't seem to be at home. I tried the door to see if it would open. It did. I let myself in placing the bread on the table. On second thought, I helped myself to a beer from his stockpile. Something told me to just sit and wait for him, after all he was talking marriage and everything. This wasn't something I would usually do at all. Quite frankly, way in the back of my mind, I wanted to see if he came back home alone. I sat there stubbornly for however long it took to down four beers. I became a little nervous when I heard him coming up to the front door. In he walked. "Oh! There you are," he said in a casual sort of way. He wasn't at all astonished by my presence because my car was right outside. His usual big chuckle accompanied the greeting.

"I've been waiting for you. I hope you don't mind."

"Heck no," he threw his coat over the chair. "I just got off work. How long have you been waiting?"

"A couple of hours, I guess."

"I see you made yourself at home," he eyed the empties.

"Yeah! I couldn't see them going to waste," I teased. "I brought you some bread I baked today. Thought you might like it."

"Thanks," he smiled taking off his sweatshirt. He started laughing loudly. "Hey, look at this!" Still laughing he exclaimed, "I'm holy!" His undershirt was full of holes!

I started to laugh, too. "You're not the only one. I have a 'holey' couch."

"Yeah, I think I caught it from you," he chuckled. Helping himself to a beer he sat down beside me.

"Hey, what happened to the holes in your shirt?" I tugged at his shirt trying to find where they had gone.

"Disappeared, didn't they?"

"Yes!" I saw that I couldn't trust my eyes. "They sure did."

"This place is spooky!" He laid his head on the back of the couch trying not to let things upset him. I got up to use the bathroom. While in there I saw a pair of his work boots. Work boots were symbolic to me of a manly male, one who wasn't afraid to get his hands dirty with hard work. To me, a laborer was the opposite of the man in the suit, who used his mouth to manipulate others, and made a living at it. "Are those your biiig boots?" I hollered at him from the bathroom.

"Yeah, their mine." His voice sounded afraid like, perhaps, I was nuts.

Then he got up from the couch as I re-entered the room. "Did you see my foot?" he asked me. "The one that got hurt?"

"No," I said, "I didn't know you had a hurt foot."

"I don't," he said. "See it?"

"I see it." I looked down at it.

"Look at it good," he ordered.

I looked again. It was all scarred on one side and the other side had stitches.

"Yes, I do see it. It looks awful."

"What does?" he snapped.

"Your foot," I pointed.

"Pat, there's nothing wrong with my foot. See, Pat? There's nothing there."

I looked again. It was normal.

"Oh. So there isn't." I tried to act nonchalantly about it, but all the time I was wondering, *have I really lost it? Is he making fun of me? Has he lost it?*"

After I joined him back on the couch I noticed a picture that was hanging on the wall up over our heads. "Does that picture mean anything to you?" he asked earnestly.

"Yes, it does. It's the same picture my self-adopted grandfather, Robbie, had hanging in his room." I got up to further inspect it.

"Oh!" He stretched out on the couch." "I'm tired. I'm thinking about moving. I have a friend that sleeps with me now and then. I don't even know who he is. He just shows up now and then. Does that mean anything to you?"

"Maybe," I answered slowly. "Maybe. I'd better go home now," I grabbed my purse. Things were getting weird, again. I quietly let myself out.

As I got out to the car, I realized that I had left my car keys on the coffee table. I crept back into the apartment. George was lying on the couch where I had left him, apparently asleep already. I grabbed my keys. Then I saw it! A grinning face laying there looking up at me. Ron's face! Now I was sure I was seeing things! I ran to my car running from the fact that perhaps I was crazy.

I tried to manage through the next days by keeping busy by fixing up the place. The curtain rods were getting wobbly, so I got out a hammer and began pounding on the nails. I heard something crash to the floor. After a moment of looking around I found the crucifix that I had hung on the wall splattered on the floor. Jesus' head was broken off. Looking back at it now I know I had flipped out. I remember crying, "Oh, no! God is dead!" I had enough sense to stop it, I knew it was stupid. I caught myself."

As time went on I became more and more angry about how George just popped in and out of my life whenever he felt like. On top of that he was driving me crazy. I wondered if he was nuts, too? I kept remembering back to how Frank, the band member who had been at my house that ugly silly night, had accused him of being crazy.

Well, I had my chance to check George out again. Another weekend rolled around. This was the weekend I had with the kids. A bright idea struck me. George did invite me to bring the kids over for a swim that time we went there for dinner. I made a quick trip to the second hand store to get them suited up. I quickly packed them up with towels, and all, and over to George's we went.

George was lying on the floor in his bathing suit when we arrived. "Hi," I greeted him. "I thought I'd bring the kids over for a swim. Is it OK?"

"Yeah," he had an on-guard friendly way about him.

"You sure?" I reacted. "You sound mad," gingerly walking over to where he lay I bent over him and came right out with it. "You don't want me anymore, do you?" I asked softly.

"I never said that," he answered emphatically. "Just don't start anything now!" His eyes welled up with big tears.

"OK," I called the kids. "Come on, we're going swimming!" I changed the subject quickly. "You coming with us?" I called to George.

"No, I just went."

It was a well-kept pool. The kids noticed little green and blue ceramic fishies that were worked into the tile around the pool. They screamed with delight as they splashed one another, especially when they caught me off guard. We had a nice swim. However, I was just pretending to have fun. I was troubled over George's upset state. "That was really relaxing," I told him as I walked back to the apartment. "Do you have a towel? The kids got all of theirs wet."

"Do I have a towel?" he ran to get it. "Isn't it cute?" He held up a big beach towel with a very cute picture of an orange tiger, the length and breadth of it. "I saw this towel and I couldn't resist it!" he declared with glee. "Isn't it the cutest towel you ever saw?" Big tears came to his eyes again.

"It is cute," I took it from him. " . . . but I wouldn't cry over it."

He sat down on the floor again. "I'm watching TV. You going home?"

"Yes, I'm going." I gathered my things and bent over to kiss him good-bye.

"Don't start anything now," he warned me again. I backed off. My eyes seemed to be playing tricks on me again. A scar came over his left eye. He was crying. Then his eye got worse. It was almost hanging out of its socket.

"Come on, kids," I called to them as I ran to the car horrified.

George's uneasiness added to my feelings of confusion and fears of becoming insane. I sat by the radio drinking beer, my usual wind-down after the kids were in bed. One night especially I was terribly troubled over these strange happenings. The radio music was softly playing as I mulled over all the recent happenings trying to figure it all out. I felt that I didn't even know who I was or who God was anymore. I no sooner secretly voiced my question when a voice over the radio spoke. *There's a woman out there somewhere who's scared and afraid. Doesn't she know that if God really loves her, He'll sneak her in the back door, somehow?* I chuckled. For some reason it made me feel better except I wondered who had said that. It was such perfect timing! I breathed a sigh of relief feeling so much more relaxed when a beautiful song started to play. I had never heard it before: *. . . and that man torn and covered with scars . . .* I couldn't help but remember how my eyes had played games with me as I had seen George's face all scarred*! . . . to bear with unbearable burden . . .* the song continued. My heart became tumulted by it. I now realized that the song was about Jesus. *. . . to fight where the brave dare not go . . .* I laid my head on the table in ecstasy. I cried out to Jesus to help me. I couldn't figure it all out.

My heart was fully open to God through my weariness. I had to go lie down to sleep. It sounded so good to just go upstairs and sleep. I dreamed of a beautiful rest as I climbed the stairs to bed. I seemed to go up, up, high into nothingness. I felt as though I were a transparent figure floating up the staircase. I was no longer just myself. There was a movement, a feeling, a wisp of warm sunlight. A voice was soothing me, "Darling, please understand." My heart went on . . .

> "He was there. He watched over me and I was aware. 'Will you not sing and dance with me?' he said, 'for I am one who has searched for love.'
>
> 'I have searched also', I answered, 'but all I have found is grief . . . except in my beloved.'
>
> 'We will dance and be ever so happy for I have found someone who knows me. We will be happy until we part. The simplicity of the beauty inside of you is what I desire.'
>
> *I have some inner beauty after all*, I thought. *He knows what's in my heart. He sees it in my eyes for I, like Him, have found nothing but sorrow.*
>
> 'You're a living doll', he said.
>
> I felt so warm. We courted. He brought beauty into my life and into my home. I felt like a child, full of beauty and grace. I made my house into a home. We exchanged moments of tenderness. There was no disgrace. 'I'll take you by the hand and lead you to the stars. Darling, please understand.'"

That night I rested a good rest. I awoke refreshed. This had been the week of my birthday. My sister-in-law had brought me a present, a lovely white slip with a large strip of lace at the bottom. It made me feel feminine, and lovely. I awoke the next morning and decided to put on the slip for I still hadn't come down from the ecstasy of feeling so close to God. Such a oneness! It was awesome. I just wanted to wear something that made me feel graceful, or exquisite. As I lay there on my bed in my new finery my little girl, Betsy, came into the room. "Mommy, here's a brush for your hair."

"Oh, thank you", I smiled a far off smile at the same time realizing that it was a strange thing for my little girl to be doing.

She had no idea what I was thinking. I was thinking that I was going to be a bride of Christ! My heart sang. All the while my brain was telling me, 'stop this, Patricia, you're going nuts!' I could feel that my eyes were sort of happily cock-eyed, sort of like having a screw loose. I had seen Ron's eyes do the same thing when he had come to visit me on his second visit. His cock-eyed look had sort of taken me aback a little that night. Now, something else began to happen which made me realize that this moment was from God not from my having lost my mind.

Little Betsy began singing, "holy, holy, holy", in the tune that is sung in church, each holy going up the music scale. This added up to something else besides craziness. *How did she know what I had been thinking about? In fact, how did she know that song? She's only three years old.* In fact, I noticed that Betsy's eyes were a little cock-eyed, too. *What's going on? I know Betsy's not nuts. There's definitely something going on here.* I began to pray as I brushed my hair faster and faster all the while thinking, *I'm so heavenly crazy.* I lay back down on the bed just sighing.

At the end of the day, again, I attempted to go to sleep hoping to find the same rest. I lie there in my bed remembering how my bed used to be arranged and how I had rearranged it when Carol had come back to live for awhile. After she had left the first time, I had moved Betsy into the third bedroom. After that I had told Carol when she had returned, "you can stay here with us as long as you're willing to sleep on the cot in my bedroom." As I lay there remembering all of these things I suddenly recalled the night I had seen the furniture flying in the window arranging itself around the room. It dawned on me. The room had arranged itself the same way it is now. It was spooky. I shivered just thinking about it. It wasn't Ron's bedroom at all, it was mine! It was a preview of these times.

As this realization hit me I heard a loud sound outside of my window. It was a car motor. I thought that someone might be coming into the house. I expected a knock on the door. I ran to the window. It was a car sitting in front of my house with no one in it! The motor was running! Instantly I remembered the night when George had come over to tell me of his dream about his car parked out front with its motor running and no one in it. It had to be George. *He must be out there.* I ran into the hallway and down the stairs tripping over a toy on the stairway as I flew to the door. I got there just in time to see the car make a U-turn, only this time it looked like the back of Ron's head as I caught a glimpse of someone steering the car. Ron was driving! I walked to the sidewalk to watch it go down the street until I saw it stop. People climbed out of it, a crowd of people came out of it! I was afraid. I was seeing things again. I shook my head. It was too much. I chose to forget about it.

The following day was another bright and summery day. I was in the kitchen cleaning up after breakfast. The kids were out of school, now. I was getting a late breakfast ready. I felt good for all of us to be sitting down for breakfast. No rush, no fussing around. I was listening to their chatter as they played outside. The radio was playing as usual. Suddenly I heard them scream, "The blimp! Hey, Mom! Come here and see the blimp!" I ran to the back porch. There were two big blimps gliding through the sky toward our street. Little Betsy was squealing in the excitement. She had never seen such a sight. Rob came running to the porch. "Hey, mom. See those blimps? That one there is going to go over the house," his arm pointed to the west, " . . . and then it is going to go way over to there and turn around and come back again over the house. When it goes over the first time," he went on, "the radio is going to stop playing. Then when it comes back, it'll bring the radio back."

"Who told you that?" I got a kick out of his excitement and his wild tale.

"I heard it on the radio, I think," he answered matter-of-factly.

As we stood there watching, holding our hands over our eyes to protect them from the glare of the sun, the blimp came on over the house. The radio stopped. I was astonished. I just told myself that the blimp must be causing interference with the radio waves. At least that's what I told the kids. I hurried to the front door to watch the blimp as it made its way across the sky. It appeared to be hovering right over, or at least, near George's apartment.

"See, mom?" I told you so. Now it's going to turn. "See?"

Sure enough. It turned. Back on over the house it came. As it glided over the house, the radio came back on. I was astonished! The radio was talking to him, too. It made me feel better for my own sanity, but I it caused me to wonder, and wonder, and wonder.

I called the neighbor boy over to baby-sit, and off I went in my old jalopy.I wondered if I was being called over to George's place. I was talking to myself determined to get over there, feeling pretty shaky. It was like I was afraid that I wouldn't be able to make it. I nervously forced myself to go on. Each block became a goal to accomplish. I don't know why it seemed so hard, but as I drove along a beautiful song took over my very being. Again, a song which I had never heard before. It was a man's voice singing, a voice that was soft and gentle. *I left this world and the joys of this life, all for the love of a girl.* That song totally relaxed me, almost in a trance-like manner. Of course, the song reminded me of Ron and my big puzzle of whether he was dead or alive. Then it dawned on me. *I don't have a radio in my car.* I was hearing things again. I got all tense and nervous all over again. Finally, I parked in front of the now very familiar apartment house heaving a sigh of relief.

As I walked up to the door, George saw me coming. He opened the door and said, "I see you made it."

"Yeah! I made it." His words stung me. It was as though he had been expecting me.

"Here's a beer," he handed me a bottle. "I'll be back in just a minute." I thought about the beautiful blue glasses I had bought especially for him. I never even had had a chance to serve him a beer in them. I knew how George preferred drinking out of a glass. I knew it didn't look too good for me to be drinking out of a bottle so I went to the kitchen and got a glass.

George came back. "One thing I know for sure," he remarked with great assurance, "there's no glass on that table." He had brought his landlady and another guy with him who were evidently good friends of his. It appeared that he had asked them to be witnesses. He took a double take. "Where did you get that?" he questioned me sharply.

"In the kitchen," I retorted. He held his hand to his mouth and sat on the edge of the couch. He then waved his friends off. Evidently they had seen what he needed for them to see.

"See that book in there?" he pointed. "Do you have some paper, or something, to put in there?"

"No." I shook my head.

"Go over there and look at it," he said. It was a dark blue book entitled, *"Blue Jacket"*.

"That's a nice book," I mumbled, thoroughly confused over his behavior. *"Blue Jacket,* huh?"

"Blue Jacket. That's right. That reminds me. Your little boy left his blue jacket over here the last time you were here." He carefully annunciated every syllable.

"Oh, thanks." I took it. "I didn't even miss it. Of course, the weather has been so beautiful he hasn't needed it."

"Now, I'm supposed to play this record." George was a little scattered, trying to follow some sort of instructions, or something. "Let's see. It's here someplace. Oh, yeah! Here it is . . . " He put it on the record player. "You sit here and listen. I'm pretty busy getting ready to move."

"OK," I smiled. I didn't bother to ask any questions. I never even thought of asking any questions. It was as if I was living a big puzzle and had to come up with the answer myself. The song played . . . *Bill Bailey, won't you please come home?* . . . it was a very peppy tune that I had always liked. I listened to it tapping my foot until it got to the part. . . . *I threw you out with nothing but a fine toothcomb.*

"Does that mean anything to you?" he asked.

"Yes, it does," I giggled, remembering that night when he got a little huffy when I had asked him to leave handing him his comb. The next song came on. *I love you truly, truly dear.*

"Gee, that's a funny combination of songs on that record," I remarked. George nodded.

"Go take a look at the record", he insisted. I walked over to the record player and peeked inside. It was a record of songs by Sarah Vaughn. "Is that the record that's been playing?" I asked him.

"That's the one."

As I scrutinized it closer I noticed that it didn't have any of those songs written on the label. George nervously took some pots and pans from the cupboard. "Now, I'm supposed to turn on the TV." He threw the utensils into a box and then nervously walked across the room to switch it on, sitting down on the couch to watch it. The title to the movie came on . . . *Miracle of the Bells*.

"That's a great old movie," I smiled.

"Yeah. Let's watch it." He sat there glued to the screen. The characters were real unusual, almost bizarre. The acting was rotten and no one made any sense. Soon I realized that the people on the TV were the same as in the picture that was hanging over the couch, the one that seemed to bother George the night we had sat on the couch talking . . . that "holey" night. I was stunned. I looked over to George as my mouth fell open with shock. He had big tears in his eyes. "Keep watching," he said.

The woman who was strangely dressed in veils appeared on the screen looking straight at me. She said, "Do you know that you were radiant?" I didn't hear her because of my state of amazement. "Hey, you!" the woman continued to look straight at me, " . . . did you hear me? You were radiant!"

I looked over to George.

He nodded his head. "You were," he affirmed. "You really were." His voice cracked from the emotion of the whole ordeal. I became afraid. George changed the subject.

"You going to be throwing a party, or something?" he continued with his strange rhetoric.

"A party? Where?" I asked.

"Upstairs, I think. You going to be pulling out some mattresses or something?"

"Yeah. Three of them," I answered smartly. Deep inside of myself I was facetiously thinking, one for George, one for Ron and one for myself. It was in remembrance of that other night when I ran out of there frightened when I thought I had seen Ron lying on that couch smiling up at me.

"I'm going to bed," George began making up his bed on the couch. "You can do what you want."

I left. "Hey", he called after me, " . . . I'll be swimming in the pool the next time you come over, or at least someone will. The next door neighbors will just be leaving their apartment when you see me swimming, or something like that."

"Good-bye, George," I walked slowly away. It was so sad, such a beautiful guy, crazy as hell". I was sure now that he was. However, I wasn't so sure I was. And if I wasn't than maybe he's not. Dear, God . . . what's happening?"

When I got home I had a hard time collecting myself. I couldn't stand it anymore. I began to cry. The tears were from the pure frustration of it all. What was all that garbage about someone swimming in the pool? It's like he knows everything what's going to happen before it happens. I kept mulling it over in my mind. The evening was still early. I decided to go over there and see for myself. He said the next time I go over there I'd see him swimming, or something. I gathered the kids in the car and went over there.

Dusk had just faded into dark when we got there. I told the kids to wait in the car. No one was around. George's apartment was dark. No one was home. I crept up to the pool. I didn't see anyone. But just then some people were leaving the apartment next to George's. I waited until the chatter subsided and the people had taken off in their car. Again all was quiet, except, I heard a splashing sound. I looked around and saw George's cute tiger towel, which he had left behind, hanging over the railing. I looked into the pool again. Someone was definitely splashing around in there. I looked again, thoroughly . . . over every inch of the pool. No one was there. *Splash!* Again I looked even harder. "Who's there?" I called out. My voice was weak and squeaky. Suddenly I felt an overwhelming Presence. It was Him. My heart pattered. It's God! He's trying to show me something! I stood there stunned. I figured that He was probably trying to tell me its been Him all along. Maybe He's trying to teach me.

I walked back to the car quietly, deep in thought.

"Hey, mom," one of my little boys greeted me from the back seat of the car. "Someone got a flat tire on the freeway."

"Who told you that?" I asked sharply.

"The radio."

"We don't have a radio!"

That night I couldn't sleep. I was too tired. I sat up listening to music once more. *It's such a lonely road . . .* came the lyrics in song, *I've been traveling alone down the lonely road . . .* I burst into tears. My heart was tormented. *Was the radio broadcast really Ron? What if he really did try to come back here for me? What if it was God. What if I'm nuts? What if . . .* I continued to listen to the songs. One song would be a love song reflecting all of the beautiful ecstasy of love. I started to put God's name in the place of the word "love". The words became beautiful praises to God. *My love (God) is deeper than the ocean, higher than the sky . . .* the words flowed filling the room. My heart melted and was at peace. But, then a song would come on which, to me, depicted the lustful yearning for unfulfilled sex. . . . *are you satisfied, really satisfied?"* The words attacked my heart. I began to reason how these songs reflected the thoughts of the society in which we live. There were those who knew of love, and those who knew only of sex and worldliness. Over and over the songs pulled and tugged at my heart, from a beautiful meaningful love song to a depressing or even sickening song filled with strife and mischief. My feelings were at the mercy of every emotion of every song. I felt like a yo-yo. I got to thinking that maybe I'm going to die of a heart attack, or something. My emotions were worn out. I grabbed a pencil that was sitting by the telephone. "If you want to see how screwed up the world is, just listen to the music," I scribbled on a piece of scratch paper. I figured that just in case I died that very night I'd have left something useful. Tossing the pencil aside I went up to bed.

My thoughts became deeper and deeper now for I was still attempting to understand more about who God was. I was also becoming reclusive. If someone came to the door I would run and hide until they left. I didn't want anybody traipsing in on my special thoughts. I tried to think back to all of the things I had learned growing up. The mystery of the Blessed Trinity stayed in my mind through all the figuring, through all the adding up of truths and subtractions of untruths which I had been learning to discern. My mind was on these deep thoughts for I don't know how long. Most of the time I didn't know what day it was, except I could tell it was Sunday when I would watch my mother driving by on her way to church. I knew she would stop by to visit my sister, then I would watch her drive by our house and go home. She didn't even want to see me. I think I made her uncomfortable. Maybe she could see I was a little weird. It made me want to cry, but I couldn't. Instead, I just went quietly about my business harboring my special thoughts.

This went on for several weeks. Then one day I remembered something. Mom's birthday! It was some time that week. Running to the calendar my fears were confirmed. I missed it. It had been the day before. The first time I ever forgot. I was afraid she'd be mad at me. I went into a tizzy. I felt I needed to explain how I had forgotten it. I walked around the house in a frantic pace, thinking. Suddenly I knew what I would do. I wrote out a diagram of what I had been thinking about. Then I could get her opinion about it. It would be like a birthday present. I made a diagram, much like a flow chart, of the Faith, Hope and Love thoughts . . . I had figured them out to be the Blessed Trinity . . . God the Father was Love, God the Son was Hope and God the Holy Spirit was Faith. Then I put the religions that matched each one. Under God the Father was the Jewish religion, under the Son was the Catholic and Protestant religions and under the Holy Spirit was the evangelists and believers. I brought them all together at the bottom of the page to unite in Unity. Once in unity it brought about God on earth. It was beautiful! I knew it was good.

As I entered my mother's house I cried out, "I forgot your birthday. I'm so sorry." I gave her a big hug.

"That's all right, dear, but I was a little worried. I was about to call."

"You don't know what I've been through, lately." I sat myself down in a kitchen chair. "You'd never believe it."

"What's been happening now?" Mom asked somewhat annoyed, or perhaps fearful of my next bit of news.

"I couldn't explain it in a million years. This will give you an idea," I handed the diagram to her. While she read the paper I held my head in my hands nearly covering my face from embarrassment.

A scared, pathetic smile came on my mother's face. "I don't know what to say. Is this what you've been thinking about? Dear, I had no idea you've been so lonely, suffering so much over this."

"I don't know what you'd call it, but it makes sense, doesn't it?"

"Don't you think maybe you need some help?" Mom reached for my hand.

"You think I'm crazy, don't you?" I flew into a rage. "I don't appreciate people laughing at me. You know, they all laughed at St. Bernadette."

"What makes you think you could ever compare yourself to a saint?" Mom was angry now.

"I'm not. I just know I'm trying. I don't always make it, but I am trying. Anyhow, all I meant was that everyone thought she was crazy, too . . . and she wasn't!" I picked up my diagram and slammed out the door.

By the time I got home my blood was boiling. Now I knew they all thought I was crazy. I slammed through the door to my house. But after I sat down and thought it over, I remembered how I had thought I was nuts, myself. I chuckled at the irony of it all. It seemed so funny how it was OK if I thought so, but I couldn't stand for anyone else to think so. Or is it that I can't stand to say it out loud?

It was only a short time later that my mother joined me in the kitchen. She had looked up the phone number to this place. I was scared to look at it. I slowly focused my eyes on it: Mental Clinic, 752-4056. I tried not to react. I thanked her although my tongue was thick, much like the feeling of eating peanut butter. My mother quietly left, just as quietly as she had come.

After that I began wondering what I should do with my stupid diagram. I scanned over it again. It still made sense to me. I still think maybe it's true. I didn't want to throw it away. I didn't want to keep it either as a reminder of everything. I wonder what George would think about it? Maybe he'll understand. That's what I should have done a long time ago. Off I flew in my car, over to George's.

Once there, after knocking on his door, I realized that there were a lot of boxes piled up. I forgot that he said he'd be moving. I prayed that he would still be there. I opened his apartment door. All the furniture was gone. There were some packed boxes along the wall. I noticed a book sitting on top of the boxes. It was that *Blue Jacket* book he had shown me. I picked it up. The title was different. It was the *Mariner's Handbook*. I didn't care. I stuffed the paper inside the book I ran out the door. I felt as though I was fleeing from a very sneaky deed.

When I got home there was a fire truck in front of my house. The hose was strung out to the backyard. I ran to the back of the house crying to myself. I had forgotten the kids. They had been next door playing all afternoon. I had taken off without thinking. They had gotten under the back porch and lit a fire! I knew that I had to get a better hold on myself. I had to think a little straighter.

After everything was OK again I grabbed a beer to wash away my fears from my own self as much as anything else. I knew that was a close call. I even remembered back to when I had heard that sermon. Something had been said to me, a silent voice, that "the fire engines were there." I guzzled down a beer trying to calm down. As I sat there thinking and listening to the radio as usual the music became louder and louder. Honestly, there were voices singing . . . . thousands of voices! They were so beautiful! They were singing, *Hallelujah, Hallelujah.* It was awesome! "Goodbye, good-bye," they sang in unison. The words soaked into my soul.

Then the voices were interrupted by a man's voice. "You will give your children an insurance policy worth at least thirty thousand dollars or more . . . or maybe for all eternity, except, maybe, for one. Signing off, this is Me, signing off." The voices said good-bye and never returned. I just kept it quietly tucked away in my heart.

As an EAGLE
STIRS up her nest
FLUTTERS over the young
SPREADS ABROAD her wings
TAKES them
BEARS them on her wings
So the Lord ALONE did LEAD

Deut 32:11-12 (KJ)

Chapter 13

Red Roses For A Blue Lady

There were a few days of an unnatural peace. Then one morn I was shocked back to reality. The kids got up and were already busy outside playing. I knew I had been ignoring their bedrooms. I really never did fuss over their rooms much ever since all the turmoil in my life. In fact, I did as little as possible, picking up their toys when it got so bad that I couldn't make it to the beds to wash their sheets. That's why this desire to straighten out their rooms from top to bottom was different behavior from my norm. I was feeling good about accomplishing that difficult feat, wishing that I could get back on track and keep things up like this all of the time.

I was interrupted by a knock on the front door. "Are you Mrs. Surina?" A pleasant tall man, all dressed up in a suit (which immediately made me nervous) was standing there. He had a buddy with him also in a suit, but not quite as well dressed.

"Yes?" I admitted. "What can I do for you?"

He pulled out a badge. "I'm with the children's protective services. It's come to our attention that we should come and look into your children's rooms to see if they're living in a proper fashion."

"Oh, yes. Come on in." I was shaking from head to foot all the time secretly giving thanks and credit to my God-friend Himself for helping me to clean their rooms that morning. I took the man upstairs. He looked around, peeked in the closet, then turned to me and said, "I don't see anything wrong here. Except, maybe you should see about those sagging springs on their beds. It looks like a nice room to me."

"Thank you." I was so relieved when they left. I finally was able to breathe deeper.

This scary happening made me decide to get help from the Catholic Services to see if I could get back on my feet. I needed to get back to a job, back into the human race instead of sitting in a melancholy state listening to the radio and drinking beer. It turned out that the only help they could give was to place the boys in a foster home run by the Sisters, and talk to my mother about letting me and Betsy live with them until I could function more normally again. There would be an opening for the boys in about a month or two.

Then came another happening. I got a subpoena to attend a court hearing. Bob and Anne were trying to have me classified as unfit mother. They didn't even know about the bad things I had done, like leaving them alone while they were sleeping, a few times. I didn't know whether to laugh or cry. It was all too much. Here, Anne and Bob had purchased a new house, Anne had given birth to their own son. Bob had started a whole new life, and had not had to pay one penny of child support even though he had been ordered to do so by the court. I did what I did best: escape. I went out that weekend to go dancing.

Again I was sitting in a booth sipping on a beer. I noticed a rather handsome young man sitting next to me with a very warm and pleasant personality. The only thing that scared me about him was that he was wearing an expensive suit. I just sat there watching him kid around with the people seeing that he was very well liked. Then I caught his eye. "Hey, there blue lady, can I come and chat with you awhile?"

Deep down I was happy to be noticed for I was definitely in a blue mood. In no time he had me laughing and feeling good about myself. His name was Glen. It was a refreshing name to me for I had never known a Glen before. He was an insurance salesman, and was going through a divorce. He took a liking to me right off. "I'll bet I could train you to sell insurance," he complimented me. He had faith in me, which was totally unearned. I immediately tried to set him straight by telling him how I was trying to get back on my feet and that selling wasn't my thing. I didn't tell him that I had almost no confidence left, but was able to fake it pretty good with a few beers in me. He even asked me for my address and phone number.

It wasn't until the music started that I discovered the pain he was going through in his divorce. The music that evening didn't help our depression at all. He started to sing the words: *Your cheating hearts, will tell on you* . . . . He would begin to laugh as the next song started up, *Please release me, let me go. I don't love you anymore* . . . I joined in with him. Our hearts were deep into the misery of it all. Finally a peppy tune got us on our feet. "Come on," he grabbed my arm. "Let's go dance this one out." By this time we were very comfortable with each other. Our outgoing personalities became a mindless combination. As the music went faster, we danced faster, almost in a frenzy. I think that the couple playing the music was getting a kick out of us livening up the whole place. Finally, we both fell down laughing. We lay there on the dance floor still singing, . . . *I could see the reflection of my gold wedding band* . . . He laughed so hard. Too hard! I could see the terrible pain he was in. "Come on . . . " he slowly quieted down as he got to his feet. "I have to go."

My day in court approached and was gone before I knew it. I was relieved for the judge had simply thrown out the case. He gave Bob and Anne a slap on the wrist for not having paid child support, especially after I had told the judge that I had made arrangements for the children to stay at the Sister's home until I could find the strength to go back to work. Bob's connection with the bowling alley and the moral squad running him out of town had made it impossible for the judge to let him have them. Anne's big complaint was that the boys needed new underwear. They were ordered to buy them some. I was very conscious, though, that I would have to make some big changes.

I was watching TV instead of listening to the radio for a change when there was a knock on the door. I opened the door to a young man who was carrying a beautiful bouquet of long stemmed red roses. "What in the world?" I didn't know what to say. "Are you sure these are for me?"

"Yes, ma'am."

I opened the card that accompanied them. It read, *Red Roses for a Blue Lady*. I knew immediately who it was. While I arranged them in a vase, the phone rang. It was Glen. "Did you get them?"

"Yes! They're so beautiful!"

"So are you". Right away my heart sank. I couldn't believe it. He had to be phony. That suit and all, and saying all the right things . . . . "How did the court turn out?"

"Good. Real good. They didn't get very far."

"Can I come over tonight? I have a surprise."

I agreed to it. I got all dressed up for I knew he was used to rather sophisticated women. I knew that when he saw my old house and shoddy furniture he'd probably take off. I prepared myself. When I opened the door to him he livened up the whole place with "Got yourself a baby-sitter? We're going out."

"No. I didn't know . . . "

"Get one. I'll pay." In his hand he was holding a bag of ice with two wine goblets in it getting chilled and an expensive bottle of wine. "Here, take care of this will you?"

I took the ice and put it in the refrigerator. Then handing him the goblets and wine bottle I exclaimed. "You do the honors. I've never opened one before."

"Here! Now, hold your breath . . . " *Pop!* "Perfect!" The sweet wine was poured out and shared. We got further acquainted sharing stories, but he never would get too personal.

The boy next door was a Godsend to me these days. After he came over and I explained to the kids that Glen was taking me dancing, we took off. Glen drove me directly to a hotel. "I have reservations . . . " he explained. "This was my surprise for you."

"I think this is one too many surprises." I refused to go in. Now I knew what he was out to get.

"Well, OK. We don't know each other very well for that, I guess . . . OK, well let's go dancing."

We did just that. There we were in a dance hall on the opposite end of town from where I usually went. As we sat there sipping on a beer I caught the shocking sight of George leaving hurriedly out the door with a woman. I could see that he had probably seen me and was trying to sneak out."Wait here a minute," I whispered to my friend. I followed George outside. There he was standing by his car with a gal in a white uniform. I surmised she was a nurse. He was purposely putting on a show kissing this woman to make me jealous. He was doing a good job of it, too. I went back in to join Glen. My lovely Friday evening was ruined. "I have to go home," I told him. He left me off on my porch offering me a sweet goodbye kiss. He wasn't even mad.

The next day was the kids' visitation with their father. Bob poked his nose in the door while they were getting ready to go. His eyes quickly gave the room a detective's scan. They rested on the red roses that Glen had sent to me. *Pow!* Out of nowhere he socked me in the mouth. "You cheap whore!," he screamed. Robert saw him hit me.

"Dad!" He shouted in horror and disbelief running up to his room. Bob followed him up to maneuver him to join Ann and himself and then whisked them off like a jet. However, it had made a big imprint on his son.

I figured that I would probably never see Glen again after that night. I felt bad because he had been so thoughtful. *I wish I had gone into that hotel room. I got blamed for it, anyway.*

I felt even worse, though, about George, now that things were back to normal. Maybe he would come back if I could just talk him into it. I still felt that we had a very precious secret that only the two of us knew about. In fact, I wondered if God hadn't been trying to tell us something. I felt that He knew about our situation as divorced Catholics, expected never to again marry. To me it made sense that those of us who were divorced should find another divorced mate. At least, we were in the same boat. We might be able to help each other out of the hole that we had found ourselves in. This was the lesson I feel that God was trying to teach us. However, I also felt that George hadn't treated the happening as special as I had, for there he was with another woman, probably practicing hobby number three. Of course, it didn't dawn on me that he saw me there with another man. The thought struck me, *My gosh, God could marry two people in person these days and they wouldn't even know it!*

Deep down inside of myself I was feeling that that's what had happened. Maybe that's why George was upset when I made him leave and handed him his comb. Maybe he felt that God had married us, but thought that I didn't think so. I was just trying to do the right thing. What had happened didn't even register in my brain until later on. Anyhow, I know now that he doesn't feel tied to me in any way. I'm so confused! I wish I knew where he had moved to. I regretted not having asked him where he was going when he had told me about moving, but things had been so crazy at the time I didn't even think to ask. I began to reason things out. I knew his father lived over on the north end of town, somewhere. Then the idea struck me to look up his dad's address. I was sure he'd be in touch with his father. I wrote in a note, "All the strangeness is all over now. Things are back to normal. You might be out playing around with little nurses, or whoever, but as for me I want something better than that."

Soon after that, I had a caller late at night. I had on my nightgown. I hoped it might be George, but it was the last person I expected. It was Glen! I could hardly believe my eyes. "I never thought I'd ever see you again," I let him in as he made himself comfortable in the chair.

"It takes more than being shot down once to get rid of me. I really like you, Pat. I understand the way you felt. Come here," he grabbed me giving me the sweetest kiss. "How's that?"

"That was beautiful." I felt like weeping.

"Then come here." He took me in his arms placing me down on the floor gently. We made love in a very natural and loving way. Being with him brought a wonderful, comfortable warmth that I had never experienced or never would experience. He left after a time as gently as he had come. I had a hard time feeling guilty about that evening. I felt that the only person I needed to be true to didn't feel that way towards me.

I laughed as I thought about it the next day. Here I had three kids, and being with Glen was my first normal sexual experience, with a caring and a naturalness about it. My mind was all screwed up on morality in general. I shoved aside what the church had taught me. I had lost all trust in their leading in such matters.

Who should appear at my front door a couple of evenings later, on Columbus Day? "Got your letter," George chuckled, his eyes sparkling even brighter than ever. He had a relaxed kindness about him. "How did you know where I was?"

"I didn't," I giggled . . . "but I do now, don't I?"

"Let's take in a movie," he suggested, no, he nearly demanded. "Call a babysitter, I'm paying."

It was early in the evening. Little Betsy came running up to him. "It's my birthday," she announced.

"How old are you?" George chuckled with delight. "How many fingers? Three?" He had her hold up the right amount. "Here," he bent down to give her a big silver quarter. "Don't spend it all in one place." He threw his head back laughing his hearty laugh that I loved so much. "Maybe you can't go then, huh? Her birthday, and all?"

"We already had her party. She'll be going to bed, anyhow. I can go."

He bought a big pizza and we settled down in the drive-in to watch the movie. It was about a couple from another planet who had crashed. They went through a bunch of survival tactics. It had a surprise ending. They turned out to be Adam and Eve. I thought it was an interesting movie with a cute twist to it, while George just became quieter and quieter. I could tell he didn't like it. I knew it was against the Bible. I decided to hush about the movie. We rode home in a rather comforting silence. "Next time you see me I'll probably have a beard. I'll look just like

Jesus. Maybe I'm one of them false prophets or something," he snickered a little nervously. I knew that he was referring to what happened, trying to make light of it.

"I know what you mean," I smiled trying to reflect back to him that I understood what he was talking about. Then I told him about my plans of living with my parents and putting the boys in a home until I could get on my feet. "Sounds like a good idea," he grinned. "Looks like we've both been doing some tall thinking." We parted with new hope for our future together.

It was only a few days later that I got the phone call to bring the boys to the Sister's foster home. I figured that at least they'll be getting some religious training. I was too confused to know what to teach them. I quietly handed my sons over to the Sisters with much trust in my heart. I needed to be free of the stress of caring for them during this time.

The final step was locking the front door to the house where so much had happened. It felt so good just to get away from the memories. There were so many memories in that house. Then I called to my mother. "Wait a minute." She was out in her car after helping me close up the house. "I'll put a note on the door in case George comes back. He doesn't know who you guys are." I hung the note on the door latch.

"Do you think he will?" my mother tried to warn me that maybe he wouldn't.

"Yes, I think so. We're getting some things straightened out," I reassured her. "Things are looking up."

The following day who should appear at the front door of my mother's house but Glen?

"Who's he?" My mother mimed the question to me behind his back. I waved my arm to her as if to say, "Shhh".

Glen wanted to know all about my plans. I was very quiet for his presence made me very confused. I really liked him, but was afraid that if I did encourage him, on top of feeling that God had married George and me, I felt that I wouldn't be able to live up to his lifestyle. My mood was very flat as we talked. "I'll stop by some afternoon and take you for a ride in my convertible," he offered.

"That'd be nice," I answered very quietly and shyly.

"Is there anything I can do for you?" he asked.

"Would you like a puppy?" Betsy had gotten a puppy for her birthday. We had to leave it behind. It was my last problem in the transition.

"Yeah," he said almost tearfully. I told him where the key was.

The next day I checked things out. Apparently he had let himself in and taken the dog. I cried inside knowing now that he was one of those "pretty birds" that I kept flying over. I wept a little baby tear.

It was that very evening that George called. "Got your note," he said happily. "I've got a problem, though, no car. I sold it to pay bills. I figured I didn't need one anyway since I've been working on the tug. I'm not in town but a day or two every two weeks."

"Where you at?" I asked.

"Down at the tavern near your old place."

"I'll come and get you," I offered. "I still have my old clunk."

"That thing still running?" he laughed. "I thought it died."

"It's still here," I answered. "See you."

George was quieter than usual, but very happy to see me. "Isn't there someplace we could go and talk?" He hailed a bartender to bring a beer to the table for me.

"Well, I have the keys to the house. My folks bought it when I got my divorce. They're going to hang on to it for me. They got a real buy on it, so I don't feel guilty about it all."

"Great!" He guzzled down his beer. "Let's go."

Once in the big old house I immediately went for the heat register. "It's a little cold, the heat's been off," I explained as I turned on the lamp so I could see to adjust it.

"We don't care," he cuddled me in his arms. "I love you," he finally admitted it, saying it with ease.

"I love you, too," I hugged him, filled with overwhelming happiness.

"Do you think it's safe?" he laughed as he pulled me to the floor, the same place where all the unbelievable happenings had started.

"I think so, I told you it was all over."

"Good." He kissed my neck.

"Don't get fresh," I teased as I crawled away from him.

"Where you going?" he crawled after me. We were like a couple of little kids: laughing and joking, smooching and teasing and making love. However, when we got to the point of intercourse, again it became an awkward experience, almost like the time we had tried to make love in the grass. It was as if we were both numb. "I love you," he said aloud. Suddenly it all turned sour. "I love you." He crawled on his hands and knees like a baby. I smiled a sick smile back wondering what was happening now? "Oh, God! I love you." He was getting very dramatic, now.

"Good!" I answered as I stared at his antics in disgust.

"I love you." He rolled over on his back. "Oh, I love you," he repeated over and over as he held his stomach. He looked like a kid who had eaten too many green apples. Then he started moaning. "Oh, God! I love her." He lay there groaning himself to a slow silence.

"Is it so darn hard to love me?" I sat there in complete disillusionment. "Are you in pain, or something?" My eyes began to fill with tears.

"Let me just lay here. I'll be all right," he calmed down. "I'm so exhausted."

"Well, I'm going up to bed. You can let yourself out." I bent down to kiss him goodnight.

That night happy memories went through my mind mixed with hurt. Evidently, he didn't want to love me. I tried to figure that night out. I knew his first wife had hurt him. Maybe he was just scared to have feelings for anyone. Then something hit me. I remembered how I had told Ron that I wouldn't have anything to do with him until he came to me on his hands and knees. George did just that. I wonder?

A couple of weeks went by real fast. I was now able to think about what I was going to do in the future. Like clockwork George called just like he said he would. "I just got in." I was so happy that he was finally calling without my having to prompt him. I had been a little afraid that he might not call after he had left the last time. "I'll come and get you," I offered. It felt so good to finally be having some sense of normalcy in our relationship. He met me immediately as I pulled up in front of his father's house. As he opened the door he suggested, "Let's take a drive down by the waterfront."

"OK," I agreed. "Do you want to drive?"

"Sure!" He climbed into the driver's seat.

We parked by the water. The waves made a wonderful sound as they swished toward the car and away again. It was a very still evening. Our hearts were at peace. Slowly, he snuck his arm around me. "What do you say we get married around January? I get some time off then."

"I don't know, George." I even shocked myself with my response. "I figure I'd better have my two feet on the ground first."

"Do you think you could manage it by then? At least one foot on the ground?"

"I'll try," I smiled shyly.

At that, George got out of the car and walked to the water. He was deep in thought. He picked up a rock or two throwing them into the rolling waves. I watched the water splash as the rock hit. I wondered what he was thinking. I worried a little. Maybe he wanted me to say "no." Soon he was back at the car. "We'll plan on it," he kissed me gently. "OK? Now, I'll be gone for a month or so because we're taking a long trip on the tug. When I come back we'll talk some more."

"Sounds good," I agreed. Butterflies were in my stomach. "While you're gone I'll try to get a grip on myself."

"Good." He started the car. "Let's go home."

. . . if our HEARTS do not condemn us
then we have CONFIDENCE
before GOD.

1 John 3:21 (NIV)

Chapter 14

When the Truth Hurts

The waiting room in the mental clinic was rather dreary. The drab yellow walls were brightly camouflaged with a couple of cheerful paintings hanging over the crack that ran in all directions. I had decided to obtain help to get back on track and find out if I was crazy or not. This was taking a lot of courage for me to do. "The doctor is a little late today," the receptionist smiled at me trying to reassure me that everything was going to be OK. *I don't know what to expect after last time,* I silently voiced my fears as I drew another puff on my cigarette. I remembered the nice woman therapist who sat in her office for hours listening to my long story. *It was the nicest thing anyone ever did for me. She listened.* I remembered back to Willie, the bus driver, who had helped me through those gray days during the tumult of my divorce as he had brought me to work each day. He had noticed the broken windows in my home and was deeply concerned. He would listen to me about my turmoil each day on my way to work. It was as if I was giving him chapter after chapter of the mess I was in. His listening had given me the strength to go to work and pretend nothing was wrong. He had allowed me my feelings and had validated the pain I was in.

I remembered how I had cried and laughed, then swore, and cried some more as the patient therapist, whom I had seen the last time I was here, had listened to me. The whole ordeal made my head spin as I had attempted to bring my story to the present day. My head felt like a big watermelon sloshing around up there. I looked up at the clock to take note of the few short minutes that had passed. On my last visit I had started out by telling her all about my marriage with Bob ending the story with huge sobbings, "I don't even trust the priests anymore." Then I started in about Ron, finishing with . . . "and I tried so hard to do everything right. I still messed up, I think . . . , then sometimes I'm proud of how I handled myself. I know I liked myself when I was with him. It's all been so hard . . . " I laughed and cried almost at the same time as in hysteria. Then I had told her about the weary days, which had followed after Ron left, how I had filled my hours thinking about him. It had become a habit, just as drinking beer day after day had been. I confessed to her that I would try to get just a little feeling of what it would be like to have him hold me one more time. I knew that I could no longer afford these habits, but they had become a priority in my life, like medicine. I assured her, though, that my children's basic needs were first on my list. After I had helped them to school, or fed them, or whatever, the time came to plug my mind in on my bondages . . . my memories. I just couldn't get Ron out of my heart. I told her about the strange radio broadcast I had heard just weeks before. That accident had bugged me to death. "I couldn't make sense of the accident that I had heard about," I confided in her. "It was supposed to have taken place on the mountain pass. It didn't add up."

For the grand finale I expounded upon my crazy romance with George. I explained how we had met and how we had many things in common . . . more than I knew then. Of course I filled her in on my friendship with Carol. "If I had known how much we had in common I probably would have run away right at first. However, I didn't run." I told the therapist of how I felt about it. "That experience was something I just didn't need", I explained to my new found professional friend, " . . . probably more than I could handle. Wherever Carol was there was mischief."

"Why did you keep falling into her trap?" I was asked.

"It seemed like a good friendship. To be honest, I think I

liked to get into a little mischief, too. Yes, I'm glad she taught me how to go out on the town. I found out what was going on out there. Let's face it, I would never had met Ron if it hadn't been for her. But then, I wasn't prepared for what's happening out there, either," I had informed her as I pointed out the window meaning society in general. "Guys think that if they are nice to you that they deserve to go to bed with you, sort of like giving them a dessert, or something. I guess that's why I loved Ron so much. He wasn't like that. He was real. Stupid, but real." I giggled to myself remembering how good it had felt to insult him.

"My mother is the one who gave me the phone number to come here", I had rambled on. "I remember she would say to me, 'Why don't you just live for your kids?' I couldn't do it," I cried. "It's like I gave it all away. There's no one there to put it back."

"Dear, you haven't had anything in life, yet," the sympathetic woman concurred. "You're completely drained!"

I had continued to explain more of what happened. I had needed to tell her more about George. "George was the one who drove me nuts," I attempted to explain. Listening about George took us way past closing time, into dinnertime. My therapist, and now trusted friend, had offered me half of her lunch.

"I rarely do this," she explained, "but I feel it is important to get all of this out in the open. You must be able to talk of these things.

"I'm sorry I'm talking so much. It's just that so much has happened!" I had apologized.

"I understand, dear. Don't worry about it. Now where did we leave off? Did you see any more of George?"

"Well, not for awhile."

I had been so surprised that she never even flinched or acted as though I had to hurry. She was so patient. I continued to fill her in on what had happened. "We started seeing the same things, and having the same dreams and stuff! Then I started to go Oops . . . raising up over myself." I laid my head down and started to sob it all out. "I am nuts aren't I?" I pleaded with her to answer me.

"I don't think so," she patted me on the back to try to comfort me. "No, I don't think so."

After having earned a huge sigh in divulging that experience I stopped to ask the million-dollar question. "Did we drive each other nuts?"

"You might be happy to know that there is a name for what you and your young man went through." My therapist had actually come up with a theory. "It's a phrase with French words, 'foille deux'. It is a word that describes a phenomenon that can happen between two people whose lives are so much the same that their lives become intermeshed with the same experiences. "She looked at her watch. "It's very late, dear. I'm going to make an appointment for you to see the doctor next week. Take care of yourself," she hugged me a goodbye. "I'm glad we stuck with it."

This bit of information had calmed me down quite a bit. Hours before I had dragged myself in there expecting the worst. Now I was dragging myself out of there feeling as though I had only been run through a meat grinder.

Now, here I was sitting here in the waiting room, holding in my hand a piece of paper with the date of my appointment with the doctor. I began to fidget around still in fear of not knowing what to expect. I wondered what that woman had told the doctor. I wondered if they'd lock me up? I prayed that the doctor was as nice as the therapist. That would be pretty hard to do.

"The doctor is ready for you," the secretary called to me as she signaled for me to walk through a door. The time had come! *Maybe I should leave*, I searched out my deepest desires. I looked out on the rainy streets. It was a drab, wet day. *No*, I caught myself. *I have to go through with it. I know I need help.*

I was ushered into a rather large room. Directly ahead of me were a desk and a chair. Several chairs were lined up against the wall. It seemed as if no one was there. I took a seat to wait. I sat there a minute or two when suddenly my eyes focused on a man sitting in the far corner of the room on a high stool. I smiled at him. "Hello".

"How are you feeling?" the strange man asked me.

"Fine," I answered calmly as if it was the most normal thing in the world for him to be sitting there on that stool. I don't know how long it was before he said a word to me. I remember thinking how silly he looked. *All he needs is a dunce cap*, I chuckled to myself. *He's weirder than I am!*

"Weren't you surprised seeing me sitting here?"

"No."

"What do you think I'm doing here?"

"Sitting there, I guess," I could feel a slow smile forming on my face.

"What do you do all day?" he asked me.

"I think."

"About what?"

"Oh, a little of this and a little of that." *I'm not going to tell him that I think about God and stuff all day . . .* My arms were waving frantically. They gave me away. He had struck a nerve. At that the man got off his stool and walked to the telephone. "I've got another one for you," he informed the person on the other end. "I'll send her over to you."

My destination was the Catholic hospital in town which had a mental health clinic annexed to it. The door was locked. As I stood there wondering what I was supposed to do now, suddenly a nurse opened the door and greeted me. "Are you from the neighborhood clinic? We've been waiting for you."

I heard the key turn behind us in the lock. It was an ominous sound*! They're going to lock me up!* my innards warned me. I tried very hard not to act afraid, walking slowly, carefully as the nurse gently led me into a large room. A friendly room it was. There were plants sitting around on the ledges giving it a homey atmosphere. A Ping-Pong table took up a large part of the room at one end. A piano sat alongside of the entrance door. "Oh! A piano!" I cheered up.

"You like the piano?" the nurse asked me.

"Oh, yes. I like to plunk on it. It relaxes me. I like that music, too." A sheet of music lay over the keyboard entitled, *I Love You Truly*. I didn't tell them about the fact that it was the song that was on the record at George's apartment that time. How did they know? I was feeling paranoid. "I like that picture, too." I pointed to a reproduction of a painting hanging on the wall over the piano.

"What do you see in the picture?" the nurse asked me.

"It's the same picture I have at home. The beautiful lady holding the baby. She looks like such a good mother. Happy too."

"Let's go to my office and have a little chat, shall we? Then you can come back out here and play the piano, or Ping-Pong or whatever you wish."

"OK". I followed her down the hall. *Maybe this will be fun!* I chose to change my fear to expectation.

The nurse signed me up to go to occupational therapy twice a week. I had absolutely no idea of what to expect that first day when I entered the workshop. "What would you like to make?" the young woman therapist smiled at me as if she actually accepted me for a friend. She was a pretty young girl with a very sure way about herself. Her dark hair and fair complexion were her strong points of beauty. "We have several projects you can start on."

"I don't think I'll be able to do them," I looked around the room very nervous, and afraid. "I've never been very good at art projects."

"Sure you can. Just start in and you'll be surprised at what you can do. Here," she picked up a little ceramic bunny. "Would you like to try to paint this?"

"I'm not very good at painting," I backed away.

"Just try." The strong sure voice sounded friendly, but stern. "You sit right here and decide what color you'd like to paint it. I'll be back in a little while." I sat there staring at the rabbit. *I don't know what color to make it,* my helpless self took over. *Let's see. Pink? No. Maybe I should make it purple. I don't like purple. Red is dumb . . .* I giggled thinking of that stupid card that I had sent to George. *Oh gosh! I don't know what color to make it!* Maybe brown. I ran my fingers through my hair trying to decide. *She's going to be back soon. What color? Oh! What color?* I was nearly in tears from the inability to make the decision. The girl came back quite a while later.

"Well, did you decide what color?"

"No." I looked up at her in confusion. "I just don't know. I can't decide!"

"You'll have to pick a color," the girl demanded. "We'll be closing up before you have a chance to paint it."

"Oh . . . oh, well . . . gray!" I picked it out of thin air. "Light gray . . . " I gained a little confidence.

"Oh! That's a pretty color," the girl raised her eyebrows questioning my choice after all that thought. "Now, here's your brush and paint. This is a little dish of water to clean your brush with."

"I don't think I can do it."

"Sure you can. Just try."

I started to shake. *I have to try,* I whispered to myself. Slowly I picked up the brush. It dripped on the figurine, and the table, then the floor. My hand trembled.

"Just relax," her firm, patient voice guided me.

"I'll start on the tail," I suggested. "Then the paint won't drip in its face." After a few strokes the paint went on easier. I began to enjoy the project. "I think that's the best painting job I ever did," I sat back to admire it. "Can I have the pink paint?"

"Sure." The girl brought me the jar. I painted little pink whiskers, pink in the ears and a little pink nose. "That's really cute!" the girl chuckled. "Now, that wasn't so bad, was it?"

"No," I smiled with pride. "Can I do another one sometime?"

"Next time. Now you can go home and decide what you want to make next."

The bunny project gave me the first sense of accomplishment that I had had for a very long time. I was so proud of it! "See what I made?" I showed my dad when he came home from work.

"Did you make that?" he was impressed. "How did you do that? Did you make a mold or carve it . . . ?"

"Daddy, I didn't make it. I just painted it."

"Oh. You just painted it . . . " his eyes welled up with tears. I knew that he had had greater expectations from me.

In only a few weeks I was becoming more stable. Living with

my folks was peaceful. Responsibilities were at the minimum. The young mother across the street babysat for Betsy when I went to my appointments. The visits to the mental clinic were helping me immensely. They told me that all I needed was a chance to gather myself together. The therapist informed me that I was "making giant strides" to recovery. With each piece of artwork that I created, she advanced me to something harder.

I became very anxious to see George so that he could see my progress. I was feeling so much better. In fact, I was beginning to wonder if our relationship was for real. It all seemed so strange and far off. More days went by, but no word. Maybe he's having doubts, too. *I think I'll go down to the cabaret*, the urge hit me one evening. *Maybe someone there has heard from him. Anyway, I feel like getting out for awhile.*

It was the same old place, the same old music, the same old stupid silly chatter, but going there was like an adventure. Each time it was like maybe I'd meet my knight in shining armor, or maybe I'd see George and find out that he was just a phony. An unusual group of very well dressed young people came prancing through the door. They were a bunch of college kids. On second glance I noticed a familiar face . . . "Charmaine!" I waved. *My gosh, I haven't seen her for years.*

"Pat!" Charmaine came over to talk. "Gee it's been a long time. Come on. Join us."

"Well, OK," I agreed. I felt a little out of place, though. They were all so perky and high functioning.

"I went back to school after my divorce," Charmaine tried to fill in the years. She was a very attractive gal with long black hair that was always in place. Her cheeks were always rosy, and her clothes always looked like they had just come out of the store. She was the daughter of my flute instructor when I was in grade school. Charmaine had played the violin. "I got a divorce you know," she clued me in. Charmaine had married right out of school like I had. "My mom is raising my son, so I figured I'd finish my schooling."

"I'm divorced too," I confided in her. Bob and I had lived a few blocks from Charmaine's parents. In fact, I had gone to their home several times for a music-fest when I was still married to Bob, during the days when he was attempting to be a public figure. Her father so enjoyed getting people together to play instruments. He could play most of them. "Do you come here often?" I changed the subject not wanting to go into my state of affairs right now. "I've been here quite a bit, but I've never seen you."

"Once in awhile." A young man was tapping her on the shoulder. Charmaine excused herself to dance. I sat there watching everyone enjoying themselves. I didn't fit into any of their conversations. Besides, they looked so young. *I wish I had stayed by myself*, I moaned to myself. *Oh, well. It's a night out, anyway.* The long evening wore on slowly. I wasn't asked to dance once. *I've gotten fat*, I thought to myself. *I guess I don't look too good lately.* Abruptly, the lights came on signaling, time to leave! Everyone jumped up to put on their coats. "You got a way home?" Charmaine asked me.

"Oh, yes." I started to get up. *I really don't, but I don't want to go with them. I'll just call a taxi.* I had finally unloaded Clarabelle to a couple of kids that wanted to tinker. Clarabelle was becoming senile, didn't have much to offer anymore. It was still cheaper to call a taxi, which I seldom needed to do, then to run the car.

Just then, a guy came walking in the door. "Gee, the place is closing already!" he scratched his head. His eyes met mine. "Hey!" he waved his arm in the air. "You."

"Yeah?" I answered.

"I just got off work. How about going with me to get a bite to eat?"

"No, I don't think so," I walked by slowly.

"Come on," he grabbed my arm softly. "Sit here a minute. Please."

He's a little different, I thought to myself, *but he seems awfully nice.* By this time he was jumping up and down, almost throwing a tantrum only in a cute way. "Please go out to eat with me.

Honest, I'm all right. I just want you to come, you know, for company. This is my only night out this week. I work nights. Come on."

Charmaine whispered to me. "You're not going, are you?"

"I think I am," I whispered. "He's pretty nice. He's sort of interesting."

"OK, if you say so," she started out the door. "Get in touch with me."

I nodded.

My new friend's name was Glenn. *Another Glenn!* I smiled remembering the last one, another special guy. It was a rather long ride to the after hours joint. He had brought me to the same place that Ron had brought me to over a year ago, that first heavenly night when we had met. It was darker, though, and the music played softly. Glenn was a quiet, friendly guy . . . the tall, dark and handsome cliche' fit him well. Candles flickered quietly as we ate our chicken. Now and then we chuckled over the way we met. "I'm kind of embarrassed now," he snickered. "I just hated to waste my only night off."

"I don't blame you," I smiled. "I'm relieved you turned out so nice."

"Who me?" he pounded his chest.

"Yes. I think this has been very enjoyable."

"Yeah! So do I. I wish I had some wine or something, but it's after hours. Hey! You know, sometimes these guys sell under the table if you pay enough."

"I don't think so," I warned.

"Hey, fella, come here," he flagged down a waiter. "Here's ten. Can you sell me some wine or something?"

"No. I can't do that," the boy backed away.

"Well, I tried," Glenn grinned. "Come on. We'd better leave." He wrapped up the leftover chicken in a napkin. "You can bring this home. I'd ask for a bag, but I think we'd better get out of here just in case that kid makes trouble."

After that night Glenn called about every other evening on his break. He never had much to say, but he just wanted to talk.

I was flattered. *I wish George would treat me right. He's never treated me that nice. In fact, Glenn reminds me a lot of Ron.* A warning began to churn inside of me. *You're getting confused again.*

On one of his nights off Glenn stopped over to meet my little girl, Betsy. Sitting her on his lap he read her a magazine full of pictures. Little Betsy was very friendly, she always had been. In fact, I used to be concerned about it. She used to know almost everyone that walked past our old house. When I would go to the grocery store, invariably, there would be someone there saying, "Oh, hi Betsy." They all knew her. Glenn was becoming a closer, and closer friend. He even made a comment about wanting to bring me to meet his family in Portland. I just took the comment with a grain of salt. My loyal mind was on George. *I promised him,* I would warn myself.

Christmas wasn't special this year. I was upset. I still hadn't heard from George. *He could've at least send me a post card,* I moped. Bob had taken the boys for Christmas, then the day after Christmas I opened up the old house for a week. The only good thing about the holiday was that my boys were home for a visit. They were tucked in bed this night. I lay on the couch watching TV sipping on a glass of iced water. I tried to fill my need to drink something, and water seemed to be the answer. Suddenly, though, as I reached for the glass my arm wouldn't move where I wanted it to move. I tried to brush the hair away from my eyes as I lay back down in a fearful daze. My hand wouldn't go to my head but went in a completely different direction. *Oh, God! What's happening to me?* I sat up holding my chest to feel my fast heart beats. My heart was beating so hard I feared it might beat right through my chest. *I've got to call someone.* I ran to the phone book. I knew my therapist's name. *Why do these things always have to happen in the middle of the night?* I swore, feverishly trying to turn the pages with my arms out of control. It was hard to dial. The minutes were like hours until I was comforted by the soft voice that always calmed me. Through tears of relief of getting some help, I explained what was happening. "Oh, dear, I'm so sorry you had to experience this while you were all alone. Don't worry about it. It's good news. Your brain has been sort of stuck in one mode, like a record that's played over and over again. The grooves in it will dig deeper, as though it's in a rut. Your brain is being used in different areas now, and is slipping out of the rut. You'll be OK."

She was right. The next day was as if it had all been just a bad dream. The reality of the following day was the boys' excitement as they busied themselves trying to find all the stuff they had left behind. "Look! My football!" Robert brought it downstairs. "You kept it!"

"Of course I kept it," I wanted to cry. *They think I've abandoned them or something . . .* "We'll all be back together here pretty soon. I promise. OK? All your stuff will be here."

"Yaaay! They ran back upstairs to their room."

Oh, I wish I could get on my feet! I had missed the boys so much! It made me feel like such a failure not being able to cope. *I need some help. Dear God, I wonder if George was just pulling my leg?* I thought over the previous weeks. *He pops up, then disappears, pops up and disappears.* I threw my cigarettes down on the table as I lit another one. A knock came on the door. *It's George!* I ran to the door. Glenn stood there shyly. "Is it all right if I come in?"

"Sure. Come on. I was just sitting here not doing much. The kids are in bed. I was feeling a little lost."

"Good. Here's a beer. I'll try to cheer you up."

After a few beers we started to get very comfy and giddy. I threw my head on his lap looking up at the ceiling. I felt the need to set things straight with Glenn. *It isn't fair to him.* I made the decision to explain how things were with me. I started to tell him about George and how we had planned to get married. "I don't care, though," I tried to make light of the whole situation. I could see him looking down at me, wondering if what he was hearing was really true. "Well, I do care, but I think maybe I shouldn't." I looked up into his face.

"Maybe you shouldn't," Glenn leaned over to kiss me.

"Yeah! Maybe I shouldn't. He's nuts anyhow. Of course, I'm nuts, too," I chuckled. "You know what? One night our bodies lit up. Honest! The whole room was dark, and our bodies turned pink. They lit up like light bulbs!"

"You're too much," he laughed. Only this time his laughter was not hearty, but it contained a nervous tone. "You are toooo much." He kissed me again. It was a passionate kiss.

"You'd better watch out," I giggled, "maybe you'll light up."

"I'm not going to worry about it," he squeezed me tight. He kissed my neck. He was breathing hard.

"I don't think we'd better," I pleaded.

"It'll be OK," Glen kept on.

"Please, Glen," I whimpered.

"It'll be over in a minute."

Soon we both lay there quietly. "Why didn't you want me to do that?" he asked me softly. "Is it because you were afraid of . . . ?"

"Yes. I don't take the pill. My doctor doesn't believe in them for unmarried people. Anyway, it's against my religion. It'll probably be OK, though."

"Well, I'd better go now. I'll see you," he kissed me good-bye.

The next morning I was surprised by a phone call from Sister. "Why haven't you brought the children back?"

"Oh! I thought that I could keep them until after New Years."

"Oh, no, dear. We can't have that. Their father wouldn't approve. You need to bring them here right away."

I started to cry. *They're treating me like dirt. I'm the one who has custody of them. He's got them all impressed with his importance like he always does. Oh, God. I've got to get back on my feet. I might lose them!* The tears flowed down my cheeks as I prayed for strength.

Just a day or two after I had brought the boys back to the foster home, I continued onward with my therapy at the clinic. I had been tediously working on a crushed glass project. It had taken much patience and time to accomplish the task. I had come a long way from painting the bunny rabbit. This time I had chosen a pattern of two knights facing each other, one on a white horse, and the other on a black horse. Their lances were pointed at each other as in battle. I carefully planned the colors using a chess game as a guide. The blanket which one knight was sitting on was checkered, so, I colored it in reds and blacks like the checkered board which the chess game is played on. I chose to decorate the white knight vibrant blues and golds. As I progressed with the picture my heart talked to me. *I know what I'll do, I'll put this in the boys' room and fix their room up using these colors. That will help them to know that I've been thinking about them all this time.* It did turn out very nice. In fact, the clinic had a day set aside each year to sell the things that were made there. I was offered twenty-five dollars for it, which to me was amazing. "No", I shook my head. "I made this for my boys."

I chose a new project of making feather flowers. While I was wrapping a stem in green florist tape, a nurse announced to me, "You have a phone call, Pat."

"For me?" I was very surprised.

"Guess who this is?" the bouncy voice sounded over the phone.

"Bill?" I acted dumb. *I think it's George,* I guessed and wished all at the same time.

"Who?" Now I knew it was him for his voice was full of suspicion.

"Brother Bill?" I repeated to regain his trust.

"Oh! Your brother! Nope. Guess again."

"Is it you?"

"Yeah! It's me, George. I'm at your folks' house. Your mother asked me to call and see if you want a ride home."

"Sure. I was just finishing up with my project. I'll be ready."

"George hopped out of the car to greet me throwing his head back in great laughter. "I surprised you, didn't I?" he bellowed.

My! What have we done to each other? my heart sank. I couldn't help but notice that his beautiful white teeth had turned green. His hair had been left to grow haphazardly and was quite long. *I'm so fat! It doesn't seem to bother him, though.*

"I'm going to stop and get the biggest pizza in the place," he put his arm around me squeezing me to himself. "This is a celebration! It's New Year's Eve, you know. I just got in on the tug. What a haul!" he exclaimed. "Clear up to Alaska and back. We had the silliest looking Christmas tree on the boat. It was fun, but I'm glad to be back."

"Me too," I snuggled up to him. "I've been accomplishing things too."

"Yeah, it sounds like it. I think I could use that place you're going to, too."

The pizza was spread out on the table looking very inviting. "Boy! Does that look good!" George hollered, "Come on, everyone, dig in!" Mom and George dug into it, but I couldn't.

"What's the matter? Eat!" George pulled me to the table.

"I'm sorry. I'm not hungry," I apologized.

"Come on. Don't be like that," he handed me a piece.

"Honest. I can't. I guess I'm just excited. I'll just sit here and watch you guys eat it."

"OK, whatever you say," he sounded a nervous chuckle. "I'm excited too, but I'm huungry!" The pizza disappeared very quickly. As we lingered there at the table George pulled out a picture. It was the first I had seen or heard about his little son. "This is Tiger!" George laughed. "Isn't he quite a boy?"

"Oh! He's darling. He looks like you. How old is he?"

"Five. Someday I'm going to send for him."

He was a perfect age to fit into my family, just two years younger than Blake and two years older than Betsy. *That's why he was in love with that "Tiger" beach towel he had, it reminded him of his little boy. Maybe there's an explanation for all of the crazy happenings over there . . .* I hoped.

"Hey! Do you think it would be OK to invite my dad over tonight? I hate to leave him alone on New Year's Eve. We can have an engagement celebration!"

"Sure! That sounds great!" Now I knew that he wasn't just

playing around. "I'm so glad you're back. I missed you so much!" I breathed my first real, deep, relaxed breath. I hope he knows that I meant the things I had said, too.

"I'll go get dad and be right back in a couple of hours." He flew out the door.

It was a short while when he returned with a little short man dressed warmly in an old sweater, a scarf wrapped around his neck. His father was a sweet elderly man. His speech was very broken. "Dad's from Austria," George began by speaking for him. "You wouldn't believe that this little guy could have a big thing like me for a son, would you?" George put his arm around the short man of about five foot four inches tall.

"Oh, go on," his dad good-naturedly pushed him aside and sat down. "I don't know what I'm to do with that boy. Where's my pipe? Ah, yes. In my pocket it is. It is nice to have New Year's Eve so nicely, though. Thank you, OK?"

My father was unusually sociable as George's father chatted on and on about who knows what. Mom was interested in getting acquainted with George who had brought pictures of when he was in the service. The most impressive one was with him wearing a parachute as a jet pilot.

The visit was interrupted by a phone call. It was for me. "Oh, no . . . " I was stunned. Some weeks ago I had gone to the bar near my home where George and I had bar-hopped, that first night we had met. I had been in a quiet mood that night. A friendly fellow began talking to me. He was evidently a person who had been born with a retardation problem. *I must've given him my phone number.* I tried to remember that evening. I did remember that he had offered to take me out on New Year's Eve. This was that date! I declined the invitation as best I could, but it was something for George to immediately suspect.

"Who was that?" he asked laughing in an I-caught-you tone of voice.

"Oh, it was nothing. It's OK, really." I didn't want to explain to him about the fellow. In his eyes he'd be labeled a nerd.

"Hey! We can't have a celebration without champagne! Let's walk to the store." George said changing the subject.

"I'll get my coat." I started for the closet.

"You'd better bundle up good. It's raining cats and dogs outside," he called after me.

It was wet, but the night air was so refreshing on the momentous occasion. "I love to walk in the rain," I lifted my head into the huge wet drops.

"We're going to look like two wet rats when we get back."

George stuck his tongue out to catch the drops. "Who cares?" We splashed through the puddles, running and laughing hand-in-hand. "I'm going to build a fifty five thousand dollar house!" George hollered at the world dancing in the rain, his arms outspread. I'm going to show those damn Slavonians that an Austrian can do it too! I knew where he was coming from. He had been raised in an area that was settled mostly by Slavonian fisherman. "I'm going to have a fifty five thousand dollar house!" I thought it strange that every guy with whom I've really been involved had parents from the Old Country. Bob's parents were from Yugoslavia, Ron's parents had come over from Italy, and now, George's parents were from Austria. *That's weird!* I shrugged off the deep thinking for this special evening.

"You got big dreams, don't you?" I laughed.

"Boy! Have I got dreams! Big ones! Long ones! Colored ones! Hey! Do you play the organ?"

"The organ?"

"Yeah! The organ."

"Oh! You saw my mom's organ, I'll bet."

"Yeah. I guess I did."

"I just plunk on the piano."

"I like to play the organ."

"Do you play the organ?"

"No, but I like to play."

He's getting goofy again. I withdrew a little. Fortunately the store was in sight now. Our hair hung down around our faces and over our faces in wet strands. Our clothes were drenched. George pulled me into the doorway of a shop. "Honey, just be true to me, and we'll have it made."

I gulped hard. *I've been truer to him than he has to me . . . that darn double standard that our men were taught. Oh, I wish that had never happened last week with Glenn,* remembering to the evening when he had become forceful. "Why didn't you at least write to me over Christmas?" I blurted out.

"There's no place to mail anything out on the sea, you know. Besides I knew I'd be back soon." I stared deep into his eyes as we held each other close. *I can be true to him, now I know he's on the level.*

The champagne was flowing. Everyone was chattering and laughing, stopping just long enough to sing *Auld Lang Syne* as the Times Square scene was coming over the TV. The old year was over, and a new one was in. "I've got to go to work tomorrow," George grabbed his father's coat ushering him to the door. "Honey," he gave me a big kiss. "I'll be getting in touch. You know, Jesus and I are pals. I'm going to do Him a favor, and then He's going to do me one." His eyes filled with tears as he said good-bye.

By the word of TRUTH,
By the POWER of God,
By the armor of RIGHTEOUSNESS
On the right hand
And on the left,
By HONOR and DISHONOR,
By EVIL report by GOOD REPORT
As DECEIVERS
And yet TRUE.

2 Cor 6:7 (KJ)

Chapter 15

There's Strength In Hope

The doctor's office was a rather busy place. One could tell that he had a large practice. Since I had just taken his name from the phone book, I had no idea what to expect. The friendly middle aged doctor set me right at ease as he invited me into his office. I could see that he had a sense of great pride in his loved ones for there were pictures of his family adorning his office everywhere.

After the exam he formed the fearful words in his mouth. "Yep, you're pregnant. As far as I can determine, that light menstrual period you described was your first month of pregnancy."

I sighed in relief. "Then it's George's!"

"What?" The doctor immediately took the hint that there was more to this story than met the eye. "There's something going on here, isn't there?" he stared through me. "What is it?"

"I'm in a bit of a mess," I confessed, "but now I'm so relieved. I'm engaged to this guy, and I goofed when he was gone. Now I know it's his. What a relief! It's only been a couple of weeks since I messed up. I'm so thankful, doctor."

"Take this as a lesson," he smiled with warmth. "I'll see you in a month, then we'll talk further."

I was so excited! I knew the phone number to call, for George had given it to me that last time he had called. The tug had pulled in for a short stay to load up so he hadn't had enough time to visit me until they pulled out again. I recalled that conversation. "You really like working the tugs, don't you?" I had asked.

"I love it," he said with great emphasis on the "love". I was happy for him that he had found something he loved to do even though I knew that I'd have to get used to his being gone a lot.

I have to get in touch with George! I couldn't wait to tell him the news! Plans went racing through my mind. I contacted the tug boat company. "They just pulled in," the man said. "I'll have him call you right back." I waited by the phone. Five minutes went by. Then ten minutes. The phone rang.

"Hi!" His calm voice was warm and sincere. "We just got in, but then we have to go right out again. Is everything all right?"

"Oh, yes," I giggled with glee. "Gee, I wish I could see you."

"I'll see you just as soon as we get back."

"George. How would you like to be a daddy?"

"Yeah. We'll talk about getting married when I get back."

"I mean a real daddy."

"What do you mean?"

"We're going to have a baby. That's why I think it's important we talk as soon as possible."

"Oh, yeah. I got to go now. I'll see you."

Time crawled by sluggishly. Two months passed. I was still faithfully going to the clinic. I hadn't told anyone about my dilemma, as yet. George didn't call like he had promised. Finally, my false hope of his return turned into great despair. "I need to talk to someone!" I told the nurse at the mental clinic. "Please! I have to talk to someone!" I was pacing the floor wringing my hands.

The head nurse walked in. "What's your problem?"

"Problem? Oh, God! Help me, please help me," I begged.

"Come on. Sit down here and we'll talk it over."

"I'm in such a mess!" I fell down in the chair. I was choking back tears. "I've got to talk to someone."

"Calm down, now. It'll be all right. We'll help you."

"No one can help me."

"It can't be that bad."

"I'm pregnant," I shouted. " . . . and George won't come back."

"I see." The nurse stroked my hair. "It's a terrible break for you. You've done so well and come so far."

"Yeah! Right smack into a bowl of shit!"

The nurse was quiet for a time. "We'll help you out through this time. We'll use this time to get you on your feet. You can keep coming here until the baby is born. Everything will turn out OK. You'll see. We'll make one decision at a time."

"I can't tell my mother!" Just the thought of it brought a torrent of choking sobs. "All I ever wanted was to make her proud of me. All I've done is disappoint her."

It had taken quite a bit of counseling just to give me the strength to go back home. I remained quiet throughout the evening not knowing how or when I could tell my folks. I even looked up live-in housekeeping jobs or babysitting jobs that were available in the newspaper, just in case my mom couldn't handle it. In my silence I suddenly realized that the house was quiet. Mom, Daddy and little Betsy were in bed. I was sitting at the kitchen table. The small lamp over the stove shed warm streaks of light over the paneled walls. I was deep in thought as I sat glued to the spot trying to figure things out. *It's been two months. I still haven't heard from him. Oh! Why did I tell him over the phone?*

My mind pondered over all the events of the last couple of months. George's father had called me during that time frightened over the fact that he hadn't heard from his son. It was then that I realized how much he depended on George to keep him company. He was the old man's major access to the outside world, now. "I worry," the elderly man had confided.

"I'll come right on over," I had offered gladly. "We'll have a little visit." I wanted to get to know the special little man and genuinely wanted to help. *After all, if he's to be my father-in-law,* I had figured, *I should learn to be supportive of his needs.* Of course, this was before I had found out that I was pregnant. As he had offered me a cup of coffee we began to exchange stories.

"Georgie is a good boy," he filled me in. "His first wife no good," he shook his head in disgust pulling right up to my chair as if to whisper a big secret. "Do you know what happened?"

"No." I admitted. "George and I haven't discussed our pasts, yet. We just know that we've both been through the mill."

"When he was in service, his wife got pregnant", the old man quickly filled me in. "He thought it was his. She let him think so. He went to hospital to see little baby. His son was little Jap! See? Best friend was Japanese guy, and he got Georgie's wife pregnant while he was overseas. It messed him up. Never been the same."

I began telling him about my dilemma. The dear old man earnestly listened, half way between caring and being nosey. "Wow! No end to trouble you youngsters get into." He had shook his head. "My, my, my."

I went home still hoping that I would hear from George. But there I had to come back to the reality of my present situation. I couldn't sleep. I couldn't even pace. I found a way to calm myself. I got into my parent's bottle of whiskey. *They won't mind if I take just one drink.* However, after thinking about the mess I was in, I decided the problem was large enough for two drinks. *Men! That's all they think of is sex.* I threw my hands up in the air as I now paced the floor. *Boy, it's different if they have sex, they're expected to. But if we mess up, we're whores and unfit mothers, and . . . .* I poured another drink. *God knows I've been trying. George, Oh, George, please come back.* I tried to choke back the tears by running to the cupboard to pour another shot. *I've got to get a grip on myself! I've got to get this straightened out! What am I going to do? I'll have to tell Mom. Oh, God! It'll kill her! What a mess. They've tried to help me. Now I slap them in the face with this! Oh, George! Please come back.*

The next morning I woke up not wanting to face the day. The very first thing that came to my mind was the fact that I drank up all of Daddy's whiskey. He and Mom religiously had one drink before dinner ever since I could remember. *How am I going to explain this to Daddy?* I wanted to just go back to sleep and forget all about it. However, then all of my other problems came to mind. *How am I going to tell Mom I'm pregnant, let alone Daddy . . . Ohhh,* I moaned. The only good thing about it all was that I didn't even have a hangover. I got up feeling physically fit. I decided to face my mother before she looked in the cupboard to find the empty bottle. *Might as well get it all over with at once, I geared up my courage.*

Mom was surprisingly calm about the baby. " . . . and I haven't heard from George since," I finished the nightmare news. I filled my mother in on all the sordid details. She just sat there shaking her head. "You know, dear, I prepared myself for this years ago when you girls were growing up. I think every mother of daughters thinks about what she'd do in such a case. I decided I would just love you and help you through it."

It was such a relief for me! But I had to press things one step farther . . . "now for the next confession. Mom, I have something else to tell you." I tried to have mercy on my mother for she was not prepared for much more, either. "I drank Daddy's bottle, last night."

"All of it?" mom looked horrified.

"I couldn't sleep last night worrying about how I was going to tell you. It killed the pain."

"Don't you feel sick?"

"Nope. I feel fine. In fact, now that I've told you I feel better than I have since I found out. Oh, I wish George would come back."

"You're going to have to tell your father."

I had to catch my Dad just as he walked in the door before he found out for himself. "Daddy, I've got something to tell you." I used all of my feminine charm that I could muster up. "I drank your bottle last night."

A look of astonishment took over his face. "All of it?" he asked.

"Yep."

"Weren't you sick?"

"Nope. Daddy I'm so sorry. I promise that I won't have my cocktail before dinner until you figure I've paid for it. OK?"

"Yeah. I guess that'll work. But that doesn't solve what we do for tonight." He walked into the front room trying to control the fact that he was feeling a bit huffy about it. I could hear my Mom talking to him in a low tone. *Oh, no. She's telling him about the baby . . . .*

"When is there going to be an end to all this . . . ?" I could hear Daddy bellowing. Suddenly, he came storming into the kitchen, grabbed his hat and coat and left. I knew where he had gone. He needed his bottle.

The terrible dread days were over with for awhile. I had come to grips with my dilemma and was enjoying a newfound peace, even though I also felt very alone in a very cruel world. One of those lonely days brought a rather surprising moment concerning little three year old Betsy. She was on the floor playing with her doll. I got down on the floor and played with her. "Here, Mommy. Put this dress on my baby," Betsy handed her doll over.

"There you go." I straightened out the little dress, "Oh, doesn't she look pretty? She's almost as pretty as you." I picked up my little girl and gave her a big hug. Everything will be all right, sweetheart." I rocked her, "Mommy will make everything all right. You know what? We'll go and visit your brothers this weekend. We sure do miss them don't we?" I sighed. "I hope you kids never have to go through anything like this." Betsy toddled off into the next room. I began picking up the room, straightened out the papers, emptied an ashtray and picked up a few toys. Betsy came back.

"Here, Mommy," she handed me a little blue book. "This is what you're supposed to use for George to come back." I know the expression on my face told of my surprise as I took the book. It was a prayer book, a long novena. This is the book Mom uses for her novenas. I thumbed through it. *How did Betsy know? How does she know what's on my mind?* My body tingled with awe. *She doesn't know. Perhaps it was God.* My mind scanned through years of muddled teachings. I remembered something about the purity of little children. *Maybe God was talking through Betsy, through her purity. No, I'm not nuts. I know I'm not nuts.*

This gave me a newfound strength in the hope of God's goodness. I started in on the long fifty-four day prayer. I was not to miss one day or I would have to start all over again. With my new found faith I resumed attending church. The first time I went it was all about novenas . . . a coincidence? The message was that the answer could be yes or no. "We must put our faith in our prayers and God," the priest explained, " . . . for He knows what's good for us. We must do our best and accept His decision. If the answer is no, we mustn't falter." My petition was, "Please let George come back."

One night a silent voice asked me, "Which George?"

I was too busy saying all the prayers. "Oh, you know which George," I giggled, stubbornly ignoring the request.

The mental clinic had assigned me to a support group of young women, who for one reason or another weren't functioning, the same as me. I was extremely nervous the first time, feeling very self-conscious. A friendly, rather large girl smiled a big smile as she sat down next to me helping me to feel more at ease. *I wonder if these girls are as crazy as I am?* the thought ran through my mind. Since I had been in the clinic I had resigned myself to the fact that I had gone crazy, even though I felt deep down that I was perfectly sane. It was easier to go along with the program. Now and then I would remark, "I get scared that I'm going to go oops again", referring to the time when my soul had risen up over my body that morning in the kitchen. When I talked like that there would be stone silence.

I was especially interested in a pretty young girl sitting on the floor in the corner. She was in a fetal position, evidently unable or unwilling to speak. The woman leading the group was a very warm, intelligent woman. She knew enough to leave the girl alone, but careful to include her in the conversation as one of the group. Another young woman, sort of a quiet person, but also very friendly beneath her shyness, always had an intelligent answer after much prodding from the therapist.

The friendly smiling girl, Diane, and I became fast friends. We found out that we were both living with our mothers during this difficult time. Our futures were very uncertain, and we both had children about the same ages (she had girls and I had boys). Betsy was the exception. Diane didn't have a little one. As our stories unfolded we both admitted to problems with alcohol.

Diane and I struck up a close friendship for a time. She invited Betsy and I to dinner at her mother's house. The best time we had together, though, was when we went on an AA overnight camping trip. It was a rough and ready group of people: couples, singles, kids from both lifestyles. A wonderful time of sharing around the campfire. They made their fires in the easiest way possible. A big log was put on the fire and moved on down as it burned. Sort of like chewing an ear of corn. Everyone was extremely unaffected and natural. It was my first real experience around a campfire and one I never forgot. Since that time a campfire signified to me a place of refuge, of communication and relaxation.

The occupational therapy room at the hospital was full of people. The project for the month was making flowers from feathers. It seemed to be a very popular one. There were so many different kinds of flowers that could be made from the brightly colored feathers. There were very large ones on down to delicate little wispy ones. One woman down at the end of the table was singing, . . . *Oh, what a beautiful day!* She danced around the vase of colorful organized phony flowers, "I feel so much better today since the rainy season is over," she explained to me as I enjoyed the little scene. "Rain makes me so depressed! I can't stand it." *Rain makes her depressed?* I couldn't believe it. *She's in the hospital because of the rain?* "Maybe I won't have to come back much longer, at least this year," the woman said prancing around the room. She then stood back to admire her creation, rearranging this little flower, exchanging it for a bigger one. "There. That's done . . . and it didn't take any rain!"

While I tediously taped together some bright orange feathers with a dainty yellow one placed in the middle to give the appearance of pollen, a younger girl walked by me carrying a teapot she had made. She grabbed three of my flowers and plopped them into her teapot. "These are the Blessed Trinity," she confided to me softly. "The teapot is collecting all their graces and pouring them over us all." She tipped the pot over my head. *She's whackier than I am . . .*, my head started to spin from all of the weirdo reactions. I suddenly realized that I could use this time to say some of my strange thoughts out loud. After all, wasn't I supposed to be crazy?

"I think I'm going to go oops again . . . " I sighed. After having tested the water I went on. "Jesus married me and George. No, maybe not. That's why I'm pregnant. No, that's not why." That last blast seemed to bother the instructor considering that the confusion was becoming contagious.

"Come on, Peggy, give Patti back her flowers and we'll go see if lunch is ready."

That episode started a whole surge of thoughts concerning the Blessed Trinity again. I would lie awake at night trying to feel what faith felt like in my heart, then hope which I was learning a lot about these days. During these little heart-drills, it was as if the door to my heart would open, it would open to a deep feeling of wellbeing, of love, the same feeling that I had felt toward Ron. Now, I realized that God was love and I would try to realize God. As I put my heart through these "exercises" I discovered that I could not feel one without feeling the other. They were all magically interwoven within one another. It was a process of opening my heart. I was afraid of becoming hardened. *There's no faith without a faith in something hoped for,* I thought a little deeper on the subject. *No hope without hoping for something desired or loved. No love without God. You can't have one without the other . . .* With this I decided that I had explained enough to myself about God and knew that I would never fully realize Him. *We can't conceive of all He is . . .*

My visits to the doctor were scheduled more often these days. I was getting well into my pregnancy. "What's the news this time, doctor?" I asked after my examination.

"Well, I've been able to pinpoint your pregnancy. You're not as far along as I thought. You'll have the baby in August."

"It can't be. It has to be July!"

"No, it's August."

"It can't be. It could be September, maybe."

"No, August." The doctor was so sure.

"It has to be either July or September." I shook my head.

"Then it has to be September," the doctor committed himself.

"Oh!" I sat back in my chair in shock. "Oh! Oh!"

"Oh, yes. There was a problem, wasn't there?"

"This makes everything different." I could feel the blood rush from my head leaving me pale. *I'm so thankful George didn't come back, now. Oh, God . . . what about that light period of just a spotting? That had never happened to me before. That's why the doctor thought I was farther along with the pregnancy. Are you playing tricks on me?*

The doctor's voice began to sound through the din of my heavy thoughts. "Have you thought of adoption?" the doctor put it very bluntly.

"No. Now maybe I will. Everything is different now."

"I'll give you the name of this lawyer if you decide in favor of adoption. He'll handle everything. You won't have to worry about bills or anything. Think about it, OK?"

"Yes, doctor, I'll think it over." *It's Glenn's baby! I can't be mad at him, I led him on. I think I hurt him. Funny he never called me back, he must've suspected that I had gotten pregnant that night. He told me where I could find him. I can't now. He'll wonder why I didn't look him up earlier. Oh, well, maybe he was just another one of them "pretty birds".*

Charmaine showed up on my doorstep one evening. "I thought you'd like to go out with me for a drink," she invited me. I was honored that someone with her apparent high-functioning ability would bother with me. I checked with my folks to see if it would be OK with them. Betsy was ready for bed. The nod of approval came.

The two of us spent the evening catching up on each other's lives. "All of those days of Bob running for public office and stuff seems like another lifetime, or something. I can't even relate to those days, anymore," I admitted.

"My mom has been helping me raise my son, or I wouldn't be able to go to school, or anything," Charmaine admitted. The more we chatted, the more we discovered those things that we had in common.

"I have a secret," I finally felt comfortable enough to divulge my pregnancy to my "new" old friend.

"Oh, Pat. You don't have to go through with it, you know. I have a number you can call."

"Abortion?" I could hardly form the words with my lips, let alone consider it.

"Think it over," Charmaine folded her fingers over the piece of paper which could free me from this terrible dilemma. I went home thankful that I had a prayer life set up for me in the novena. Afterward, with great fervor, I threw away the paper. *Dear God, I promise that one good thing will come from all of this: my little baby.*

At the mental group I decided that the young girl who refused to speak was just afraid. She was sitting on the floor. I sat there on the floor with her sitting squaw style during the session. I attempted to zero in on her opinion as topics unfolded in conversation. I pushed the right button. I mentioned the place where I had gone to dance that first night when I had met Ron, down in skid row. "Do you go there?" the young woman asked.

"I usually go dancing closer to home, but I've been there."

"Oh! That's where I met the guys I'm staying with. I have five kids. They live with a foster family. I want them back." Her whole story came out so fast that it surprised even her. With that she decided she had said too much and became mute again.

However, that was the start of a friendship that began to remind me of the incident with Missie. We went dancing. Darlene ended up with a bunch of trampy guys, leaving me alone. Then she went one step farther: "If I could just store some of my stuff in your house . . . " she had suggested. I backed off.

"I think I created a monster." I said to our therapist.

"You've done a super job. You've opened her up. I can handle it from here."

"Can you tell me what they call my condition?" I asked.

"Well, when you first came here we had you down as manic-depressive, but now we've changed it to "acute mental exhaustion.""

"Oh! Then I wasn't nuts?"

"No, not in the usual sense. Could I ask you one thing, though? What's all this business about you going "oops," you keep referring to?"

"Oh, I can't explain it. I was sitting at the table and I went up out of my body once, that's all. I found out that material things aren't all that important . . . "

"Oh, well, you learned from it anyhow . . . " I could tell that it made my therapist do some thinking, too.

"Will I always be like this?"

"Perhaps, to a degree, but you probably won't ever get this worn out again. You'll know the danger signals, and know when to get help or get away from the problem."

"All I know is that I have a hard time sleeping at night. I tried some pills that the doctor gave me, but they knocked me off my feet. My mother had to carry me to bed."

"Is there anything that does help?" the woman asked.

"Beer. It takes about a six pack. But then I can sleep."

"Well, dear, you're not sick enough for the strong medication, you might as well continue with that as long as you keep it under control."

As time went by, I found that my mental attitude had been helped by walking a lot. I took the bus to the hospital that was several miles away. When I would go to take the bus I was too nervous to just sit and wait. Gradually, starting on down the avenue from one bus stop to the other I found that I could easily walk all the way, and it made me feel better. So now I left a little early with full intention of walking all of the way.

As I sauntered along this day, I turned on to the little shopping area, which alerted me to the fact that I was getting close to the hospital. Then I noticed a familiar face from the past. It was Bob's sister! The one I didn't get along with. Oh, no, I felt warning flags waving inside of me. *That's all I need is for them people to find out. I haven't gained any weight, though. I'll just hold in my stomach and keep walking.* As we passed each other we completely ignored the existence of one another. *Whew!* I let my stomach out. *I'd better pull in my rear now, though, just in case she turns around. Someone's protecting me,* I thought to myself quietly thanking God for getting me past that situation. *I really don't think anyone can tell, yet. I was scared I'd have to hide out, but here I am. In fact, Mom told me the other night a neighbor had commented about how much thinner I looked. I guess my prayers have been doing some good. Just think, I was praying so hard for George to come back, now I'm glad he didn't, since I talked to the doctor.* I could just barely see the hospital up ahead. *This walk is pretty far.* I wiped the sweat from my forehead. The noon sun was hot beating down on me. *I'm going to adopt the baby out.* I had made up my mind. *It's best for the kids. Bob will just try to make more trouble. He took the boys out of the home for the summer, but I'm getting them in September. Oh, my God! How am I going to do that? Now I know the baby is going to be born later than I thought! I'm supposed to take the kids back that month! Oh, no! What am I going to do? Bob will get them! God, please help me . . . .*

The street became shady under a long line of trees whose branches waved over the sidewalk bringing a cool breeze. *This feels so good,* I sat down on some steps to rest a minute. My thoughts got deeper. *I wonder if George knew the baby wasn't his.* I remembered back to how angry Frankie had been that night at my house. He had perfectly described this predicament, from George's own words. *He had said that he thought George was talking about himself . . . it sure fits. Then when he had told me about the deal Jesus had made with him. Maybe that's why he wept. He knew! Somehow he knew! Oh, God, I'm so sorry . . . but you knew what was going to happen.*

I was so thankful for the lawyer my doctor connected me with. Very quickly and painlessly I arranged for the adoption. I would not see the baby (for I knew if I did I would never be able to give him or her up). The only decision I was asked to make was, "What religion preference do you have for him to be raised in?"

I didn't say Catholic. Instead I said, "I want him to be raised a Christian, so he'll know why Jesus lived and why He died."

Spiritual matters seemed to be very popular in the mental clinic. People who were confused about God, or just plain misunderstood by others, seemed to be a top concern among those populating the mental wards. It was another day of the same, tying feather flowers together. It took a lot of them to make a bouquet. A little nun was sitting across the table. She was quietly working, then decided to share a thought. "We all have our little mysteries in our hearts," she assured me. "I would like you to have this. It's a scapular, a relic from St. Theresa, my patron saint. St. Theresa will help you." She pressed it into my hand.

"I can use all the help I can get, Sister. Thank you.

After lunchtime was over, everyone resumed their projects. The room looked like a florist's shop as the bouquets grew. Soon a nurse flew into the room. "Has anyone seen Sister? Has anyone seen Sister?" She ran from room to room. "She's disappeared! I can't find her! I hope she hasn't gone to the Chapel! I'm supposed to keep her out of there. She thinks she's talking to God."

"Maybe she is," I suggested.

The nurse gave me a dirty look. "They don't make saints anymore," she snapped.

Why not? I wasn't convinced even though we had been taught that very fact at the Catholic School. *That little Sister is the most humble little person I've ever seen.* It wasn't at all unusual to see the little nun picking up after others, emptying wastebaskets, wiping off tables, etc. *She's given her whole life to God, for heaven's sake. Sometimes I wonder who are the "nuts", the nurses or us?* It wasn't long before Sister came quietly walking into the room.

"Where have you been?" the nurse sternly demanded.

"I've been in the garden," she winked at me.

"Oh! That's a relief!" the nurse sighed. "I thought maybe you were in the chapel," she shook her finger at Sister.

"Oh, no," Sister smiled. "you told me not to go there anymore. I can talk to Him in the garden just as well."

I had gotten away from the feather flowers and was now finishing up painting a ceramic fruit bowl. I was busy painting the yellow lemons. There were many of them. My therapist suggested, "Why don't you make some of them limes . . . you know, lime green."

"I hate green, "I shook my head. I had seen one like it at Diane's mother's house and was trying to make it like that one.

About this time an interesting letter came in the mail for me. Granted I had gotten over my anxieties very well, but, this surprise was too much. It was postmarked Viet Nam. Lonnie had evidently written the letter under great distress. *"I'm holed up here on a hill. Everything is quiet now, but we are expecting an onslaught any minute."* My heart cried out for his safety as I read it. But then he went on . . . *"Pat, I've been thinking. When I get out of here maybe we could get married and take the kids back to Tennessee. I know I could support you and the kids. Now, I know this sounds kind o'far out. Please answer me. I don't care if you tell me to go to hell. Just please answer me."*

I just sat there holding my head in a daze, as if I had a big headache. It certainly was a big heartache. *Oh, no! Just when I just started getting things figured out. If I accept his offer then I won't give up the baby. But, what if I do that and he gets killed or something? Then I'll be in a heck of a fix.* My stomach churned as though I might throw up. *I can't face this decision, now. Oh, Lonnie, Lonnie . . . I'll write to you after everything is done. I need time to think.* I pushed it out of my mind unable to face the decision. I never wrote that letter.

I told my therapist about how upset this letter was making me and not being able to make any kind of decision. She could see that I was faltering and needed to be very busy at this time. "Here's a ceramic stein," she offered me my next project. "They're very popular".

I had noticed several of them being painted by higher functioning ladies who came in just to paint. Most of them were painted in brown tones. *I want mine to be different* . . . I stepped out into more dangerous territory with my decision making. This was about as dangerous as I could handle. *I'll color the background green,* I smiled thinking about how then I could use yellow and red hues over the green to create an autumn effect for there were hunters on the stein. Autumn it had to be! My therapist was shocked when I said I wanted to paint it green.

"You've got to be kidding." She couldn't believe her ears. "Do you remember when I suggested making some of the fruit on your fruit bowl limes instead of lemons? Do you remember what you said?"

"No. What did I say?"

"You said that you hated green!"

The two of us arrested our frustrations by laughing until we cried. It was so ironic.

In my strangeness I was finding my friendships to be too much to handle along with my other problems. It seemed with each friendship more problems were presented to me to solve. I was amazed one evening when Charmaine stopped over very excited. "Pat, we have to go some place and talk." When we got off by ourselves Charmaine confided, "I've met someone that I'm really interested in! I just have to tell you about it. I love the way he dresses, kind of classy," she continued describing him with big goo-goo eyes. "He wears big thick glasses, though, probably half blind, he doesn't even have a job. The thing that sort of worries me is the night I met him he stood in front of my car saying, 'Please help me, I need you.' Now, I need some help. Please help me, Pat! What do you think I should do? I really do like him a lot!"

I didn't know what to say. "Seems like you need somebody that can help you a little." But then I remembered back through the years that I had known Charmaine and her family. She was quite an eccentric person in her own right as was her father, an eccentric musician. I could remember how he had held a long cigarette filter between his teeth as he would listen to me play my lesson on the flute. He wore those fancy two-toned white and brown shoes with little holes in the toes that were only fashionable among snazzy musicians. I didn't know what to tell her. *Now that he's passed away, maybe Charmaine needs someone eccentric in her life.* "Charmaine, only you can answer that question." All I knew was that, as for me, I needed someone that would be able to help me out a little. *Maybe Charmaine is more self-sufficient . . . no, her mom has just handled a lot of her problems.*

My mother helped me to help myself. She surprised me with a gift one day. "Dear, I've saved up the money I receive playing the organ for weddings and funerals. I want you to have it to buy whatever you need to get the house ready for you and the kids." I pounced on that offer real fast! Within hours I found myself on the avenue with Betsy, hanging on to her hand wondering, *now how can I stretch this money?* The first item on my list was a davenport. The one I had was full of holes. Then I wanted to fix up the boys' room for them and hang my picture of the "chess knights." I had looked up the whereabouts of a couple of second hand stores downtown in the phone book. Little Betsy ran along beside of me trying to keep up with me. I was in high gear. I came to notice that each shop seemed to have certain things that were their specialty, but no davenports, at least none that I could afford. But, to my amazement, after much digging around, I found two very sturdy desks. That's what the boys' need in their room. Desks. They've outgrown their toy boxes. One was fifteen dollars and the other ten. They weren't much to look at, but I was finding that with paint a little creativity could go a long way. "My brother-in-law will pick them up," I told the man.

Even though I was happy with my find, I still hadn't found a couch and we were getting tired. We stopped to have a cup of soup and a Coke. As we finished up our lunch I remembered about the Good Will which was only twenty blocks or so away. *They had some nice couches there for cheap the last time I was there.* "Come on, Betsy," I coaxed the tiny girl to try to be enthused along with me. "We're going to buy a davenport!"

We started on the long trek. I had been used to walking long distances, but little Betsy was getting mighty tired. Finally she stopped. "Mommy, I don't want to walk no more."

"Come on, honey, it's just a little farther."

"Mommy, I'm tired! She then put her hands on her hips. "Do we have to carry the davenport all the way home?"

The humor was precious, but it was a flag to cool it for the day. As we finally entered the Good Will, there in front of our eyes was a soft overstuffed davenport. It wasn't the most fashionable one, but it didn't have any holes, and it was comfortable. More than that the price was right. Thirty-five dollars. "I'll take it," I told the man. I was even more excited when I found out they would deliver it. "Now we can go home, honey"! I took my tired and very relieved little girl by the hand and slowly led her to the bus stop.

My mother became very enthused in my project when she found out how much I had bought for my money. The two of us busied ourselves painting the boys' room. Mom painted the desks red. She had taken some springs off of her old chaise lounge that was falling apart and repaired the sagging springs in the beds. I painted the walls a deep blue that matched the fabric I had been able to purchase with the money which was left. I had bought enough material to make bedspreads and curtains to match. I had hoped to find some blue material with a splash of red in the design, but the best I could do was to buy a red and white denim with a design of blue boats in it. The final touch was the red football helmet which I carefully placed under the desk.

Time was running out. "What are you going to do about the boys? The baby won't be here when school starts." To Mom it was becoming an impossible situation.

"I'm going to go home with them when school starts," I answered full of confidence.

"You can't do that, can you?" My mother was baffled at the decision. I had done some deep thinking about the situation. Mostly I had faith that my prayers were going to help me through this, so I decided to pretend that nothing was wrong and go through with accepting the boys home in September.

PAT BRAHMAN

The big moment came. The car pulled up in front of the house. I ran to the porch, my arms outstretched. They ran to give me a big hug. "We're home!" I held them to myself in very long bear hugs.

"I hope we're never separated again," I kissed them.

"I plan on seeing them every other weekend, bitch," Bob approached me. I was wearing a mou-mou type dress so that he couldn't see my dilemma. I had been very lucky to have gained only a few pounds. Probably all the walking had helped along with the fact that I had been overweight before I got pregnant.

"We'll see," I grabbed the boys. "Come on, kids, let's go see the surprise mommy has for you." Their eyes sparkled with excitement when they saw their new room.

"Wow! They jumped on their beds, bouncing and shouting. "This is neat!"

"I planned for this day for a long time," I smiled. "I'm all better now." I picked up Betsy and gave her a kiss. "We're going to be a family." *Now if the baby would just get here. I wonder how I'm going to get through that mess without their knowing.*

"You had a beautiful boy," a soft voice whispered as I was coming out of the anesthetic. "He's a real football player type!"

I opened my eyes to the kind face of my doctor. "You didn't think I was going to give that nice couple a pip-squeak, did you?" I smiled groggily. I felt so proud.

"You'll probably be able to go home tomorrow if you follow instructions."

"Really? That's great!" I perked up in disbelief. I had always stayed in the hospital at least three days with my other children. "I'll just tell the kids I had a hemorrhoid operation. That'll be perfect." That was not far from the truth because I was suffering terribly from them.

"You rest now. "I'll see you tomorrow." As the doctor walked away he remarked, "Keep your chin up."

There were four girls in the room. *Oh, I hope they don't bring the babies in,* I hoped to myself. *It'll nearly kill me to see a baby right now.* The girl across from me introduced herself. "I'm Shirley. You had a boy, huh? I had a girl. Sue over there had a boy and so did Karen. I guess I'm outnumbered."

"When do they bring the babies in?" I asked.

"I don't know." Shirley became quiet.

"You haven't seen your baby, yet?" The other girls sat up listening.

"No," Shirley said slowly.

"Hey, what's going on here?" A woman who was sitting across the room remarked. "There's something fishy here. Don't you girls know that you're all in the same boat here?"

"Are you adopting your baby out?" Shirley asked me.

"Yes. I was so scared to think that they might bring a baby in here."

"If they brought a baby in here, I'd walk right out that door," Karen piped up. "I just want to get this over with. It's been a nightmare!"

"OK girls," the woman tried to calm everyone down. "Now you can all talk it out and get it out of your systems."

The rest of the day and into the night we chattered a million miles a minute explaining what had happened to us. I remained somewhat quiet for I didn't want them to know that I was crazy. In the morning, the papers were signed and I went home looking forward to a future with much hope in my heart. *I got through this with your help, God, now, please, give me the strength to do better.*

It is of the
LORD'S MERCIES
That we are not consumed . . .
Because
His COMPASSIONS
Fail not.

Lam 3:22 (KJ)

Chapter 16

To Know Sorrow

My sister-in-law, Joyce, and brother Bill aided the transition period for my starting all over into a fresh new existence. They moved in with the kids and me while I was getting back on my feet. They had a new baby. I was concerned that being with a new baby would upset me, but I was so happy to be back home with my children and back on the road to a new life that fortunately it didn't upset me. I had the spirit of a surrogate mom, I guess. At least I psyched myself up in that manner. I felt a pride that I could hand over a beautiful child to a childless couple. I named my little gift-child, Raynold.

The fact that I told my children that I had had a hemorrhoid operation was very believable. Dear Joyce helped nurse me back to health. The window seats in my old house came in very useful. There she placed grandma's very large old stainless steel pan filled half full with tap water and with the boiling water from the whistling teakettle heated it up to a very hot sitz bath temperature. There I sat several times a day. We laughingly called it my throne. "Oh, I see she's on her throne again," my brother would laugh as he wearily came through the door after work. Joyce was tired after taking care of not only my needs but also those of the kids. She, too, was exhausted at the end of the day. One night Bill asked her if she had washed his pants for work. She had washed them but they weren't dry (I still had never owned a clothes dryer).

"Here blow on them," she cried. We all got a laugh out of it, but it was then that I realized just how much it had taken out of them to help me at this time.

I made my last visit to the clinic to thank them for helping me through a very hard time and to show off my new me as I unveiled my new figure . . . or old high school figure . . . which had come back very nicely. Now, it was just the kids and me against the world, again. However, I was also fearful once more. I was finding that my greatest fear was to be stuck in the house with no connection with the outside world. I had my children and friends, but no life of my own. I had become very shy in groups such as PTA, etc. for I felt I had nothing in common with the parents there. I felt that I was very low functioning and being a divorcee made me nervous around married women. It upset me when they complained about their little headaches of "what size sleeping bags they were going to buy this year" or "Susie has too many clothes, I'll have to have another closet built for her."

My only friends were those who were in the same boat as I was, and they had just as many problems to share as I did. This time around, though, I was less depressed or at least was handling it a little better, except for one thing. The past was still not completely past. I was bogged down by the slight chance that George just might come back. Deluded by the hope that he had known what was going to happen and therefore might be waiting for things to get back to normal, I couldn't shake the off-chance that just, maybe I had had faith in my novena which I had finished without missing a beat. Yet, I had the sense to know that this hope of mine was extremely far-out. I couldn't help myself, though. My faith was almost all I had left to go on.

To start my new life off I was given a gift of encouragement. The bookkeeper at the hospital called. *Oh, no,* I moaned under my breath, *I'll never be able to afford it, whatever it is . . .* The woman was anxious to inform me, "We've been looking into your situation and found that you were more help than you were a problem, therefore we're giving you an 80% discount." The full amount of my bill was $80! "Thank you," my heart was a'hummin'.

I wish I could go to school to work in that field. I think I could make a difference.

The kids and I fell back into our normal routine. The kids were back in their own school and we all had a new sense of hope for a brighter future. One night there sounded a strange knock on the door. I had been expecting no one for I had cleared all of the late night doorknockers out of my life. It was Kevin, Charmaine's boy friend. They had spent quite a bit of time together until now. Charmaine had made a big decision to find a job since she was no longer going to school. "Have you heard anything from Charmaine?" he asked nervously. I could see his red swollen eyes, in spite of his ultra-thick glasses, signaling to me how troubled he was.

"Yes. I got a letter last week." I clued him in. Charmaine had answered an add in the paper for a secretary job in the Aleutian Islands off the coast of Alaska. She felt that she needed to get away and think.

"Did she say she was coming back?"

"No," I stated bluntly. "Did you guys have a fight, or something, to make her pick up and leave?"

"I don't know what happened." He paced the floor.

"She told me she loves you, if that helps any." I tried to calm him down knowing how much it hurts to get left behind.

"Did she really?"

"Yes, she did. She'll be back, Kevin."

"Boy, am I glad I came here. That makes me feel a lot better. How have you been doing?"

"Real good." I positioned myself on the couch to relax. "Sit down, take a load off your feet," I pointed out the overstuffed comfortable chair. "I've been doing some thinking, though. You know that guy I was going with before? George? Well, I've been thinking of getting in touch with him. But I don't know how. I don't want to call him at work. He's not at his dad's."

"I went to school with him," Kevin announced.

"You're kidding." I could barely believe it.

"We were in the same class. I'll bet I can find out."

"Do you think you could?" It seemed like fate to me.

"Watch me." He went to the phone book and called George's father. He found out where George was that easy. He called the number his father had given him. A man's voice answered. "Is George there?" Kevin asked.

"No. He should be back pretty soon."

"Who am I talking to?" Kevin winked at me. He held his hand in an OK gesture.

"His roommate. Can I give him a message?"

"Yes. This is Kevin. We went to school together. I'm on the planning committee for our high school reunion. I'd like to talk to him."

"Sure. I'll have him call you back as soon as he gets here."

"Good deal!" I laughed. "That was neat! Clever, boy, clever!"

"That guy said it would be awhile," Kevin explained. "I'll run down to the store and get a six pack of beer. We can have a few while we wait." Kevin left. He had no more than made it a block away when the phone rang. *Oh, no!* I trembled. *He called back too soon. What'll I do? I'll just have to answer it.* I gathered myself together. *Here goes,* I picked up the phone.

"Hello?" I said softly.

"Hello, is Kevin there?"

"No, he just stepped out for a minute."

"Who is this?" his voice asked suspiciously.

"Hi, George," I sighed. "It's Pat."

"Oh! Hi." There was silence. "How've you been?" he asked with much tenderness.

"I'm doing pretty good. You know, George, you did the right thing not coming back. I just wanted you to know."

"Oh. Yeah. Well, thanks for telling me."

I became fidgety. "Do you have any feelings for me at all?" I blurted out.

"No. Not one," he admitted.

"Well, I figured that's the way that would be," I sighed, "but do you think we could have a talk sometime?"

"Yeah. Sometime," he moaned.

"George, are you still nuts?"

"Yep. I'm nuttier than ever."

"Oh," I trembled.

Kevin came walking through the door. "Did he call already?" he whispered to me. I nodded back. "Here, let me talk to him," he grabbed the phone. The language was terrible. They were fighting over the phone. "Do you have any idea what this girl has gone through because of you, you S.O.B?" Kevin hollered. I walked to the front room. That's a boy, Kevin. *Kill it. Stomp on it. Kill the last ounce of hope,* I muttered. It was over. Finally.

Too soon, though, the relief turned to frantic pacing. *I knew it. I knew it. Why should it be such a shock?* I walked around the room, wringing my hands. *If only he'd see me one time, I could explain. He could explain all that weird stuff that happened. What should I do?* It was as if I didn't know where to rest my heart. My maternal emotions were healed after I got my family back, but I had a spiritual void for my relationships had taken on a spiritual overtone. I threw my hands up in the air feeling so helpless!

"Calm down," Kevin came into the room. "There's other fish in the sea."

"I know. But I can't kill the hope. I've lived on it for so long."

"He's no good for you anyhow," Kevin assured me.

"I know what I'll do. I'll open the Bible. Sometimes it helps me to just open it and read right where my finger lands. See?" I held it up so he could witness what happened. I closed my eyes. My finger went down the page and stopped.

He is gone. He shall not return. The words stared me in the face.

"You'll never believe this," I showed Kevin.

"That's spooky," he shuddered.

"It's true." I limply sat in the chair. "It's true."

Knowing that I needed some kind of help immediately, the very next day I looked up an article in the paper that someone had told me about and called the number. It was a Parents Without Partners group. Luckily their monthly meeting for new members was that very night. At the meeting I discovered that there were groups which met at all different nights of the month. In fact, their calendar was pretty full, something happening almost every night. I tried to get active in a support group and attend those functions where you bring your children. Once a month there was a Friday dance that was most popular. Almost everyone tried to attend. It was a time to mix and meet one another in a more personal way. The focus was supposed to be on family, but the dance was one night out just for mamma or daddy.

The first function that I attended I brought the kids to a swimming party. It was a little awkward, though, because I didn't know anyone. The second function I went to was a dance. Before the music even started I heard a "yoo-hoo". It was an old friend of my sister's. Just as we sat down together to catch up on stories of our broken lives, I was asked to dance by a handsome young man dressed in a gray suit. It surprised me that a suit didn't bother me that much any more. *I guess I've accomplished something,* my heart sang. I found out that he was a schoolteacher and lived close to where I did. After a couple of dances he invited me to take a walk around the block being as how it was an unusually warm fall evening. The big maple trees with their red-golden leaves umbrellaed the sidewalk where we paused long enough for him to plant a warm friendly kiss on my hungry lips. We slowly strolled around the block chatting a little about our lives, both of us careful to leave our skeletons in our closets. At the end of the evening he asked if I would like to go home with him. I didn't want him to think I was easy, now that I was trying to turn over a new leaf. Besides I had my own car. "No, I think I'll go home by myself," I answered.

He got a little huffy and walked off.

He left me sitting at the table nursing a drink. *Why did I say no? I really don't know what to do anymore. I don't know what's proper or improper.* A friendly older man, Wayne, sat down next to me noticing that I was nervous. He seemed harmless enough and was full of empathy and understanding. He was good tonic for me, as I attempted to be for him. I felt safe giving him my phone number and address for he simply needed companionship as I did.

Even though I had still rid my life of late visitors, another strange knock came to my door. It was late at night. *I thought I got rid of the doorknockers.* I moaned. "Hi!" Barbara greeted me. "Did I disturb you?"

Barbara was an old friend of mine. In fact, she had been a bridesmaid at my unfortunate wedding. She had married a fellow who had also given her a bad time in their marriage, "peeping tomming", and more. She was a beautiful little thing, blonde hair with big dimples, and a complexion of snow. She was divorced several years before I was. I hadn't seen much of her in recent years. Barbara always found out where I was through my mother.

"Come on in," I ushered her into the front room.

"Gee, your place looks nice, it looks like you really care. I know this is a bit unusual, coming over at this hour, but I just got the strongest urge to Ouija. Would you Ouija with me?" She pointed to the box she had under her arm.

"I've never done it before," I warned.

"Come on, let's try it," Barbara walked to the dining table. "Come on."

"OK", I sat down. "What do I do?"

"Just put your hand lightly on the marker. Like this." We settled in with working with the board just to get the feel of it. Suddenly, the marker started to move. R-O-N it moved around the board. I-S . . . Barbara repeated the letters. D-E-A-D . . . the marker spelled out. "Ron is dead," Barbara said out loud. "Does that mean anything to you?"

Barbara knew nothing about the happenings in my life in the past few years. I had cold chills all over my body. "Yes. It does. How did you know about that?" I snapped.

"I didn't do it. It moved by itself. It's kind of scary, isn't it?" she remarked slowly. "This board has never worked for me before, I just felt I had to try it tonight for some reason."

We just looked at each other, aghast, trying to get a grip on ourselves.

"Do you want to tell me about it?" Barbara asked me.

"Oh, I just got it in my mind that Ron, a fellow I was seeing over a year ago, is dead. That's all. I didn't know whether to believe it or not."

"Oh. That really is spooky," Barbara stammered. "Let's try it again. Ask it something."

"O.K." I closed my eyes to think. Then . . . "Will I get married?" Our hands were on the marker. It wiggled a little this way and then that way.

"You're moving it," Barbara accused me.

"No, I'm not. What's it doing?"

"Nothing yet." Barbara stared at the board. "Now just relax." The marker slowly moved to the S. It wobbled to the O. It moved wildly for a minute then back to the O. Slowly it crept over the N.

"Soon," Barbara squealed. "It said soon!" Boy, if you get married before me, I'll be mad," she shoved the board across the table at me.

"Oh, come on, Barb," I laughed. "That's silly. I don't even know anyone."

"Well, it makes me mad."

"Come on, you ask it something," I coaxed.

"Let's see," Barbara hesitated. "What's going to happen to me and Don?" she blurted out. The marker was still for awhile. We concentrated harder. A-M . . . it moved directly. E . . . it swirled around the board and landed on an S. It circled the letter, then slowly sat on top of it. "A mess," Barbara cried out. "Did you move it?"

"I didn't move it, Barb."

"A mess!" Barbara repeated.

"Do you think this thing is from the devil?" I asked her.

"I don't know, but I'm never playing it again." She gathered up her ouija board and stomped out the door.

Wayne, the older man I had met at PWP, called on me the very first week. We mainly chatted and got acquainted. He showed me how to make a delicious hot toddy . . . right up my alki alley. It wasn't long before we both discovered that we had a deep belief in God, a personal knowledge of Him and His wondrousness, but neither of us had a good insight into Biblical truths and had a dislike for religion. It was then that I found out the depths of Wayne's pain in his fight to understand God's dealings with His people. As he explained about his wife's illness with cancer and the helplessness and hopelessness he had felt during those last hours with his wife, he frightened me . . . maybe he had a screw loose!

"I could've healed her!" he cried aloud. "I put my hands on her body. I could feel the heat radiate from my hands! If there's anything I can't stand it's for someone to call me a healer!" His face was red with anger. "She died!" he cried out.

He's got things all screwed up, I winced. *God is the one that does the healing. I think that this experience made him crack up a little.*

I tried to console him with whatever words I could. I told him, "If we didn't feel sorrow, we couldn't feel joy. There are mountains and valleys." I didn't know exactly where the words came from, but he was impressed.

"I think it's very refreshing to find someone with the wisdom you have at your age. Maybe that's why I love you." I felt like crying. *He's so good to me, but I don't love him, what am I going to do?* I just ignored his little comments and clung to his friendship.

My friendship with Charmaine, which had been on hold since she had gone to Alaska, stared me in the face when Charmaine showed up on my doorstep one day just back from the Aleutian Islands. "Would you come to the airport with me? I have a friend who's coming in with the rest of my luggage. I had too much, so, he offered to take my trunk because he was traveling light." Fortunately it was over a visitation weekend when I was free.

I was impressed with Charmaine's jet-set type life style. I was even more impressed when I saw her friend. He was a bright, successful, handsome man obviously with eyes for Charmaine. They were good friends. Charmaine had no romantic interest in him at all. *She must be as crazy as I am,* I tried to figure it out. We were left free to chat as her friend departed on his next flight. "I got your letter about Kevin spending the night," Charmaine glared at me. That was convenient for you, wasn't it?"

"Oh, Charmaine. I let him stay on the couch. He had helped me so much! He did kiss me, though . . . on the hand." At that we both started to laugh.

"Isn't he something?" Charmaine's eyes sparkled when she talked about him. "Who do you know these days that would kiss your hand?"

"How was it in Alaska?" I was all ears to hear about it.

"Dangerous! Pat, I was working with the Mafia!"

"Oh, you're exaggerating," I only halfway doubted her. I knew how eccentric she was. Maybe it was true.

"No. Really! Those guys had guns in their desks, and they wanted me to be their mistress. When they started that kind of stuff, they even promised me my own little island. Can you believe?" She shook her head. "I high-tailed it out of there. Actually I snuck out. I'll never answer an ad like that in the paper again!"

My nights had been free of things floating around the room and voices talking, etc. It was a relief to know that those experiences were from the past. Even though they were interesting and, yes, beautifully exciting, I didn't want the problem of trying to figure out such things. I just wanted normalcy in my life. It was the middle of the night. I had been sleeping comfortably when suddenly I was awkwardly awakened by a vision of Wayne at the foot of my bed chatting with me. It was a few moments until I realized that he wasn't really there. I sat up so that I could see him better as he said, "do you want to see something very few people have seen?" The vision came closer as he extended his arm to show me his hand. It was full of blood! The dark red substance slowly dripped from his palm. It was grotesque. As the blood fell in drops his hand then turned to blue and green hues and withered away. "Oh! It makes me sick." I groaned. Hiding my head in my pillow I moaned my way back to sleep.

I was awakened by the telephone ringing. Daylight had crept through my window alerting me to the fact that this was another day. I got to the phone just in time. "Patti, guess what?" It was Jeanne, my sister. "I have a friend who works at the vocational school. She says that she just took down a note from their bulletin board advertising a car for sale for thirty-five dollars!"

"Oh! Thirty-five dollars! Tell her to hang on to it for a day or so until I see if I can come up with the money! Thirty-five dollars! It's a miracle!" I was dancing around the room before I even hung up the phone.

That evening who should show up but Wayne. I was still all in a dither about the car. "I'll loan you the thirty-five dollars," he offered without even wincing. "Better yet, I'll give it to you if it's a good deal."

"I can't accept that from you," I declined. "By the way, guess what I dreamt last night?

After I told him exactly what I'd seen, he was deeply moved.

"You know what that means?" he asked me. "Trust me. Let me buy you that car. Trust me."

The very next day he drove me to the elderly woman's house. She was too old to drive it. It was a '47 Chevy, just like Clarabelle was, only it was in better shape. The only thing wrong with it was that the battery was dead. Wayne took it out. "I'll get it recharged. You talk over the deal with the owner. I'll be right back!" Off he went. It took no time for him to get it back into the engine. It purred. We drove it around the streets a little. Wayne became very excited! "Look at the pick-up this thing has! It's like a new car! I'm going to buy it if you don't!"

That statement almost persuaded me to let him help. Up to that point I was still holding back on allowing him to help me in that way. I wanted to feel independent and not beholden to him. However, my mind was fully made up when I saw the woman's name on the registration. Unabelle Stark! Stark had been my grandmother's maiden name on my father's side. And Unabelle . . . well, it was going to be the name of the car. Unabelle. Clarabelle's twin!

Charmaine was fast becoming like Carol's twin. She showed up one evening. "Pat! Can you come with me? Let's go out someplace different. Kevin is driving me nuts."

"What's the matter?" I asked as I tried to figure out a way to get a sitter for the kids.

"I don't know. Maybe he's in the occult, or something. I can't explain it. I swear, it's like I feel like some kind of spirits are there sort of watching us when we make love. It's weird."

"I had some weird things happen, too," I snickered in disdain.

"How do you get out of these things once you're in them?" Charmaine asked me. "It seems that if you follow the path of your life, you can't change the direction no matter what you do."

"I know," I nodded. "Sometimes I feel like a puppet, or something. It's like it's already planned out ahead of time."

"Let's go out on the town and forget about it."

Charmaine and I took off after the boy next door came to baby-sit. We went to the downtown area hoping to find a place to dance. As we headed down to the usual places we heard some fantastic music coming from one of the side streets. "Let's follow it," Charmaine suggested as she began to play detective. We ran toward the area where we could hear music coming from. "It's up one more street," she pointed. "Come on." Running up the hill to the next street and down half a block we came upon the spot. "It's coming from in there."

It was a small tavern. The music was live, a three-piece combo that really knew how to play the blues. We shyly sat down in a booth before we realized that we were in a black bar. A couple of guys were in the booth next to us. As we waited for our pitcher one of them came over to introduce himself. "Hey! Can we join you?"

"Sure!" Jim sat next to me and Zach sat next to Charmaine. They were very good conversationalists, which made getting acquainted with them a lot of fun. Nothing was ever said about the blackness or whiteness of one another. We just had a very enjoyable time. It didn't seem very long at all that the place was ready to close, though. "Hey, girls. How about coming to a night spot with us?"

"You promise you stay with us?" I was a little nervous about it.

"No problem, babe," Jim took me by the arm and the four of us climbed into a car that was parked down the block.

On arriving at the joint we were greeted by a guy at the door checking to make sure he knew whoever was coming in. The room was very large, tables jammed in. The place was packed. We sat down to order some food. While we were waiting we were served bottle beer. Suddenly, out of nowhere a very drunk big man came over to our table. "Did I hear someone say the word nigger?" he bellowed, his fists ready to take aim. Jim tried to push him away. I couldn't believe that this big black guy would start something with no provocation at all.

"The only one in this place using that word is you," I pointed my finger at him.

Jim looked at me as if to say, "Cool it, babe." It was decided that we should leave before there was any more trouble. "He's just drunk," Jim explained. "He's really a nice guy."

The next stop was his apartment. Charmaine and Zach were in the front room listening to records and getting better acquainted. Jim and I lay on his bed looking at pictures. "This is the picture of my ex-wife. I met her when I was stationed in Germany when I was in the service." I could see that he was proud of her beauty. "It didn't work out . . . "

"Yeah, I was married once. I've got three kids. It's been rough."

"Hey! Would you consider marrying me?" Jim asked me.

"Are you serious?" I couldn't believe my ears. "You don't even know me."

"I know you . . . " he gave me a very sweet meaningful kiss.

"Jim, it's inviting. But to tell you the truth, I have so many problems. This racial thing would be just one more problem that I don't think I could handle at this time."

"Well, here's a magazine with my name and address on it. If you change your mind just write me a note. OK?"

"Uh-huh," I nodded. "Now I need to go home."

After that night I thought about him from time to time. *He was such a nice guy, probably one of them "pretty birds".*

A few nights later Charmaine and Kevin appeared at my front door. "We've decided to get married," she announced. "Can you come with us and be our witness? One of the guys in Kevin's apartment house is going to be his witness. We've got the license. Now all we need is a ring of some kind, even if it's just a cigar band." I remembered my old wedding ring in my jewelry case.

"Here. It's a wedding present for you. The only thing is, it has had bad luck."

"Oh, I'm not superstitious." The wondrous bride slipped it on her finger just as though it were made for her. "Come on, let's go."

Kevin's friend, Tom, was a really cute guy. He had offered the use of his car along with an offer to chauffeur the bride and groom to wherever they wanted to go within city limits. Kevin and Charmaine sat in the back seat. "OK, where are we going?" he asked for directions. Kevin ushered us in and out of the judge's chambers . . . a very quick service. "Now where to?"

"Now, we're going to the cemetery," Kevin began giving the instructions on how to get there.

"The cemetery? On your wedding night?" Tom looked over at me as if to say "Are they for real?"

"Take him there," Charmaine ordered. "You said you'd take him anywhere he wanted to go."

"What's he going to do there?" Tom was a little nervous.

"I want to ask Charmaine's father for her hand in marriage."

"What are you going to do if he says no," Tom kidded. "You've already tied the knot." At that, Tom and I took a quick glance at one another choking back the laughter. Feeling as if we were being real good sports, we went along with it.

At the cemetery the beautiful grounds didn't have any kind of spooky feeling to it even though it was late at night. The grass and trees shown of deep dark hues of greens turned to bright greens. Streaks of light from the moon shot down through the trees revealing bright colored flowers here and there much as a spotlight would do. "Stop right here," Kevin ordered. "Now which one was it?" he asked Charmaine.

"It's over there," her patience was wearing thin.

Kevin got out of the car making his way through the trees and graves until we could no longer see him. Then we heard it. "I love Chaarmaaine . . . I love Chaarmaaine . . . "

"Oh, for crying out loud," Charmaine didn't know whether to laugh or to get mad. The three of us tried not to notice the spectacle he was making out there in the graveyard. We began telling jokes. Anything to get our minds off of the strangeness of what was happening.

Suddenly through our laughter Kevin showed up at the window. "You guys are laughing at me," he cried. "I'm serious. I respect her father. I just wanted him to know that I'm trying to ask him for her hand, that's all. It's not funny."

"We weren't laughing at you, Kevin," Charmaine grabbed his jacket and pulled him in the car.

"Now where to?" Tom was almost afraid to ask.

"We have to take Pat home."

After the usual beer stop we ended up having the "reception" at my house. I was relieved. At least I was home safe. Tom and I sat on the couch getting acquainted, laughing at the ridiculously funny evening we were experiencing. The soft romantic music was a wonderful background. Kevin and Charmaine were sitting together in one chair smooching. Something happened. They began to quarrel. "Don't give me that, Kevin . . . " Charmaine was yelling.

"Charmaine! I'm sorry. I love you."

"Sure, Kevin."

"I love you, Charmaine," he pulled her of the chair.

She pushed him. "I love you too, Kevin."

Tom and I were wishing we were invisible for we couldn't help but laugh at what was happening just a few feet away. "Do you hear some rather awesome music?" he kidded.

"Awesome," I giggled as I sipped another slug of beer.

"Kevin, that's enough!" Charmaine screamed. Kevin tackled her by her legs. *Splat!* She hit the floor! By this time Tom and I weren't surprised at anything those two did. We just ignored what was happening. Pretty soon Charmaine started crying. "We've got to leave," she whined. "I think he broke my arm or collarbone, or something."

We felt bad. "Oh! You were really fighting?" Tom asked.

"Of course we were fighting! You guys just sat there and let him beat the crap out of me!" Charmaine screamed. Kevin carefully and angelically laid her coat over her shoulder so as not to hurt her arm. "Thanks, Pat," she said snidely. "You going to take me to emergency, Tom?"

"OK if I stop by sometime?" he gave me a little kiss.

"You think that Patti is a great gal, don't you?" Charmaine painfully made waves. "Do you know that she got pregnant, had to adopt the baby out because she didn't even know who the father was?"

Tom looked at me in surprise.

I nodded. "It's true."

"Oh." He left with the already bedraggled newly weds. I knew he wouldn't return.

After that, I was happy to see Wayne. He was a wonderful friend. "Get the kids ready," I opened the door to an enthusiastic man who appeared 20 years younger than he had when I had met him. "We're taking the kids skiing for the weekend. You don't have any plans, do you? I'll take you to my house on the way. We'll stop there for dinner and sleep so that we can get an early start in the morning!"

His home was a modest house that he had built himself. I found out that he was a contractor. "I was really down and out," he explained to me. " . . . . then out of the blue it dawned on me, I can do anything that anyone else can do. So I bought this property real cheap. I built this house first, and now I have contracted to build those houses over there." He parted the curtains to point them out to me. Sure enough, there were several houses in different stages of being built.

On his piano was the song, *How Great Thou Art.* "Oh!" I exclaimed. "I love that song." I sat down on the piano seat and attempted to play it. I was able to somewhat plunk it out on the keys. Wayne was impressed. "You play it better than I do." Then he handed me a precious book. It was a book which society was just beginning to take to its heart, a book of spiritual love, but a book without Jesus. It revolved more around the universe as being heaven. Society was in stages of flirting with the eastern cultures probably because Christianity had become stale from incomplete teachings. The title of the book was *The Prophet*. "Read this", he placed it in my hand. "Keep it."

After dinner and a visit with his older daughter, we left off his younger daughter at a friend's house. She was a little older than my boys were. When Wayne finally brought me and my tired little brood back to his house, he had already figured out the sleeping arrangements for our little family. Wayne also had a son about my age whom I didn't meet. In the deep night Wayne came tiptoeing into the bedroom where I lay. "What do you want?" I wiped my eyes. "Is it morning already?"

"No," he carefully placed his body laying on the very edge of the bed. "How about a kiss?"

"No," I squirmed. "Wayne, you told me there wouldn't be any hanky-panky."

"I know. You don't have to do anything," he smiled. "You can't blame a guy for trying. I have a question to ask, though." He lay there in deep thought. "What is adultery?" he asked almost reverently. "I've been trying to figure it out. Isn't that when a married person has intercourse with someone?"

"Yeah, that's right." I was intensely listening to his reasoning. "Well?"

"Well, what?" I asked.

"Are you married?"

"No."

"Neither am I." We looked at each other, wondering about that. "I don't know the answer," I admitted, " . . . but I still think it's wrong."

"OK." That was that.

The following day went smoothly. The boys were delighted as Wayne fixed them up with skis. He owned one pair, and he rented the other. He had a little sled to pull Betsy around in. The snow was fresh on top of well-packed snow. It was perfect for skiing. The boys ran up the slopes in delight. Betsy pooped out quite quickly so we sat with her in the car quite awhile, watching the boys getting used to the tow. We watched as the little lads came spilling down the slope, picking themselves up then getting themselves back up to try again.

It was a day well spent. We also had a very worn out crew as we headed home. However, when we got close to home I decided that it wasn't fair for me to lead Wayne on into thinking that anything more than friendship would arise from this. I felt that he was getting some ideas that I had no thoughts of at all. Suddenly he became a maniac. "I'll drive the whole bunch of us off of this bridge," he screamed.

"Wayne, don't be like that," I pleaded. "I just wanted a friendship, nothing else. I never promised you any more than that."

"You're right. I'm sorry I lost it." He was most apologetic and sweet as he helped carry Betsy in the door saying good night to the boys as they barreled up the stairs to their rooms.

I had so appreciated that special weekend. I felt badly that I had hurt Wayne. The book he had given me was a book that I still cherish for in it Kahlil Gibran had so poetically voiced values of the spirit that I could understand. The principles were the same as the ones I had been learning by my own experiences in real life. However, with my Catholic Christian upbringing I had been taught to beware of any spiritual teachings that didn't include Jesus and the Holy Spirit as well as the Father. It truly helped me at this time, though, to understand what I was going through. I wrote in the margin my own interpretation of what the words meant to me at this time:

> *Love makes you pure, but together—not apart.*
> *Love directs you—not you it.*
> *To love is to be happy to be happy is to know sorrow*
> *to know sorrow is to know love.*

Christmas time was on us. I had saved a goodly little sum for my Christmas shopping. At least it was enough to buy everyone on my list some thoughtful gift. My sister, Jeanne's family had increased fast . . . six children in all. I drove my little old Chevy to shop at the mall prepared to completely wipe out my list. I bought my sister a pretty waste–basket and filled it full of goodies, one for each child and something for her husband, Corky. I bought the boys the Creepy Crawler set they wanted and Betsy the little oven she was so anxious to cook on. It really did cook, with a light bulb, no less. I had found something special for my parents, and then for my brother and his wife I had decided to make some pillows for their new (second-hand) davenport. All I needed to do was to buy the stuffing. I already had some very colorful splotches of material that my mother had given to me when I had learned to make pillows at the mental clinic.

I had all the gifts piled up in old Unabelle's back seat. Just as I was leaving the mall I remembered that the pillows had to have some tassels on them. *I'll just run into the store real fast and grab some yarn. The gifts will be OK.* Unabelle's door wouldn't lock. *Dear God please protect the gifts . . .* I mumbled in haste as I flew into the store. It was a fast transaction. I was back out to the car quick as a flash, or so I thought. As I opened the door I looked into the empty back seat. It didn't even dawn on me for a moment. It was as if my mind wouldn't let me believe what I was seeing. *It must be a mistake!* First I checked to make sure I had the right car. Then I continued into the car. *I must have put them in the trunk . . .* Then the denial released its kind hold on me and allowed the reality of the situation to sink in. *I've been robbed! Oh, no! I've been robbed!*

In the numbing emotional shock I dutifully went to the auto store which was closest to the parking lot and reported what had happened. "Do you know how to get in touch with security?" I went through the whole story several times answering questions from whomever came along to play detective until finally there was nothing more I could do but to face the fact that my Christmas was ruined.

I didn't want to go home even though I knew that I needed to pick up Betsy soon. I simply needed a few moments to regain my composure. I decided to go see my friend Barbara, the ouija board dropout, to just share the experience with her. Barbara was the only other person that I knew who had as much bad luck as me, and would have the empathy without all the phony "you poor little thing" stuff that most people dole out. "Who would do such a thing?" Barbara was infuriated at the idea of it. "Anyone could tell that you didn't have much money. Just one look at that car would tell them that." We both laughed through the misery of it all. Then suddenly, I got a bright idea.

"I know what I'll do, I'll make pillows for everyone!" With that brilliant idea I left the shelter at Barbara's side and went for it. I busied myself making pillows: big ones, little ones, flowery ones, gold ones. The only problem was affording the stuffing for all of them. And then, there were the kids. Pillows were not exactly anything they'd appreciate.

Out of the blue, sister Jeanne stopped over. "Patti, I heard about what happened to your Christmas. An anonymous person asked me to give this to you. It's not me, now. I'm not supposed to tell you who it is." She handed me fifteen dollars. It was like a million bucks. It was just enough to rebuy the Creepy Crawler set (which was on sale this time) and the oven and the stuffing for the pillows. Christmas was on!

It was only a couple of days before Christmas. I had been so busy making pillows that I had forgotten all about getting a tree. It was a good thing because I didn't have the money anyhow. Again, Providence helped me out. One of the guys from PWP came bouncing in one evening leaving off a tree for us. He was a friendly little redheaded fellow. A true extrovert. We had become good friends from talking from time to time on the telephone. He was left with three little kids to raise by himself and was stuck at home a lot so he talked on the phone quite a bit to alleviate the lonely hours in the evenings. It helped me a lot, too. He plopped the tree down, waved a hello and a goodbye announcing, "I have five more of them to deliver," and off he went. We had that tree decorated and fully laden with the array of pillows underneath. I had made Wayne a pillow, too. And had bought some bubble bath for his little girl. I knew he'd bring me a gift. I was prepared. Wayne was so shocked. "You shouldn't have," he scolded.

I just smiled, "I wanted to."

Then Wayne got the idea again that there was hope for a more permanent relationship. Again, I tried to drive the fact home to him that I wasn't romantically interested in him, finally adding: "I'd like to meet your son." I figured that was one way to get the point across without abandoning him completely. I knew that his son was about my age and was going through a divorce.

"OK," he agreed without batting an eye. "I'll invite him to come to the New Year's Eve dance," which was one day before New Year's Eve.

Wayne not only arranged a blind date, but made it a double date. I was pleased with my blind date for Dave was a rather handsome fellow. Black curls crowned his head. His eyes twinkled with warmth as well as did his smile. His stocky build was much unlike his father's stature, which was frail and thin. We hit it off immediately. *Now, I don't want him to get serious like his dad did,* I started right off making it clear to him that I was only interested in a friendship, nothing more.

But, then I noticed the schoolteacher whom I had met at the first dance. He appeared to be by himself. Partly because I wanted Dave to know that I wanted to be independent at these functions, I decided to take it on myself to ask my schoolteacher friend to dance. I was surprised, though, and a little embarrassed for when I got to his table, his date was just joining him, probably returning from the powder room, or something. He was kind enough to dance with me, though. I tried to warm up to him to let him know that I wished I had gone home with him that night. He was kind but unresponsive. "Keep your shoes on," he finalized things. At that, I knew that our relationship was a dead end.

As the four of us left we walked right by my schoolteacher friend. With great gusto I blew the New Year's blow-toy at him making a loud raspy noise as if saying, "Good-bye forever one and all!" The evening ended with the four of us snacking at a greasy spoon and then we each returned to our lives.

I had decided to stay home with the kids the following night, the real New Year's Eve, no big deal. I was surprised by my mother's phone call. "Dear, if you'd like to go somewhere tonight I'll be willing to put the kids to bed over here so you can go. "This was highly unusual. It was the first and only time that my mother had offered to baby-sit without having been asked.

"There's a PWP party I could go to. It's at a private home. It would give me a chance to get better acquainted with some of the people in the club. Thanks, Mom."

I became frantic. I had to act fast. First I had to get the kids ready to stay the night, then I had to bring a dish. Something quick, something I had all the ingredients for. *Good old Spanish Rice! That's what I'll make.*

I pulled up in front of this gorgeous split-level home in my "new" car, Unabelle. Cars were parked all around. I giggled to myself as I parked my old clunk next to the newer cars that were there. As I made my way into the brick entranceway, the hostess gave me a most friendly welcome and introduced me around. As I was being walked around in the large family area where the party was beginning to happen, there was a guy who was obnoxiously making himself noticed. He followed behind the people I was being introduced to waving at me from behind their backs, making a total pest of himself. As I was introduced to the last person he walked up to me saying, "Where've you been all my life?" Now, he was dressed in a suit. This added to my dislike for his phony behavior. He was handsome though, or maybe the word was cute, about in his thirties, some important pluses.

I stiffened at his phony remark. *He's probably in love with himself.* I stuck my nose up in the air starting up a conversation with a couple who were sitting in the corner. Their chairs looked through a huge picture window overlooking the patio that was colorfully decorated with lush flowers hanging from baskets. "It's such a beautiful place, isn't it?" I smiled at the couple.

"Yes. It really is nice. Nice party, too."

My obnoxious friend piped up waving his arms wildly. "It's a fifty-five thousand dollar house! A fifty-five thousand dollar house!"

"It is not," I snapped at him. "It's nice, but it's not a fifty-five thousand dollar house."

"Oh! I thought it was. Anyhow, I like to play the organ." At that I was on the alert. *What is going on? That is what George was rambling on about last New Year's Eve . . . he mentioned about the organ, and was screaming about a $55,000 house.* I began to tremble. "Come on," my new, rather forceful friend took me downstairs. "What's your name, anyhow?" he asked me as he showed me to the Ping-Pong table there.

"Pat."

"Mine's Dick," he picked up a Ping-Pong ball. "Now, the idea is to hit the ball." He handed me a paddle.

I started to laugh. "You're a nut, you know."

I slammed the ball at him. We were able to play a rather mean game of Ping-Pong.

"Soooup's on" a voice came shouting down the stairs.

"Come on. Let's join the party."

We heaped our plates with food and walked over to the room divider that was decorated with ivy plants entwined in the latticework. "This is a cheerful spot," Dick said. Out of the blue he shared, "I live on faith," muttering, as he chomped on his food.

"What kind of faith do you live on?" I asked sarcastically.

"Well, it's like this. Either you and I will get married, or we won't get married. That's right, you know. Either we do or we don't." He stared at me very seriously. "That takes a hell of a lot of faith, you know."

I was becoming nervous. *What a line,* I thought to myself. "I live on childlike faith, myself," the words gushed out.

"Oh. That's real interesting." My statement had really caught his interest. "What's that kind like?"

"Well, when you think you can't go one step further, something always breaks, something good happens. It's awfully hard to explain."

"That makes sense to me," he laid his plate aside. "Come on. Let's join the party."

"Who owns that old Chevy outside?" A voice came bellowing through the crowd. I blushed.

"I do," I confessed to Dick.

"We have to move it so these people can get out."

"Give me your keys," Dick ordered. "I'll move it."

"OK, but don't be too shocked when you see it," I laughed.

Dick came back into the room shortly. "Hey, Pat. Does your house need painting as bad as your car?" He teased.

"Almost. Not quite," I smiled. "You know, I thought you were a phony, earlier," I confessed.

"Boy, you really know how to hurt a guy, don't you? I don't ever like to give that impression. In fact, I bought a truck instead of a car just so I wouldn't make that kind of impression."

I giggled. "There's only one thing worse than a fancy car to make that impression. That's a camper truck."

"Boy, you really know how to hurt a guy. That's exactly what I have, but not because of what you think. I just like to go hunting and fishing." My heart raced to the past to Ron, this time. His words were still smoldering in my brain. "If I ever come back here I'll be driving a camper".

"Hey, you guys," said a girl handing out hats and noise blowers. "Hurry! It's almost zero hour. Get ready for the blast!"

After the celebration was over Dick walked me downstairs to get away from the people. "I have a dinner reservation at this nice restaurant. My date stood me up," he commented.

"I can't go." I was afraid of taking off with him in that camper and leaving my own transportation behind. We sat down on the daveno. The room was dimly lit. I leaned my body against his, our heads together just listening to the piped in music or pretending to listen to it until we found ourselves in each other's arms, a sweet time of caresses and kisses. Nothing heavy. Of course as all good things have got to end we had to go, leaving me to feel just like Cinderella.

"I'll call you," Dick assured me as we walked to our cars. My heart was feeling a little heavy from the beautiful evening having to end. I stopped for a red light a few blocks down the road. I was shocked by a hand knocking on my window. "Hurry up! Roll down the window!" Dick stuck his head in. "Hurry up. Give me a New Year's kiss!"

Be AFFLICTED
And mourn and weep:
Let your LAUGHTER
Be turned to mourning
And your joy
To HEAVINESS.

James 4:9 (KJ)

Chapter 17

It Must Be Him

I now had two frequent callers, both Wayne and Dave: a father and son team. I was in a quandary as how to handle this situation that I had stupidly gotten myself into. Wayne had stopped by "just to chat" one evening when there was a very important phone call. It was Dick, My New Year's Eve romance. "Hi! I was wondering if I could stop by tonight."

"Oh!" I was caught completely off-guard. First, I thought of the dirty dishes in my sink. Then worse than that I thought of this very possessive older man who was sitting in my dining room. On top of that, I couldn't talk freely.

"Gosh, Dick . . . I have company right now . . . "

"Oh! Well then, I'll give you two or three days. Maybe more . . . " he answered snottily. I was shaking in my boots as I hung up the phone. *Now I've gone and done it,* I moaned secretly.

That whole week I prayed each time the phone rang that it would be Dick. A song on the radio was even expressing my feelings . . . *It must be him, it must be him, or I shall die . . . Hello, hello, it must be him, Oh, God, it must be him . . .* I couldn't believe that someone had actually written a song like that especially at this time. I entertained the thought, *It must be a thing of the times . . .* I had become more and more amazed at how the new songs on the radio so fit into my life at the exact moment that I was experiencing the same emotions that the writer was evidently experiencing. It made me aware that songs are very good temperature takers of the emotions in our society.

That weekend there was a PWP roller skating party. I had it all planned that I would run into Dick there with his kids and get better acquainted. Friday night Dave, Wayne's son stopped over. "Are you going to the skating party tomorrow?"

"Well, I thought I'd go with the kids, alone."

"Good! I'll pick you up about 12:30."

"No, that's OK. We can get there on our own. There's no need," I didn't want to hurt his feelings. I really did like him.

"No bother. It's a date, OK?"

"Yeah, OK."

Just as I had wished, I saw Dick when I went up to the counter of the roller rink to get my skates. "Hi!" my heart thumped.

"Hi!" his eyes sparkled a friendly warm smile. "I've got to get these skates on the kids. See you later." He waved me on.

Dave was very attentive, hanging on to me like a leech. The first couple's dance, and he was right there. I kept trying to find Dick. Finally, halfway into the session who did I see but Dick barely rolling along in the most awkward manner. *Oh, oh. He doesn't know how to skate,* I giggled. Later I saw him hovering around his little daughter at the end of the rink. I decided to go down and see if I could help. "Can I help you?" I zipped up to them trying to show that I could handle myself quite well.

"No, thanks. We're just getting used to standing up on these darn things," he laughed.

Suddenly Dave zoomed up to join us. "Everything OK here?" he latched on to me. "Come on, let's make use of this music," he nudged me to join him. I frowned. Dick looked disgusted.

"Go on," he told me.

I was getting upset with Dave. We had words something to the effect of: "You know, Dave, I like to meet other people, too. I'm trying to get acquainted with the members."

He took off in a huff. I caught sight of Dick edging his way across the floor of the rink trying very hard to sway to the music in a cool fashion. I went out to join him.

"Wanna dance?" I grinned.

"Isn't the guy supposed to do the asking?"

"Oh, not really," I laughed. I could see that Dick was embarrassed at his inability to skate. I took the hint to bug-off.

I needed to get my mind off of this man-dating mess I was in. Something was beginning to gnaw at my very soul. It was the fact that I didn't have a copy of my book that I had sent off to Ron about one year ago. *I was told to write down my experiences . . .* I remembered the words clear as a bell that wondrous day when I had received an assignment from my very bosom, from the Holy Spirit. After I had mailed it off in haste that morning when I had so feverishly mailed it off, I never even stopped to think that I didn't have a copy of it. *I have to recreate what I wrote . . .* I shuddered to think of the work it would be, having to relive all that all over again as I wrote it down. I also knew that if I were to write down all of the strange happenings it would help to relieve my mind. I borrowed a typewriter from my mother. I was very rusty with my typing, but I decided all I could do was the best that I could do.

Dave came over one evening as I was tediously trying to get the story down. In his arms was a box full of groceries. "Just thought I'd bring some food over and help feed the kids while you're working." He cheerfully lay the box on the kitchen table. "I have two more sacks . . . " He flew out the door. When he returned he ordered me, "You get back to work, I'll take care of the kids." *He has got to be a gift from God,* I blessed his generosity as I continued to work for many hours. *Make sure you tell the truth, the whole truth the best you can,* I reminded myself. Some of it was very embarrassing to divulge.

Silent utterances came to me monitoring my words. I attempted to write up to the present time. The closer I came to the present, the more difficult it was to write. The emotions and the uncertainties caused me to barely tell the happenings. I still didn't have the hindsight to be able to figure things out. I finally finished it off with a scenario about how "each one of us are like stars, each have a path to follow. We pass one another along the way, sometimes colliding, sometimes travelling together . . . the Creator in charge of it all". I was finally finished! *Ta-da!* I proudly showed Dave my masterpiece. He had been dying to read it. He anxiously scrutinized it.

Finally he came forth with his truest comment, "Pat, this is terrible! The writing is horrible!"

"I know it needs improvement, but can't you look beyond that? I'll learn to do better. There's quite a story there. At least I'm getting it all down."

He shook his head. "You've got a lot of work to do on it." He never again asked about it.

It was just a few days later when my childhood friend, Mary, came to visit. She had traveled abroad and had many glamorous accomplishments: a master's degree in music, she had been a beauty princess, was almost as eccentric as Charmaine only in a more wholesome way, and had paid some of her way through college from publishing stories in magazines. Her experience in this field was what I mostly looked up to her for at this time. She was like a Godsend to me, just as Mary's husband had been a Godsend to her. She had married a photographer who understood her eccentric ways. Her creativity was the most important thing .in her life. As the two of us caught up with what was going on in our lives, I divulged to her not only that I had had a baby whom I adopted out, but that I also had another child . . . my book. Mary looked it over. "Hmmm, interesting . . . " She started to laugh almost uncontrollably. "You've got a good story here. I like the simplicity with which you write. But, Patti, have you read the last line on the first page? It read, *He was a boy and she was a girl.*

I started to laugh. It was funny and embarrassing all at the same time. "You can see where I was coming from being as how Bob was gay," she dried her eyes from laughing so much.

"I know", Mary shook her head in amazement, "I guess that's what's so funny. It makes sense that you would write it."

"Oh, my God. No wonder Dave thought it was awful. Now I see where he was coming from. Mary got back to the book. She more than scanned through the pages. She could see the plot. She could see the creativity in writing even though the writing was jerky and splotchy. "Anything I can do to help?"

"Well, I was wondering how a person gets past reliving everything. I get sort of high sometimes, and sometimes I get depressed, like I'm reliving it."

"First of all, you need to decide what person to write it in. You go back and forth from one person to another. You know, first person is the most difficult to write. I think you might try writing it in third person. That way you can keep yourself from not getting so involved emotionally. OK?"

"Yeah. Thanks." I was smirking to myself . . . *and Dave thought it was useless . . . hrmmph.*

"Keep me posted on what happens. You've got the right idea. When you go back to it someday you'll see the spots that need the work. You can do it."

During this time I was also trying to get out into the world on my own without having to rely on men to keep me in touch with society. Brother Bill's wife, Joyce, had told me how to apply to take a civil service test. I had followed through with this information, and lo and behold the military reservation near us, the very one that Ron had worked at, gave me a call. "We just noticed your name on our register. You have IBM tabulating experience? I can't believe it. Boy, can we use you!"

I was hired.

"Hey, kids!" I was almost too excited. "Mommy found a job! We'll be living like real people!" I threw the sofa pillow up in the air.

"Hooray!" the boys screamed. The three of us danced around in a circle, hand in hand all excited, jumping up and down with little Betsy clapping her hands in the middle of the ring. I hung my coat on a hanger. "Nothing's going to stop us now!"

Now I was feeling that I had things well in hand for the first time since my divorce. I had already gone to a lawyer to make Bob pay support. It hadn't made much difference when I wasn't working, all the support money would've gone to the state, anyhow. But now that I was going to be earning my own money, it made a big difference. The lawyer had sent for Bob's police records. "Boy, that's some stack of papers . . . " he had commented. "I socked it to him!"

He was a fresh young lawyer, evidently an untouchable by Bob's "secret squad." Bob was ordered to pay two hundred fifty dollars a month, more than the original divorce decree along with the six hundred eighteen dollars I would make after taxes.

I had already arranged for a new babysitter, the quiet girl I had met at Group Health. She had mentioned to me that she was looking for a job. I kept her in mind for she was a very straight levelheaded girl . . . sort of the prim and proper variety. Not only did she baby-sit, but she did my housework. I wished I could pay her more, but I had a lot of things I needed to catch up with such as the clothes for the kids and things for the house that were needed badly. The first thing I bought was a good vacuum cleaner. And, for the first time I was getting well stocked up on food.

I still had a very strong desire to make it to PWP functions alone so that I could get better acquainted with Dick. I went to a dance by myself. Dick didn't show up. It was a rather boring evening. I did sign up to work behind the scenes, though, in the kitchen and taking tickets. I felt it was a good way to make friends. I then went to the next dance with Dave. Dick was there with someone else. Through the evening I was rather sullen, trying very hard to have a good time, but I kept eyeing Dick and his date trying to figure out just how serious it might be. *He probably wonders the same thing about Dave and myself.* I slowly sipped on my drink with a pasted smile on my face trying to be polite to Dave. Finally, just before the evening was over, Dick came and asked me to dance. *I'll bet he wanted to see if I was going to goof and ask him to dance,* I glided around the floor in his arms happy that we finally had a chance to talk. "I just got hired at the Fort,"

I tried to impress him that I was building a life and wasn't helpless. He was happy to hear it.

"Who is that guy?" he asked pointing to Dave.

"Oh, just a friend. Actually, the son of a friend," I tried to make light of it.

Naturally, though, I went home with Dave being as how we were both with someone else. *Why am I so mean to Dave?* I wondered. *He's a really sweet fellow. He really cares for me. His dad likes me. Why do I treat him this way?*

Mid-week as I was doing up the dinner dishes, a knock came on the door. "Dave!" I squealed. He stood there proudly, all dressed up.

"How do you like my suit?" he gleamed as he handed me a box of candy, and some flowers. "Guess what! We're getting married!"

"Who's getting married?" I stammered.

"We are." He gave me a big hug.

"What makes you think that?"

"I had a dream. I dreamt I was right here in this house." He pulled me by the arm back into the kitchen. "It was that very faucet. See? That's the faucet all right. That was the faucet in my dream!"

"Yeah?" I chilled. "Then what?"

"I don't understand the rest of it. Maybe you can explain it." He walked me into the front room. "I was drinking water from the faucet. I was drinking and drinking . . . like I couldn't quench my thirst."

"Oh! I know what it means . . . " I was surprised at myself as I explained it.

"Explain it to me," he coaxed.

"Well, it doesn't mean we're getting married. It means we're not getting married."

"Why does it mean that?" he said angrily.

"Dave, I can't marry you. For one thing you're not even divorced, yet. For another thing, I don't love you like that."

" . . . but you're my goddess . . . " He fell to his knees dramatically. "You're my god!"

"Dave," I put my hands on his cheeks. I could hardly believe what I was hearing, and the awful dramatics! "Dave, don't ever say that. Those kind of feelings belong to God, alone." I had learned that lesson myself the hard way.

"I thought we were going to get married," he started to cry. "That is what the dream means. Thirst. That is what it means, isn't it? I'm going to thirst." He held his hands over his eyes weeping.

That kind of dramatic behavior was one of the very things that frightened me about Dave, and his father, too. *It sure runs in the family*, I sighed wondering how in the world things had escalated to that point. *They're both so sweet and would give you the shirt off their backs.*

Dave now decided to impress me with his psyche. He claimed that he could control anyone's mind if he wanted to. "Yeah? How do you propose to do that?" I prodded him.

"I can mentally transport my thoughts into your thoughts. I'll tell you what. Tonight when I'm driving my cab, I'll use my mental telepathy and you'll be able to see me."

"What if I don't want you to?" I smirked.

"I will, wait and see."

I was sound asleep. It was about 10 o'clock at night. Something in my mind was nudging me to wake up. Slowly a dark shadowy vision became visible in my thoughts. I could see him! He was in his cab driving! I could see him clearly, the windshield wipers were going back and forth. *This is freaky!* I got up and moved around the house to clear my mind. It made me very uncomfortable to think that someone could force his thoughts on me against my will!

The next day he called. "Well, did you see me?"

"No," I lied. "See, I told you you couldn't control me."

"What the heck? I wonder why it didn't work? It always does."

The next Friday night I snuck off to the dance by myself hoping to see Dick there. Just one time I wanted a chance to see him again without Dave butting in. As I sat at a table barely getting my bearings I felt someone behind me. I turned to see.

"Oh, Dave!" I was shocked to see him. More than that, I was angry.

"I brought you a bottle of the best whiskey there is," he plopped down beside me.

"Dave," I pleaded. "I told you I wanted to come by myself."

"I know, but I thought I'd keep you company."

"Dave, I'm interested in someone else," I tried to be as explicit as I could.

"He's not even here," Dave strained his neck to look around.

"He is too. He's right over there." I pointed at Dick who was sitting up against a wall across the room.

"That's him, huh?" Dave got up. "I'll be back in a minute."

"Oh, no!" I hid my face in my hands. *I'm so stupid. He tricked me into telling him who Dick was. Dang him . . . he's going over to talk to him!*

Dave then walked back to the table. "He's not interested in you," he announced. "Now get some sense."

"I have to collect tickets at the door in five minutes," I excused myself. "You shouldn't have done that, Dave," I swore at him as I left. I wasn't there at the ticket table very long when Dick sauntered up to the ticket table.

"Don't drink too much," he grinned at me.

"Yeah. Sure," I blushed. "So what?"

"Take it easy," he walked away. I went back to the table after my hour of ticket taking was over. "Don't get too drunk," Dick goaded me again as I passed his table returning to my seat beside Dave.

"Here. I mixed you a stiff one. You probably need it."

Don't drink too much, I stubbornly repeated Dick's message to myself. I slugged down the drink. "I don't give a damn," I bellowed. "He's too much like a guy I used to know, anyhow. He nearly drove me nuts." I proceeded to get drunk. Dave kept me well supplied. Through the fuzzy thoughts and narrow sight I saw a familiar face from the past which brought me out on the dance floor to greet. It was one of the guys who had given Ron and me and Carol a ride to the night spot that first night I had met Ron . . . one of the guys who had nearly run Carol and me over earlier that same evening.

"Hi, there," I patted him on the back. "Long time no see."

"Yeah!" He was staggering drunk. "I'm not doing too good," he mumbled.

"I'm sure glad to see you," I shook his hand.

"Yeah! I got to sit down before I fall down," the guy swaggered into a chair. I looked up toward the door. Dick was standing there glaring! I stared back. *So I'm drunk!* I swore at him silently. Dick shook his head. He turned and slammed out the door. "Goodbye," I whispered. *You're too much like George, anyhow.* I gathered myself together. "Come on, Dave. Take me home now that you fixed everything."

When HE the
SPIRIT OF TRUTH
Is come,
He will GUIDE you into ALL TRUTH
For He shall not speak of Himself;
But whatever He shall HEAR
That shall He speak
And He will show you THINGS TO COME . . . .

John 16:13 (KJ)

Chapter 18

A New Life

Emotions were no longer discernable. Was it anger? Was it despair? It was as though I was hanging in mid-air from a hopeless yearning, a huge cavity that could not be filled. I was docile, obedient to my friend, or was he my foe? Dave was crying as he knelt by the side of my bed holding a sack. I was sick from the ordeal of the evening, the games, the trickery, the drunkenness. Yet, I was thankful that Dave had stayed with me for I was sicker than I had ever been from drink. On the other hand my mind was saying as my head was spinning. *It's the least he could do after spiking my drinks all night.* He knew it. His tears were tears of guilt and remorse for his behavior. My body retched with huge heavings. From somewhere in the recesses of my mind it was symbolic of throwing up all of the ugliness of the past few years. It was a symbol of getting rid of the old and on with the new, whatever that might be.

My body simmered down. Dave was exhausted from the emotions that had brewed all night in his heart. He asked if he could lie next to me. "I promise I just want to lay here for a few minutes." It was the least I could do in friendship. After all, his main fault was the fact that he cared for me in a way that I couldn't return to him. He was a faithful friend in spite of the awkward situation that had permeated most of our friendship. *I wonder if I hadn't gone to that New Year's Eve party and met Dick if it might've been different between us?* I lay there pondering over what might've been.

After we had rested for a time Dave, just like his father had done, began to pressure me to accept some sexual advances. "I don't want to go all the way," he insisted, "I just want to hold you, to make you feel better . . . " I had no doubt that he felt that way, but I had started a new life. In fact, that new life had started months ago.

It was when I was still at the mental clinic. The occupational therapy had been very helpful in enabling me to function again. The group therapy had helped me share my disappointments and longings with others who had felt the same way and gone through many of the same experiences. But the greatest hurdle was the inability to rid myself of the guilt I had felt from my cheap lustful dealings . . . sins that had gone so far as to even cheat me from the experiences of raising my little son whom I had adopted out. I had secretly named him Little Raynold, in honor of the great love I had felt for Ron. My problem had been, *How could I confess things that were of such confusion? How could I decipher between the right and wrongs between me and George? What if I tell them about what really happened? Maybe they would lock me up* . . . Sometimes I felt guilty about everything, almost guilty for having been born, guilty of the overwhelming stigma of my weaknesses.

There had been a nurse at the hospital who was extremely understanding. As the pain of not being right with God welled up in my heart, I had finally turned to the passionately empathetic woman. I took the chance and confided my deepest secrets and feelings to this nurse whom I felt more and more that God had placed there for me at this time. "I know of just the person for you to see," the nurse joyfully exclaimed. "This priest will do just the trick for you. He's seen many of our patients. He's very understanding!"

As I had entered Father's office I felt a comfortableness. His office was pleasant, nothing fancy, but it had a nice flavor to it. Even more than that I could tell in an instant that he was a very caring soul. He had a gentleness about him. He greeted me cheerfully offering me a seat directly across from him. He had a way of making one feel secure, giving me the impression that no matter what I had to tell him, no matter how strange my story or even my behavior might be, that it would be OK with him. He took nothing for granted, not even the fact that, perhaps, I was insane. It didn't matter. It was a perfect opportunity to voice some of the strange happenings between myself and George. It was the first time that I had had an opportunity to divulge our "secrets" without fear of someone making a big issue of it. He quietly nodded in understanding as I recited my story. "Now, just what is it that's bothering you the most?" he gently tried to steer my ramblings on to the subject at hand.

"I suppose the fact that I got pregnant, but it's so hard to confess. I really had no intentions of being that intimate with the baby's father. I was lonely. In fact, it was just the opposite. I was trying to do the right thing . . . just trying to set Glen straight about the strange relationship I was having with George. I was trying to be truthful. He didn't like that, I guess. Glenn was a really nice guy, Father. He did force himself on me in anger, no, it was more from aching with hurt . . . Oh . . . . " I groaned. It was all such a mess! "I get so confused," I began to tremble as I rubbed my hands together, then wringing them.

Father could tell that I was unable to make too much sense of any of it. "It's OK," Father tenderly tried to console me. "It's not so much what happened that's the point here." He picked up a pencil and started to doodle. His brain, or perhaps his soul, went into a deep trance, perhaps coming in contact with the Holy Spirit. "It's what you do after the fact. You must learn from your experience. Then go on ahead without looking back."

"That sounds so good!" I heaved a massive sigh of relief.

"Now, we'll go to the confessional. You do your best to tell me what you want to. You can keep it short being as how I know the whole story. We'll get all of the heaviness off your chest."

I quietly knelt by the little door in the little darkened room waiting for that ominous sliding sound of the door allowing in a little light, and the sound of a gentle voice on the other side. I carefully formed the words, trying to make it brief. Father helped out cutting me short here and there, guiding me through the steps. After he closed the little window that ended the ordeal, Father came out of the confessional box. From experience he knew that his arms and shoulder would be needed. "I wish you a blessed future . . . " he extended his arms inviting me to a hug. Tears streamed down my cheeks as I fell into his loving arms. His shoulder was all wet from my tears. I could hardly breathe between the heavy sobbings. Father held me close patting me on the back as a parent would hold a child. It was one of the most comforting things that anyone had ever done for me. He had wanted nothing in return.

Since that day I had been able to continue my life with more confidence, a stronger feeling of alliance with God, and able to keep my nose clean. Now, here I was with my friend wanting me to throw away my peace of mind that I had received that day. "No, I shook my head. I can't . . . " My eyes begged him to understand.

"Pat. If you don't use it, you'll lose it . . . " he repeated a very popular version of the outlook among the singles in the society of the times.

"I don't agree." I held my ground. "I know some friends who got married in their mid-thirties. They didn't lose anything. In fact, they gained. They waited and they're happy."

"I can't argue with you . . . " he smiled. "It's OK."

After that, Dave cooled it. He no longer forced himself on me, but seemed to be keeping a comfortable distance from me.

I was a little shaky from that night, wondering just what my belief system was concerning pre-marital sex. I decided to look it up in the Bible, but the problem was, where? All I knew was that Moses gave us the ten commandments. I also remembered seeing all kinds of laws in Deuteronomy. I scanned through the pages until finally I found something involving sex in Deut. 27:20. "Cursed be he that lies with his father's wife; because he uncovers his father's skirt . . . Cursed be he that lies with any manner of beast . . . " *Oh, for heaven's sakes,* I slammed the book shut. *I can't hack this book.* I just shook my head with disgust for either the contents of the book . . . or my own stupidity. I didn't know which. On I went walking the treadmill.

Talking of stupidity, I felt very stupid one day when my supervisor at work decided to play a joke on me. I had been doing well on the job. My supervisor was probably ten years my senior, a retired sergeant. Art was a quiet but friendly man. He was not at all the stereotype of the loud sergeant ordering his troops around. He quietly oversaw the work, quietly gave orders, and treated his workers with respect. One day he approached me with a new job. "We've decided that you're just the person to take over the telephone billing." Up to that point they had given me very routine work. Now they were giving me more responsibility. *This is great!* My heart was floating with pride that they had acknowledged my good work. "They will bring the cards in to you sometime this morning. Here is the procedure to follow. You might want to look it over while you are waiting."

I went over to a quiet corner to study it. There seemed to be no problem. It appeared to be just the normal routine type of stuff. After a bit my supervisor tapped me on the shoulder. "The cards are here."

"Oh, wonderful!" I was anxious to get started on my new job. There in front of me stood a soldier who had pulled a dolly up beside me. It was overflowing with huge boxes.

"Where do I put these?" he asked.

"I don't know, ask Art. I'm busy now." I looked around for the stack of cards that was supposed to be sitting around there somewhere.

"I did. He told me to give them to you. Where do you want them?"

"What's in those boxes?" I know a look of horror overtook my face.

"Cards", the young soldier explained, " . . . lots and lots of cards!"

Art peeked around from behind one of the machines. "Those are the telephone billing cards. You'd better tell him to pile them up on this table here which we reserved for you, plus these two sorters here are yours. Good luck. The corporal, here, has to get some more so you'd better get busy." He then walked off with a sneaky grin on his face.

I knew this was a test. He was halfway teasing me, and halfway seeing what kind of stuff I was made of. I stood up straight, rolled up my sleeves after kicking off my shoes, and attacked the job as one would attack the ball carrier on the football field. *I'll show him,* I swore, then giggled to myself. *I sure fell into this one.*

It was a two-day process just sorting the cards. Art did come to my rescue giving me a hint on how to make the best use of two sorters instead of one. I filled every card rack in the place. Fortunately, as I collated them into sections, they had diminished to a job of about five boxes . . . something easier to handle. The rest of the cards had been boxed up. They were the refuse or waste. From then on the job became very interesting and fun. I began to look forward to my monthly challenge with the IBM card monster.

I had been discovering in the last few years that just living on this earth was a constant challenge. The society in which I lived was in a period of gross change and the churches were feeling it to the point that they, too, were floundering. One Sunday afternoon I was watching a TV program called *Challenge.* I was finding that I enjoyed a challenge as long as it was within the realm of possibility. *Challenge* was a show that had three ministers who talked over issues concerning religious affairs. One was a rabbi, one was a minister and one was a priest. This one day they were talking about women and how the Bible pertained to them. The rabbi mentioned, "Sometimes I wish that we could get a little more insight on the spiritual experiences of women."

The minister added, "Yes. It does seem that the Bible is usually written from the male point of view. It would be helpful to have a woman's input."

"I agree," the priest said. "I know a lot of what they think from the confessional, but of their spiritual needs I know very little. I don't know what goes on in their little heads."

"We're married and we still don't know . . . " the other two kidded Father as they all three joined into gleeful laughter.

This little scenario settled into the depths of my very being. It was soothing to me. It was a reality. It was a verification of the importance of what I had been doing in writing my story. There was a need. I was filling it ever so secretly.

There came news from far away of my friend, Wynne, who had waited until later in life to marry, and was now getting married. She was a high school friend of both Mary's and mine. In fact, she was the one who had gone with me to drink a hot rum on Christmas Eve, the night that sickening political buddy of Bob's tried to seduce me. Wynne was a very tall, willowy girl who had gone through college to become a teacher. She had decided to be adventurous and took a teaching job in Germany. There had been a time of despair in her life when she had written to me concerning her own loneliness and wondering if she would ever marry or have a family. Now she was bringing home her prize, a young man from the air force. Wynne was one of the last of my schoolmates to marry. Her fiancée was not only a good catch career wise, but also socially and financially. He was also of the same religion, Catholic. My first thoughts after I opened the invitation consisted of my knowledge of the Nuptial Mass. *There will be communion. I need to go to confession about getting drunk, and . . . and I haven't been going to Mass, and . . . what a relief! I've been to confession over all the hard stuff.*

I reverently and dutifully went to church with my mother the next Sunday. Father was hearing confessions that day. I did my best filling him in on my life as a divorcee . . . tackling the newer problems which didn't seem to bother me quite as much as the older ones. *I hope that I haven't forgotten anything,* I feared as I signed off. Father answered rather unusually, "This has been a good confession." I left the confessional feeling very blessed. Only one thing bothered me. *How did he know that it was a good confession? Was the Holy Spirit talking through him? I wonder.* I felt so content. Now I would be able to truly receive communion and offer it to God in prayer to ask for a life of blessings for my friend.

On the wedding day, after the bride had entered in regal splendor and the nuptials were said, I found myself kneeling there at the communion rail patiently waiting for the priest to reach me. It was the same priest with whom I had had my "God is love" discussions. In fact, he was the very priest to whom I had sent a copy of the latest version of my book. Here he was on this very special day. Apart from it being Wynne's wedding day, for some reason I was feeling as if I were stepping into a new era of my own life. Father was slowly making it down the row of persons receiving the little white host who in their hearts were receiving the body and blood of Christ. I reflected on how lonely I had been living in spiritual death and how close I felt to God since I had joined the land of the living (in Christ). I reflected on how communion was the covenant between Jesus and the brethren in Christ and how awesome to think that down through the ages those people who believed in Him and loved Him all partook of this covenant. Finally, Father reached me. Quickly a soft excited voice whispered into my ear. No, actually the voice was talking to Father. "This is her. Listen to her." Father made a loud grunting sound as he was pushed backwards a little. Then, calmly he gathered himself back to the task at hand and gave me communion. I was stunned and elated. But then, maybe I was disappointed that perhaps I was still hearing things. No, more than that: *maybe I'm still crazy!* The fear tinged my soul. Little did I know that this was the last time that I would receive communion for 14 years. What a special day it was.

. . . let us also LAY ASIDE
every WEIGHT
and SIN which CLINGS SO CLOSELY.

Heb 12:1 (KJ)